How It Works®

Science and Technology

Third Edition

Marshall Cavendish
99 White Plains Road
Tarrytown, NY 10591

Website: www.marshallcavendish.com

Third edition updated by Brown Reference Group plc.

Library of Congress Cataloging-in-Publication Data
How it works: science and technology.—3rd ed.
p. cm.
Includes index.
ISBN 0-7614-7314-9 (set)   ISBN 0-7614-7326-2 (Vol. 12)
1. Technology—Encyclopedias. 2. Science—Encyclopedias.
[1. Technology—Encyclopedias. 2. Science—Encyclopedias.]
T9 .H738 2003
603—dc21   2001028771

Consultant: Donald R. Franceschetti, Ph.D., University of Memphis

Brown Reference Group
Editor: Wendy Horobin
Associate Editors: Paul Thompson, Martin Clowes, Lis Stedman
Managing Editor: Tim Cooke
Design: Alison Gardner
Picture Research: Becky Cox
Illustrations: Mark Walker, Darren Awuah

Marshall Cavendish
Project Editor: Peter Mavrikis
Production Manager: Alan Tsai
Editorial Director: Paul Bernabeo

Printed in Malaysia
Bound in the United States of America
08 07 06 05 04   6 5 4 3 2

Title picture: Enlarging a print, see *Photographic Film and Processing*

How It Works®

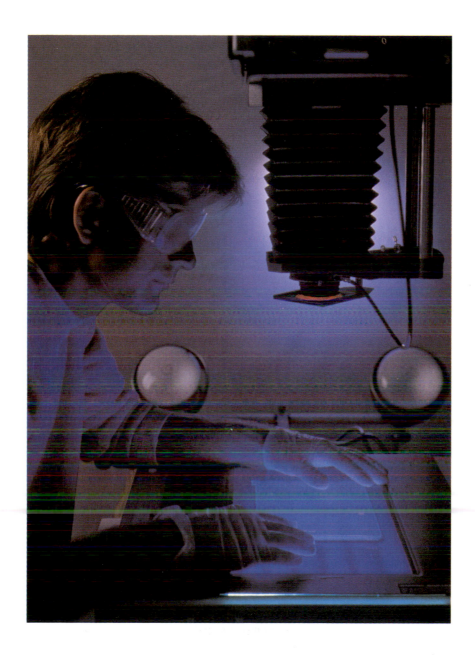

Science and Technology

Volume 12

Ophthalmology

Physics

Marshall Cavendish

New York • London • Toronto • Sydney

Contents

Volume 12

Ophthalmology

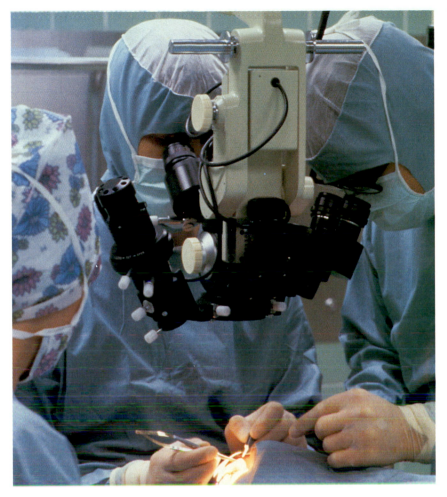

Ophthalmology is the medical specialty concerned with the diagnosis and treatment of eye disorders. All ophthalmologists are physicians. They are sometimes called oculists but should not be confused with optometrists, who are people who test vision and prescribe glasses and contact lenses. Optometrists are not primarily concerned with eye diseases.

The range of equipment used by ophthalmologists has increased greatly in recent years. It includes slit lamp microscopes to examine the outside and front interior of the eyes under high magnification; automatic refractors to check whether glasses are needed; various kinds of ophthalmoscopes to examine the insides of the eyes; visual field analyzers to check how far the field of vision extends outwards and to see whether there are any defects in the visual fields; ultrasound eye measurement equipment to work out the power of lens implants needed after cataract surgery; lasers to treat a range of conditions and to seal holes in the retina; cryopexy equipment to freeze parts of the eye and secure attachment of detached retinas; and diathermy equipment to control minor bleeding in the eye.

▲ A surgeon uses a binocular operating microscope during an eye operation while a student follows the operation's progress using the other set of binoculars.

Diseases of the eye

There are many conditions that affect the eye, some of which respond to drug treatment and others requiring surgery. The outer eye is suspect to inflammations of the lids, cornea, and lachrymal ducts that can arise through scratches from foreign bodies or infections of the sinuses or eyelash follicles. Most of these conditions can be treated with antibiotics or under local anesthetic to remove small growths or abscesses.

One of the most common ailments that impairs vision is the development of a cataract, which causes the lens to become opaque. Cataracts are mainly a consequence of aging but can also be found in infants whose mothers contracted rubella in early pregnancy. Exposure to certain drugs or radiation can also result in cataracts forming as can wounds that perforate the lens. Removing cataracts today is a straightforward procedure that uses a small ultrasonic probe to shatter the lens into fragments that can then be sucked out. An artificial lens is then inserted into the eyeball, or the patient is prescribed special glasses or contact lenses to enable the eyes to focus.

The most serious problems with the eye are those affecting the retina and the optic nerve at the back of the eyeball. The retina is a thin layer that contains the rod and cone cells that provide color vision and has only a limited ability to repair any damage sustained. Small holes or tears can occur in the retina from physical injury and are common among nearsighted people, whose larger eyeballs may stretch the covering layers of the eye. As a result, the vitreous humor leaks through the retina, detaching it from the pigmented layer behind. Today ophthalmologists repair such tears using a laser, effectively spot welding the retina back in place.

The retina is also subject to degenerative diseases that can be hereditary or senile in nature. Retinitis pigmentosa is a hereditary condition that causes progressive loss of the field of vision until only a small tubular field remains. By contrast, in old age there can be a loss of vision from the central part of the retina owing to a decrease in the blood supply to the macula. Neither condition can be treated satisfactorily by drugs or surgery, though some improvement can be made by using corrective lenses.

Damage to the optic nerve can occur as a result of brain swelling from tumors or head injury. Pressure must be reduced quickly to prevent atrophy, which often leads to blindness. The

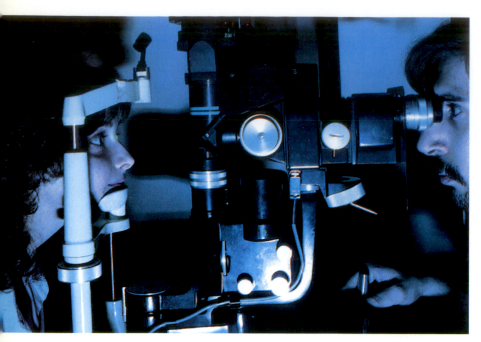

who are nearsighted have corneas that are effectively too strong for the length of their eyeball, so the image of distant objects is brought to a focus in front of the retina and appears blurred. They can, however, see close objects clearly.

The excimer laser uses a mixture of argon and fluorine gases to produce a narrow, concentrated beam of intense but invisible ultraviolet light. This light energy does not generate heat in the tissues but vaporizes them with great precision.

To treat myopia, the cornea is flattened by removing a thin layer of tissue centrally—up to about 10 percent of the thickness. The laser beam does not penetrate the cornea, and there is no danger to the internal parts of the eye. The surgeon has to estimate the amount of tissue removed from the cornea with great care in order to correspond to the previous focusing error.

Once the surgeon has reduced the curvature by just the amount needed, the image of distant objects falls exactly on the retina at the back of the eye, so the patient can see them clearly. Near objects are focused by the normal process of accommodation, using changes in the curvature of the internal lens.

After the operation, which takes about ten minutes and which is performed painlessly in the surgeon's office using anesthetic eyedrops only, the patient feels some discomfort for about 24 hours. After about three to six months the eye's focusing becomes fully stabilized, but from the time of the operation most patients can see clearly without glasses or contact lenses.

optic nerve can also become inflamed, leading to a condition called optic neuritis. The sufferer loses vision in the central region of the field and experiences pain on moving the eye. Function is restored following an attack, but the condition may return after a period of remission.

Eye operations

Eye operations have always called for great skill. Today, new equipment means that not only is it easier to carry out basic operations, but new operations are possible that were once only dreamed of. Microsurgery, using binocular operating microscopes and instruments of remarkable delicacy and precision, is now established, and almost all ophthalmic surgery is done using the operating microscope.

As in any operation, the eye surgeon wears sterile operating clothes and gloves and must not touch anything other than sterile equipment and instruments. The surgeon controls the basic movement of the operating microscope by a panel of pedals; most surgeons kick off their rubber boots when they are comfortably seated at the microscope. The pedals control axial and other illumination, focus, zoom magnification, and up, down, and sideways position shift. The microscope and the latest operating instruments, such as diamond scalpels, allow a degree of precision that would otherwise be impossible.

The excimer laser

The excimer laser is one of the most recent developments in ophthalmology. It is an instrument used to reshape the surface of the external lens of the eye (the cornea) in order to abolish nearsightedness (myopia) and other focusing errors. People

▲ A diabetic patient having damaged blood vessels in the retina repaired by a laser beam. Lasers have replaced conventional cutting tools because they can be applied precisely by computer and cause little damage to surrounding tissues and structures.

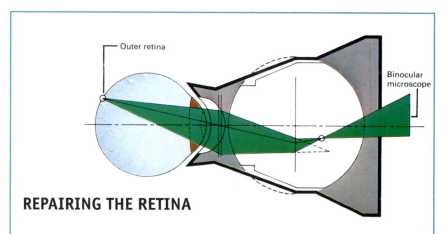

REPAIRING THE RETINA

Tears and holes in the retina at the back of the eye can be repaired using an argon gas laser, which is beamed through a binocular microscope. The beam travels through the cornea, lens, and vitreous humor before hitting the retina, where the radiation is absorbed and converted into heat. Retinal blood vessels absorb the heat and are closed down as a result, healing the retina.

SEE ALSO: CONTACT LENS • EYE • LASER AND MASER • MICROSURGERY • OPHTHALMOSCOPE • OPTOMETRY • SPECTACLES • SURGERY

Ophthalmoscope

The ophthalmoscope is an optical device used for examining the interior of the eye by looking through the pupil, the tiny black window surrounded by the iris.

Before the invention of the ophthalmoscope, it was impossible to see inside the eye. It was believed that the blackness of the pupil was due to the total absorption of light rays by the eye, but the German scientist Herman von Helmholtz discovered that most of the light entering the eye is reflected back and can be intercepted by an observer. Helmholtz investigated the speed of nervous impulses, color blindness, and other subjects, but he is most famous for his *Handbook of Physiological Optics*. In 1851, he had the idea of directing a beam of light into the eye with a mirror in which there was a tiny aperture through which an observer could look.

For diagnostic purposes, it is important to obtain a good view of the fundus, that part of the cavity of the eye that can be examined by looking through the pupil. This enables the observer to detect abnormalities and pathological changes in the eye; some diseases, such as diabetes, manifest themselves in the eye before symptoms appear elsewhere. The fundus, however, cannot be examined by a perforated mirror alone; it gives only a red reflex. Helmholtz found it was necessary to interpose a condenser lens, with about a 4 in. (10 cm) focal length in order to obtain an inverted image, magnified five times. This combination of mirror and handheld condenser was called an indirect ophthalmoscope and was used until about 1920.

Today, ophthalmoscopy is carried out by a direct method with a handheld instrument. From a tiny lamp powered by dry batteries that are located in the handle of the instrument, a narrow beam of light is directed through the pupil and into the eye of the patient by means of a prism or a perforated mirror of steel or glass. The image, magnified 15 times, is viewed through the sight hole in the mirror and brought into focus by a revolving magazine of lenses rotated by the index finger of the observer. It is interesting that the power required to focus the image represents the refractive error of the eye and gives roughly the power of the eyeglass lens required to correct the vision. This coincidence is incidental to the real function of the instrument, which is the examination of the interior of the eye in order to detect abnormalities.

Many instruments are fitted with a variety of filters, such as red-free and polarizing screens,

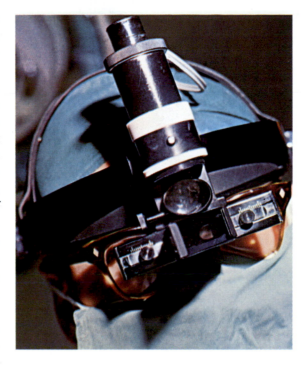

◀ This binocular ophthalmoscope uses mirrors and forms an inverted, three-dimensional image.

that show up conditions not visible with white light. Cross-line graticules can be projected onto the retina so that a particular point can be given a grid reference. There is also a new type of ophthalmoscope that projects a laser beam; it is used in eye surgery to coagulate the tissue around a detached retina. For clinical research and a more detailed study of the eye, there is a large binocular ophthalmoscope that is framed in a headband. With this instrument, it is possible to obtain a large stereoscopic picture of the fundus magnified from four to eight times.

A further development is the use of lasers to scan the surface of the retina to produce images that may then be used for diagnosis.

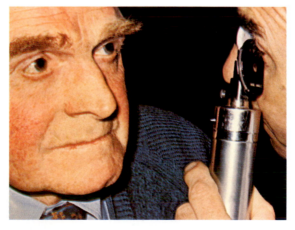

◀ A physician examining the eye of a patient using a handheld ophthalmoscope. A narrow beam of light is directed through the pupil and into the eye.

SEE ALSO: EYE • LIGHT AND OPTICS • MICROSURGERY • MIRROR • OPHTHALMOLOGY • OPTOMETRY • PRISM

Optical Scanner

▲ Drum scanners are high-level image-input devices used by reprographic companies. They use photomultiplier tubes, which are more sensitive to light than the sensors used in flatbed scanners. The image is mounted on a glass drum, and light is passed through it as it revolves. Drum scanners give better image resolution, making them ideal for fine art reproduction.

An optical scanner is an input device that can convert visual images and text into digital information that can be read by a computer. It works by converting the dark and light areas of an image into zeros and ones, which are resolved as pixels on a computer screen and which can be output as dots by a laser printer.

Scanners work either by reflectance from an image or transmission of light through it. Most desktop scanners made for the home market use reflectance; the more specialist drum machines used by reprographic companies and printers are capable of scanning by reflectance or transmission. Transmission is mainly used for scanning transparencies and slides.

To scan an image, it is first placed on a glass screen or drum and covered to prevent light from escaping. In a flatbed scanner, the light source and sensor are mounted on a carriage that travels the length of the scanner; in a drum scanner, the light source is beamed through the glass drum to a sensor located in the center. Early scanners, which used fluorescent bulbs as the light source, had a disadvantage in that the heat they produced would distort the optical components inside the scanner. They have now been replaced by cold-cathode bulbs, which operate at much lower temperatures and are more reliable at producing a constant white light. Xenon bulbs have recently begun to make inroads as scanner light sources because they can provide an extremely stable full-spectrum light, though they have a higher power demand than other bulbs.

Light is directed to the sensor by a system of lenses, mirrors, and prisms. In high-quality scanners, these devices are made of glass and coated to minimize diffusion. Cheaper models use plastic lenses, which can lead to poorer definition and chromatic aberration of the image.

Sensors

Three types of sensor are currently in use, depending on the sophistication of the scanner. Most desktop flatbed scanners use thousands of charge-coupled devices (CCD) arranged in a thin line along the length of the sensor. CCDs are electronic devices that convert light into a voltage, which is passed through an analog-to-digital converter to turn it into a signal that can be read by a computer. To pick up the different colors that are present in a photograph or a piece of artwork, the light is shone through a series of red, green, and blue filters and reflected into the CCD array by the optical system. Other systems use three colored tubes and a single CCD to collect each color. The difference in operation is such that filtered CCDs need only one pass of the scanner head, whereas a single CCD system requires three passes to pick up each color.

A cheaper alternative is the contact image sensor (CIS) system, which uses red, green, and blue light-emitting diodes (LEDs) to produce white light. The CIS system requires no mirrors or lenses, as the sensors are arranged close to the glass supporting the image. CIS scanners are therefore much thinner and lighter, but the resolution of images is not as good as with a CCD scanner.

To achieve the quality of resolution needed for printing, most reprographic companies use a drum scanner. Drum scanners use photomultiplier tubes (PMTs) as the sensor, because they are more sensitive to light than CCDs. The image is mounted on a glass drum and rotated at high speed around the sensor. The light received by the sensor is split into three beams and passed through a red, green, or blue filter before it is collected by the PMTs and converted into a voltage. The lack of optics in a PMT system prevents any refractive problems, and their lower sensitivity to electrical noise gives a better resolution of tones than do flatbed scanners. However, they are slow to use and more expensive to buy and maintain.

Image resolution

How well a scanner picks up the detail in an image is determined by its resolution, measured in dots per inch (dpi) or pixels per inch (ppi). Each CCD picks up one pixel, so a typical 8.5 in. (22 cm) wide, 600 dpi flatbed scanner will have 5,100 CCDs arranged across its scanning head. The scanning head appears to move across the image in a single continuous sweep but actually makes a number of stops every inch to sample the light. While the resolution is usually given as the number of CCDs multiplied by the number of head stops, for example, 600 x 600 dpi, much depends on the quality of the optics, motor control, and electronics. As the current maximum number of CCDs that can be arranged on a scanning head is 600 per inch, higher resolutions are obtained using a computer technique called interpolation, by which software calculates the likely color of spaces between the dots and fills them in.

Another important element in image resolution is the bit depth of the scanner, which determines how much information is picked up from each pixel. The simplest black and white scanners, such as those used to read bar codes, are known as 1-bit scanners, because they can determine only whether light is on or off and therefore record black or white. To achieve gray-scale (a number of tones between black and white) scanning requires at least a 4-bit (16 tones) or 8-bit (256 tones) scanner. Color scanners are a minimum of 24 bits, using 8 bits for each of the three scanning colors. In theory, these scanners have a range of more than 16 million colors; the process is known as true-color scanning.

The dynamic range is another factor that affects image resolution and indicates the ability of the analog-to-digital converter to screen out any problems with the light source, filters, and electrical noise. It is measured on a scale between 0.0 (white) and 4.0 (black), and most desktop color scanners have a rating of 2.4. Higher quality flatbed scanners range from 2.8 to 3.2, though drum scanners top the range at 3.0 to 3.8.

Whatever the resolution capabilities of the scanner, it is rarely necessary to scan an image at the maximum possible. Instead, the resolution should be set according to the output device and the paper it is being printed on. For an ordinary

◀ An optical character-reading machine. The document-feeding mechanism is seen to the right, with the machine's reading area to the left. The video camera above the reading area scans the documents. Typical applications for this type of machine include the reading of charge-card documents, and processing forms containing computer-printed customer account names and numbers and the processing of gas or electricity meter readings.

ink-jet printer capable of 720 dpi color printing onto glossy paper, the scanner should be set to scan at 240 dpi. For ordinary paper, this figure would need to be halved again to 120 dpi, because of the dithering technique, by which ink-jet printers scatter color, and the absorbency of the paper. Images to be displayed on a computer screen are limited by the size of the monitor and the processing ability of the graphics cards installed. A suitable resolution is around 72 dpi.

Storing images

Once the image has been scanned, it must be saved as a computer file. The high resolution of modern scanners often results in very large files, typically 30 MB (megabytes) for an A4-size image. A number of different formats are available: bitmap files store images as full color without compression or as 256-color images with simple compression; TIFF (tagged image file format) files can be stored either for displaying on-screen or for printing and can be compressed without any loss of quality; GIF (graphics interchange format) images are stored as 256 colors indexed for each file and as a result produce smaller files. Another file format,

JPEG (joint photography experts group), can be compressed, but the loss of detail makes it suitable for on-screen images only.

Scanned images rarely look the same as the original whether viewed on-screen or printed out, so a color-matching system is used to improve the color. Several proprietary software programs have been developed for end users that require close color calibration, such as printers and graphic artists. The software standardizes the colors throughout the system so that the image looks the same on-screen and printed.

Captured images do not have to remain true to the original, however, as software packages, such as Adobe PhotoShop, can transform pictures in ways that would have been impossible using photographic techniques. Wrinkles and flabby chins can be eliminated, apples and bananas turned blue and orange, and new elements added without any obvious outlines showing.

Optical character recognition

Optical character recognition (OCR) is the name of the automatic process of reading machine-printed or hand-printed text. Character-recogni-

◀ Transparencies for scanning are mounted onto the glass of a drum scanner. Drum scanners work by transmission of light through the image, where it is collected by a sensor located at the center of the drum.

tion machines are used mainly for the input of data to computer systems. When scanned, a page of text is converted to pixels, but standard word processing packages are unable to recognize the images as text, so it has to go through a complex software transformation to turn it into a form that can be manipulated for other purposes.

Character-recognition technology has been around since the 1950s, but until the 1990s, it was unreliable and limited to work with particular typefaces and point sizes. One of the first systems used stored bitmaps of fonts such as Courier, Times, and Helvetica, which it compared with the bitmaps of scanned letters to determine the most probable candidate. The main problem with this matrix, or pattern-matching, system was that it could not read multifont documents, proportionally spaced fonts, or sizes beyond those already programmed.

Progress came with the ability to match features of the letter shape, a process called feature extraction. This approach established rules about how the circles, arcs, and straight lines of characters were linked to each other so that a letter could be identified whatever the typeface. For example, the letter "a" is defined as a circle with a short line on the right-hand side and an optional arc over the circle connecting the two. If the software detects these characteristics on a scanned letter, it is coded as an "a."

While feature recognition improved the range of typefaces that could be read, in practice, it was no more accurate, as printing faults and blemishes in the paper could cause letters to be wrongly identified. Much effort was put into ways to remove this background "noise" so that fragments of type could be interpreted as individual letters.

Most modern OCR programs use a combination of pattern matching and feature extraction backed up by powerful software programs that make intuitive guesses as to what a letter might be based upon the word containing it. These programs have given OCR a 98 percent efficiency in capturing texts. Noise is eliminated because the program compares the millions of different ways the bitmaps in a word can be arranged and then calculates the probability that the right interpretation has been made. Much of this progress has come from research into artificial intelligence and cognitive sciences and discoveries about how the brain recognizes images.

Other types of recognition

Magnetic-ink-character-recognition (MICR) equipment is used by banks for sorting checks using the coded information printed in magnetic ink at the bottom of each check. The characters

◀ An optical reader eye with five lines of 72 photodiodes arranged on a silicon chip.

are specially designed to be read easily by machine and are printed in magnetic ink. The characters are magnetized just before passing under the scanner, which is similar to the tape head used in a tape recorder, and are recognized as a series of bars of varying width or spacing. The visual appearance of the characters is similar to that of ordinary characters. This technique has the advantage that dirt and other unwanted artifacts are usually not magnetic and therefore go unregistered by the machine. MICR characters can also be read optically.

Though not strictly using character recognition, OMR (optical mark recognition) machines were the first type of machines to be able to process hand-printed forms directly. OMR machines work by detecting the position of marks made by pencil or pen in boxes on prepared forms and perform no recognition as such. The performance of OMR machines depends on how carefully the marks have been made and positioned by the person completing the form. OMR is often used in applications where one set of options has to be specified, such as survey polls.

Handwriting is much more difficult to read and interpret and has had limited success in OCR applications. Several machines are available that will recognize numerals and a limited number of alphabetic characters, but their speed and reject rates are significantly worse than those for machine print. To achieve even moderate success, the writers have to print the characters carefully within boxes printed on special forms.

SEE ALSO: CHARGE-COUPLED DEVICE • DIODE • FILTER, OPTICAL • LENS • LIGHT AND OPTICS • PHOTOMULTIPLIER TUBE

Optometry

▲ External features of the eye, such as the cornea, are assessed using a slit lamp microscope, a variable source of light that projects an image of the slit onto the eye. Sometimes drops are put into the eye to shrink or dilate the pupils or to show up scratches and other defects on the cornea.

Optometry is the science and practice of testing the sharpness of vision and, when necessary, prescribing the appropriate spectacles or contact lenses. The term comes from the Greek words *optos*, meaning "seen" or "invisible," and *metron*, meaning "a measure."

Many people are uncertain about the difference between an optometrist, an optician, and an ophthalmologist. An optometrist is a person trained and qualified to measure the optical power of the human eye and to prescribe correcting lenses. There are two kinds of opticians. An ophthalmic optician is the same as an optometrist; a dispensing optician is legally permitted to fit spectacle frames and may fit contact lenses but may not prescribe the power of lenses. An ophthalmologist is a medically qualified doctor and surgeon who has specialized in the disorders of the eyes.

Ophthalmologists are skilled in eye testing, but most hospital ophthalmologists rely on trained optometrists to perform this work.

Visual acuity testing

Visual acuity means "sharpness of vision," and it is measured by asking the patient to read a well-lit chart with lines of letters of diminishing size set at a measured distance of 20 ft. (6 m). The chart is set at an exact distance for two reasons: distance determines the apparent size of the letters, and a distance of 20 ft. ensures that the patient will not be tempted to focus the eyes. In people with optically normal eyes, focusing is required only for close viewing. The letters are read with each eye in turn, and the optometrist makes a note of the lowest complete line that can be read correctly.

Near the foot of the chart is a line of letters that everyone with normal vision can read with each eye separately. A person able to read this line is said to have 20/20 (or 6/6, measured in meters) vision in each eye. This ability is called the visual acuity, and it is a measure of the size of letters that can be read at 20 ft. (6 m). Many people with normal visual acuity can read letters smaller than those in the normal line.

A person who can correctly make out only those letters of twice this size is said to have a visual acuity of 20/40, and a person who can read only the top letter of the chart has an acuity of 20/200. The top letter is ten times the size of the those on the normal (20/20) line. A person with normal vision can make out the 20/40 line at a distance of 40 ft. (13 m) and can read the top letter of the chart at 200 ft. (65 m). At distances of 20, 30, 40, 60, 80, 120, and 200 ft., the apparent size of the letters on the appropriate line is the same. At each of these distances, the images of the letters formed on the retinas of the eyes are the same. Visual acuity is recorded as 20/20, 20/30, 20/40, 20/60, 20/80, 20/120, or 20/200. It may also be recorded as "better than 20/20" or "worse than 20/200."

Refraction

The natural light-focusing power (refractive state) of the eye is called refraction, and the same word is used for the process of determining this power, which can be done in various ways, depending on the skill of the optometrist. A simple but not ideal method is to put an empty spectacle frame, known as a trial frame, in front of the patient's eyes and to insert lenses of different power until the optimum degree of sharpness is achieved. This method requires the cooperation of the patient and may result in prescription of overly strong lenses in the case of near sight (myopia) and unduly weak lenses in the case of far sight (hyperopia). Such errors will occur if the patient is allowed to focus the eyes during the examination.

The definitive method of determining the refraction is known as retinoscopy or, sometimes, skiaskopy. Retinoscopy does not mean "examination of the retina" as is sometimes thought. It is an objective method of measuring the optical power of the lenses of the eye—the cornea and the internal crystalline lens—and the effective distance of these from the retina. It requires only that the patient keep his or her eyes open and look into the distance, and it can be used on all patients with clear lenses, including small babies and uncooperative adults. Retinoscopy is a difficult technique, but it is extremely accurate when performed by a skilled examiner.

Retinoscopy is performed using a simple, self-illuminating instrument called a retinoscope, which projects a fine beam of light into the eye. The optometrist is able to look along this beam and works at a standard distance, usually 30 in. (75 cm). Light reflected from the patient's retina is observed by the optometrist as the beam is moved slightly from side to side. The direction in which the emerging light is observed to move, relative to the movement of the retinoscope, is determined by the refraction of the eye. Light emerging from a nearsighted eye moves in the opposite direction from light emerging from a farsighted eye.

In retinoscopy, trial lenses are held in the proper spectacle position in front of the eye until the movement of the emerging light ceases. This point is called the neutral point. The required spectacle correction can then be easily calculated from the power and type of lens required to achieve neutralization.

Retinoscopy would be easy if the refraction of all eyes was like that of a perfectly spherical lens, but this is seldom the case. The greater part of the optical power of the eye is provided by the curvature of the cornea, and corneal curvature is seldom the same in all meridia. In many eyes, the curvature from top to bottom is significantly steeper (of lesser radius) than the curvature from side to side. This difference in curvature causes a reduction in visual acuity of a kind called astigmatism. The situation is further complicated by the fact that the meridian of maximal steepness of curvature is not necessarily vertical. It may lie at

▼ A patient undergoing optometric testing. The optometrist is able to change the strength of the lenses placed in front of the eye until the patient can read the letters on a chart 20 ft. (6 m) away.

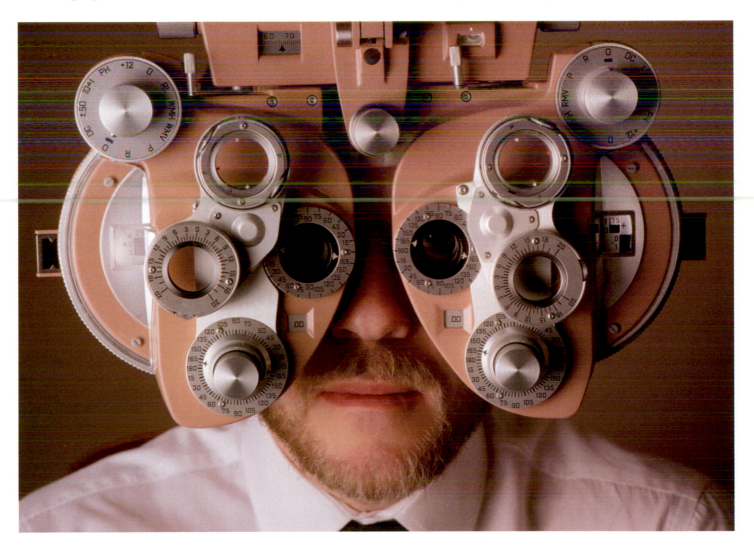

any angle. For accurate prescription of correcting lenses, the angle (axis) at which the steepest curve is set must be known. The axis of the flattest curve is always exactly at right angles to that of the steepest curve.

For these reasons, an optometrist performing retinoscopy must start by determining the angle of the two axes of curvature. This angle is found by moving the light in all directions and noting the effect on the emerging beam. In the higher degrees of astigmatism, there will be a considerable difference in the power of the lenses needed to neutralize movement in the two meridia. It is not uncommon for one meridian to be nearsighted and the other farsighted.

Having determined the two powers and the axis of maximum curvature, the optometrist is able to calculate the appropriate prescription. This prescription is set up in a trial frame, and the patient is again asked to read the chart. Small adjustments to the prescription or to the axis of the additional curvature used to correct the astigmatism may be made at this stage.

Machines known as automatic refractors have been developed that can perform retinoscopy rapidly and accurately, and the best of them perform as well as a skilled retinoscopist. Some machines use an infrared beam. Many of these machines will print out the appropriate spectacle prescription for the patient.

Once the basic refraction is determined and an accurate correction for distance vision known, the prescription of glasses for near vision is a simple matter of adding the required amount of plus power (weakly magnifying lens power) to compensate for the deficiency in the patient's own ability to focus. Optometrists are careful to prescribe the minimum additional plus power needed to allow comfortable reading. Overprescription unnecessarily limits the depth of field of clear near vision and will often cause dissatisfaction with the glasses.

Disease diagnosis

In addition to prescribing glasses, the optometrist has a responsibility to try to determine whether the patient is suffering from any ocular disease or from any other condition that manifests itself in the eyes. It involves checking that the eyelids and external aspects of the eyeballs and their covering membranes are healthy, that the optical media— the cornea, internal lens, and internal fluids—are optically clear, that the retinas show no visible abnormality, and that the pressure of the fluids in the eyes are within normal limits. Optometrists will also check that there are no obvious restrictions of the fields of vision—the areas of visual perception surrounding the point at which the person is looking—and no obvious gaps in the fields.

In many cases, initial diagnoses of ocular, neurological, and more general diseases are made by optometrists. They require that the optometrist carry out an external and internal examination of the eyes. The latter is done with an illuminating instrument called an ophthalmoscope and may require the use of eyedrops containing a drug that widens (dilates) the pupils. Conditions commonly diagnosed by optometrists include inflammation of the external eye membranes (conjunctivitis), corneal opacities and ulcers, internal lens opacities (cataracts), abnormally high internal eye pressure (glaucoma), diabetes and high blood pressure from characteristic changes in the retina, and brain tumors and strokes from visual-field defects and retinal changes.

If any ocular or general disorder is found, the optometrist has a duty to refer the patient to a doctor for further examination and treatment.

FACT FILE

- Color blindness is an inability to distinguish one or more of the colors red, green, and blue. The condition arises because sufferers lack the normal number of cones on the retina capable of detecting these wavelengths of light. Red-blind people confuse red and green colors, green-blind people cannot see green, and blue-blind people have problems with blue and yellow.

- Color blindness is caused by a recessive gene that predominantly affects white males. One in twenty men suffer from this condition, which bars them from certain professions, such as the police, fire service, printing trade, medical practice, and flying aircraft.

- Color blindness does have some advantages. Sufferers are better at seeing outlines, and some flew in spy planes during World War II to spot camouflaged German camps. They also tend to have much better night vision than the rest of the population.

SEE ALSO: COLORIMETRY • CONTACT LENS • EYE • LIGHT AND OPTICS • OPHTHALMOLOGY • OPHTHALMOSCOPE • SPECTACLES

Orbit

An orbit is the path of a body under the gravitational influence of another. It is the balance between the inertia of the moving body and the strength of the gravitational field and can be illustrated by a bullet being fired horizontally: a bullet from a normal gun will eventually fall to the ground, but if it could be given a high enough initial velocity, the downward curvature of its path would become equal to the downward curvature of Earth's surface. It would stay at the same height, although falling continuously.

Strictly speaking, the gravitation of the bullet must affect Earth as well, and the orbit of the bullet is not about the center of Earth but about the center of gravity of the two bodies (the barycenter). Although this correction is negligible for something as light as a bullet, it is important when considering the orbit of the Moon, the mass of which is ⅛₁ that of Earth. Both Earth and the Moon orbit about their barycenter, which is 3,000 miles (5,000 km) from the center of Earth, only 1,000 miles (1,600 km) below its surface.

Shapes of orbits

Sir Isaac Newton showed in 1687 that as a consequence of the inverse square law of gravitation, all orbits must be one of a group of curves known as the conic sections, and in fact about 80 years earlier, the German astronomer Johannes Kepler had found that the planets move in elongated circles called ellipses (which are conic sections), the Sun being at one of the two focuses. Kepler also discovered that a planet moves fastest when at its closest to the Sun (perihelion) and slowest when farthest away (aphelion). The average speed of the planets decreases with increasing distance from the Sun: Mercury, the innermost planet, moves at 108,000 mph (174,000 km/h), Earth at 67,000 mph (108,000 km/h), and the outermost planet, Pluto, at only 10,800 mph (17,400 km/h).

The other conic sections are the circle, the parabola, and the hyperbola. Circular and elliptical orbits are called closed, because the orbiting body returns to its starting place; parabolic and hyperbolic orbits extend to infinity and are open, that is, the orbiting body never returns. Periodic comets have elongated, elliptical orbits, whereas the orbits of nonreturning comets are generally parabolic, although a few appear to be hyperbolic. The orbits of the planets are mainly in the same plane as Earth's orbit.

Spacecraft

The principles governing the motion of the planets about the Sun also apply to the orbits of artificial satellites around Earth. The lowest orbits possible are about 125 miles (200 km) above Earth's surface, because at lower altitudes the drag of the atmosphere slows down the satellite, and it spirals downward until it is destroyed by friction with the dense lower atmosphere. At a height of 125 miles the orbital period is about 90 minutes and the speed 18,000 mph (29,000 km/h). A particularly important Earth orbit used

▲ An infrared view of Saturn showing its orbiting rings made of chunks of ice. The rings are separated into several different bands labeled A to F. The chunks of ice in the F ring are prevented from straying by the gravitational attraction of two small moons—known as shepherd moons called Pandora and Prometheus.

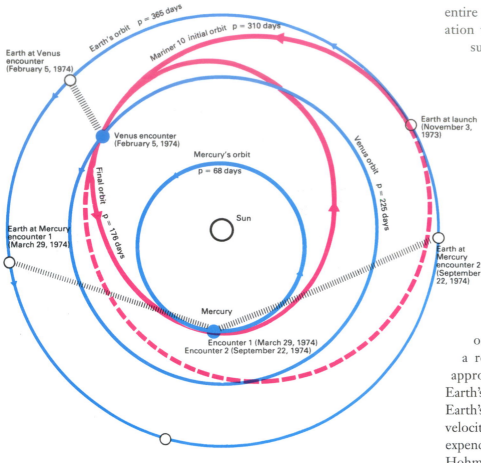

entire surface is covered—an important consideration with some applications, such as military surveillance and meteorological sensing. However, considerably greater launch boost is required to reach orbital velocity for a polar orbit.

A spacecraft traveling at 25,000 mph (40,000 km/h) will escape from Earth's gravitational influence and move into an orbit around the Sun. Planetary probes are put into orbits of this kind: for example, a spacecraft to Mars would be put in an elliptical orbit whose perihelion is at Earth's orbit and whose aphelion is at Mars' orbit. This Hohmann transfer ellipse is achieved by accelerating the spacecraft along the direction in which Earth is moving in its orbit. As a result, the probe starts with the orbital velocity of Earth and requires only a relatively small increase. The alternative approach, namely, to accelerate outward from Earth's orbit directly toward Mars, would not use Earth's velocity as a contribution to the spacecraft velocity and hence would require a much greater expenditure of fuel. The disadvantage of using the Hohmann ellipse is that the journey takes a long time—260 days for an Earth-to-Mars flight.

for satellites is at a height of 22,283 miles (35,860 km), where the orbital period corresponds to the rotation period of Earth so that the satellite appears to remain stationary over a particular spot on the surface.

Spacecraft are usually launched eastward so that they start with the velocity of Earth at the launch site—about 1,000 mph (1,600 km/h) at the Kennedy Space Center, Cape Canaveral—and so need less of a launch boost to reach the orbital velocity. This approach puts the satellite into an orbit either along or inclined to Earth's equator.

When an orbit is inclined at 90 degrees to the equator, it becomes a polar orbit. With such orbits, Earth rotates at right angles to the movement of the satellite so that, over a period, the

▲ Mariner 10 in orbit. It flew past Venus in 1974 and used that planet's gravitational attraction to change course.

▼ Satellites put into orbit at high speed are pulled by gravity into a downward path that keeps them at a constant height above Earth's surface.

The most economical method of traveling to the two planets between Earth and the Sun—Mercury and Venus—is to use rockets to slow the spacecraft to a speed less than Earth's: it will then travel in an ellipse with the distance of Earth as aphelion. In any of these transfer ellipses, the target planet must be at the right part of its orbit when the probe arrives there, and hence, the launch date of the spacecraft is restricted to a few days each year (the launch window) when Earth and the target planet are suitably placed relative to each other.

FACT FILE

■ Orbiting debris introduced into space poses a threat to space missions. A small chip in one of space shuttle Challenger's windows has proved on analysis to have resulted from a collision with a fragment of paint from some other project. Much of the orbiting junk is large enough to cause serious damage.

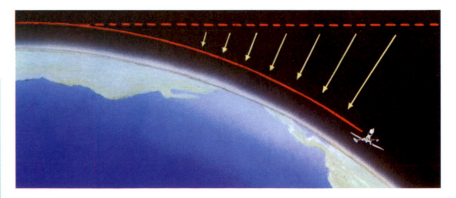

SEE ALSO: EARTH • ENERGY, MASS, AND WEIGHT • GRAVITY • INERTIA • NEWTON'S LAWS • ROCKET AND SPACE PROPULSION • SATELLITE, ARTIFICIAL • SOLAR SYSTEM

Organ, Musical

In theory, the pipe organ is a simple musical instrument; in practice, however, its design is complex. Not only is it the largest instrument, but it is also one of the most versatile, in terms of the loudness and variety of sounds it can produce as well as its range, from low notes, which are felt rather than heard, to notes so high that they are almost beyond the range of normal hearing.

The organ works on a principle similar to the pipes of Pan, which were bundles of hollow reeds bound together. A tune is produced by blowing across the tops of the reeds, each of a different length and producing a different note. In an organ, a mechanical bellows provides more wind than can be produced by human lungs, and another mechanism delivers the wind to the selected pipe. Unlike the wind instruments of the orchestra, where one pipe is adapted to play many notes, the organ has a separate pipe for each note.

Early organs

The earliest-known pipe organ, the hydraulus, was made in Greece around 250 B.C.E. and was operated using water pressure. Crude bellows organs existed during Roman times, and by the Middle Ages, organs began to be used in churches to accompany choral singing; they had only one row of pipes, called a rank, with a range of about

the same as that of the human voice, a range smaller than that of the modern piano. (The keyboard of an organ is still smaller than that of the piano: 61 notes as against 88.) This range is known as unison pitch, and the rank that sounds it is called the eight-foot rank, after the length of the open pipe, usually the largest in the rank, that sounds two octaves below middle C with a frequency of 64 hertz (cycles per second).

An open pipe of four feet, half the length, will sound an octave higher; two feet, another octave higher; and so forth. Similarly, doubling the length of any open pipe will make it sound an octave lower. Throughout the world, the sound (pitch) of a rank is always indicated in measurements of feet and fractions of feet.

On the early organs, there was not much variety of tone available because the note always sounded the same whether the key was touched lightly or heavily. When extra ranks were added, the appropriate pipes from each rank all sounded together when the key was pressed, making a loud brilliant noise. For quieter passages, a smaller organ was added, tuned to two feet and played from a separate manual (keyboard). Gradually, the instruments were combined and the keyboards set one above the other as in many of today's organs.

▲ The Lowrey MX-1 electronic organ employs two synthesizers and a microprocessor to give a choice of 12 fully orchestrated backgrounds.

At about the same time, to save wind (which was then generated by muscle power) and to give variety and greater control when the organ was used as a solo instrument, a mechanism was devised to allow the player to stop off certain ranks and select the ones to sound. These controls, usually draw knobs placed on either side of the manuals, are called stops. Four main types of pipes have evolved, made of metal or wood according to their tonal quality: diapason, the original organ sound; flute; string, imitative of a string instrument such as viola da gamba; and reed, which can vary from a very loud trumpet tone to the softer sounds of the oboe and the clarinet stops. Many organs have several varieties of reed tone. Types of pipes as well as ranks can be selected and combined using stops.

Since the 14th century, a pedal board operated by the player's feet has been used to control the longer pipes. During the 18th century, another pedal was incorporated to help control the volume of sound by operating shutters on a swell box

◀ An organ in Netley, Britain, on which the German composer Felix Mendelssohn played.

enclosing the pipes of one or more manuals. A coupler mechanism is used to combine manuals or to connect manuals to pedals.

Modern pipe organs

Each rank has the same number of pipes as there are keys on the manual, usually 61. A medium-sized organ with 30 stops on three manuals and pedals will have no fewer than 1,656 pipes. (The pipes that can be seen on an organ are only a small proportion of the total.) Organs of this size and larger were common in the Netherlands and northern Germany in the 17th century and were the subject of great civic pride and competition. (In 1705, the German composer J. S. Bach is said to have walked from Lüneburg to Lübeck, over 200 miles [322 km], to hear the Danish organist and composer Dietrich Buxtehude play the organ.) These 17th-century instruments are still used when making recordings of the music of the 16th to 18th centuries, and many musicians believe they have never been surpassed for tonal quality. Yet they were built before the Industrial Revolution and rely for their virtual airtightness on the quality of their mainly wooden construction. The oldest organ still in use was built in about 1380 in the church at Sion, in the canton of Valais in Switzerland, and many of the characteristics of modern organ building are present in this ancient instrument.

The mechanism required to control these instruments must be light, quick acting, and trouble free. The pipes are wider than the keys, so mechanical means must be used to spread the vertical motion of the keys to ranks of pipes that can be many feet wide or even on the opposite wall of the church.

Construction

Console is the name given to the assembly of keyboards and controls. The traditional mechanical action between key and pipe system is called a tracker action; it is a system of cranks, rods, levers, slips of wood that push (sliders), slips of wood that pull (trackers), rollers, and valves. When a key, mounted on a fulcrum, is depressed, the other end rises; a rod transmits this vertical motion to an arm on a roller, which in turn transmits it laterally to a similar arm below the pipe that is to sound. This second arm draws down a tracker, which opens a spring-loaded pallet valve; through this valve air passes to the chamber on which all the pipes controlled by that key are mounted. The pipes that sound depend upon which of the stops have been selected. When the player releases the key, the spring closes the valve again, and the air supply ceases.

The action of the stop is transmitted, again by rods and cranks, to a glider mounted between the air channel and the base of the pipe. When a drawstop is pulled, the slider moves so that a hole in it lines up with the foot of the pipe and allows the pipe to sound. Today many organs operate the valves and stops by means of solenoid switches actuated from the console or by compressed air, methods that simplify transmission of motion. Many recitalists still prefer tracker action, and many organs are still built with it because of the more intimate control it provides.

A plentiful supply of wind (air under mild compression) is essential, and the pressure must not fluctuate. For centuries, leather bellows were used to raise the pressure, at first, of the simple blacksmith's forge type but developing into a powerful pump with twin bellows alternately feeding a large pleated leather reservoir. Weights placed on top of the reservoir provided sufficient pressure for the numerous pipes.

The bellows were driven by the muscle power of several people working long levers or treadles. Human power was supplanted by steam at first; today the wind supply is generated almost universally by electrically driven blowers.

Electronic organ

The electronic organ, once regarded as the poor relation of the pipe organ, has developed since the 1960s to the extent that modern models bear little resemblance to the earliest ones.

The electronic organ may be voiced either classically or to suit light music. The stops on the first type are named in a way similar to those on a pipe organ, for example, rohr flute, gedeckt, and bourdon. An organ voiced to suit light music is the type of electronic organ with which most people are familiar, and it is often referred to as a home organ or entertainment organ.

The home, or entertainment, organ may have one, two, or three keyboards, or manuals. The size of the manuals in terms of octaves varies according to price range. The organ is also equipped with bass pedals, which are played with the foot, and they may consist of 13 foot pedals, in which case the instrument is termed a spinet organ. Larger models are equipped with a full pedal board, which radiates below the organ bench. The spinet pedal board can play only one note at a time, even when two pedals are depressed, whereas the full pedal board can be played by both feet simultaneously as with the pipe organ pedal board.

Volume is controlled in all cases by one of the pedals, which is operated by the right foot in the manner of an automobile gas pedal.

▶ Some manufacturers design organs that can be assembled with a minimum of technical knowledge; many enthusiasts reduce costs by assembling their own organ from a kit of components.

Each organ has its own built-in amplification, although there is normally a facility for connection to external speakers.

Electronic methods

The electronic organ has progressed in tone generation from using electrostatic and electromagnetic methods through multiple electronic oscillators, multiderivative dividers (to improve tone and keep the organ in tune, as used by Hammond and others), and analog filters to more sophisticated means of sound reproduction. The two major methods in current use are pulse-code modulation (PCM) and frequency modulation (FM), although some electronic keyboard manufacturers still use analog filters in their organs.

PCM is a form of digital recording and playback whereby the waveform of an instrument (for example, a trumpet) is sampled and the information then passed through an analog-to-digital converter (ADC) where it is digitized before being stored in the instrument's memory bank. On playback, the information undergoes a reverse process via a digital-to-analog converter (DAC) to convert the coded information back to sound.

The development of the FM method of sound reproduction is attributed to Dr. John Chowning of Stanford University in California. His extensive work on the effects of FM on musical tone production and the theory of mixing tones to produce sounds resulted in findings that were eventually adopted by various electronic musical instrument manufacturers. At the heart of FM synthesis lie operators and algorithms. Operator is a collective name for modulators and carriers, and a combination of such operators is termed an algorithm. FM is a method of producing complicated waveforms by the interaction of modulator sine waves with carrier sine waves. Modulators and carriers have pure digitally produced sine waves, and by increasing the output of the modulator, a disturbance is caused in the output of the carrier. The fluctuations produced in the modulator sine wave in turn cause a stretching and compression of the waveform that results in tonal change.

The player recalls these preset sounds from the instrument by pressing various buttons, some of which are allocated to each manual and others to the pedal board. Usually the manuals can also be linked to each other to increase the capacity of the organ. Most electronic organs are now equipped with built-in rhythm units that offer various prerecorded rhythm patterns incorporating a wide range of nontonal instruments, such as drums, cymbals, and claves. In some instances, sounds such as hand clapping are available, and some instruments are preprogrammed to produce voicelike exclamations, and others can reproduce the sound of a choir, albeit by use of vowel sounds only. Key scanning and tone management are controlled by microprocessors, while digital displays advise the player of various functions, including the chosen registration, time signature, and rhythm speed.

Other instruments

Many electronic organs are preset with sounds during manufacture, but they also incorporate a synthesizer section that gives the player the facility to manufacture specific sounds. The synthesizer, however, is an instrument in its own right. Evolving in the main from the FM method of sound generation, it enables the player to compose an almost limitless range of sounds.

Closely allied to the multikeyboard is the single keyboard, which although having only one manual, can be attached to a portable pedal board to extend the bass section or linked to a multikeyboard to provide an additional manual. Usually the single keyboard is capable not only of being played as a conventional manual but also of being divided to give the player the effect of two shortened but separate manuals on which melody and accompaniment can be played with differing registrations. As with the larger organs, single keyboards have a diverse range of easy-play features, including light-emitting diodes, which indicate chords to help the learner, automatic chords, key transposers to vary the key that is being played, and arpeggios to avoid the need for quick fingering.

◄ The electronic organ is a versatile instrument that can be used to mimic the sound of an acoustic piano or be employed for its own musical characteristics.

New developments

Musical instrument digital interface (MIDI), invented by the electronic instruments company Roland, has become a universal language adopted by many major manufacturers. Any instrument equipped with MIDI can be connected to a computer or to other similarly equipped pieces of peripheral equipment, for example, keyboards, sequencers, computers, drum machines, and synthesizers, and can be used to control the peripheral items from the one source. In effect, the MIDI allows suitably equipped instruments to talk to each other digitally, and because the same system of interfacing is used by various manufacturers, the equipment of these various sources is compatible.

RAM-ROM packs are also used on electronic organs, single keyboards, and synthesizers. The RAM (random-access memory) pack is a cartridge that is slotted into the control panel of a suitably equipped keyboard. It allows the player to prerecord settings or whole performances for playing at a later date. After preprogramming, the player can insert the RAM pack into the slot and push a button, and the instrument will load the information and set the registers automatically.

SEE ALSO: Amplifier • Analog and digital systems • Oscillator • Piano • Radio • Sound • Sound effects and sampling • Sound mixing • Synthesizer

Oscillator

An oscillator is a system that exhibits periodic behavior: its state changes in a regular, repeated manner. Pendulums, tuning forks, piano strings, and tuned electrical circuits are examples of systems that can oscillate if stimulated.

The behavior of an oscillating system can be described by plotting against time a variable such as the displacement of a pendulum from its neutral position or the potential difference between two points in an electrical circuit. In many cases, such a plot is sinusoidal (having the form of a sine wave), and the system is then a harmonic oscillator. More complex oscillators, notably some electronic types of oscillators, have plots that are square or saw-toothed waves.

Pendulum

A swinging pendulum is a simple oscillator, but it serves to illustrate properties that are shared by more complex oscillators. At the center of the swing—the neutral point—the pendulum has kinetic energy due to the motion of its mass.

At the top of each swing, the mass momentarily comes to rest, and the kinetic energy of the pendulum falls to zero. That energy has not disappeared, however: it has changed into an additional amount of potential energy that the mass has gained by rising above the level of the neutral point in a gravitational field. When the mass starts to fall again, it starts to lose potential energy and gain kinetic energy until it reaches the neutral point and starts a new upswing. Hence, the oscillation of a pendulum is associated with a repeated exchange between two forms of energy.

Gravity is the agent that causes a swinging pendulum mass to repeatedly decelerate, change direction, and accelerate. More specifically, it is the component of the mass's weight that acts at right angles to the pendulum string. This force increases with increasing displacement from the neutral point and acts in the opposite direction. A force that changes in this way is called a restoring force, since it tends to restore the mass to its neutral position when displaced.

Amplitude, period, and frequency

Oscillations are characterized by three properties: amplitude, period, and frequency. The amplitude of a pendulum is the maximum displacement at the end of each swing. It depends on the initial energy input that sets the pendulum in motion.

The period is the interval of time between consecutive instants when the system is in the same condition. For a pendulum, period is the time taken between two instants when the mass is moving in the same direction at the same point in the swing. The period of a pendulum swing on Earth depends only on the length of the string (it is proportional to the square root of the length).

Frequency is the reciprocal of period, so whereas period is the number of seconds per swing, frequency is the number of swings per second. The unit "per second" is otherwise called the hertz (Hz). A pendulum that has a swing period of 0.5 seconds has a frequency of 2 Hz.

Damping

An ideal pendulum in a vacuum would continue to swing forever as its energy switched back and forth between kinetic and potential forms. In practice, air resistance absorbs some of the energy of the pendulum with each swing. Consequently, the amplitude of a pendulum swinging in air diminishes until it comes to rest.

The effect of air resistance on a pendulum is an example of damping. In more general terms, damping is any phenomenon that tends to diminish the energy, and therefore the amplitude, of an oscillating system. When it is desirable to keep vibration to a minimum, such as in a vehicle moving on an uneven road surface, the energy of an oscillator can be dissipated using devices such as damping springs and shock absorbers.

The effects of damping can be overcome by pumping energy into the system at a sufficient rate. In the case of a pendulum, pushing the pendulum at an appropriate point would replace the energy lost to air resistance.

▲ A tuning fork is an example of a mechanical oscillator. Striking the base of the fork on a hard surface provides the energy that sets it oscillating at its natural frequency. That frequency can then be used as a benchmark for tuning instruments.

Resonance

As discussed, a pendulum has a frequency at which it oscillates—its natural frequency—that is determined by the length of its string. The swing amplitude increases if a repeated shove is applied at that natural frequency. A shove at any other frequency will coincide with the swing direction on some occasions but oppose it on others. Over time, the amount of energy transferred to the swing will average to zero.

In general, a system that is capable of oscillating will absorb energy from a stimulus that oscillates at its natural frequency. This phenomenon can be seen when rubbing the rim of a wine glass to make it ring. The vibrations of the finger on the rim consist of many frequencies, but the glass absorbs energy only from vibrations that coincide with its natural frequency, at which it rings.

Resonant circuits

A resonant circuit is an electrical circuit in which electrons move back and forth in a manner reminiscent of a pendulum. The key components are a capacitor and an inductor. A capacitor consists of two conducting plates separated by an insulating medium; an electric field exists in that medium when the plates carry opposite charges. An inductor is essentially a coiled conductor; a magnetic field passes through the loop when current flows through the conductor.

At one end of the "swing," electrons collect on one plate of the capacitor and positive charges collect on the other. The energy of the system is then stored in the electrical field between the two plates. During the swing, electrons pass from one capacitor plate to the other via the inductor, creating a magnetic field that stores energy. The restoring force of the system stems from the potential difference between the capacitor plates.

At the point that is analogous to the bottom of a pendulum swing, there is no charge difference between the capacitor plates, so there is no electrical field and no potential difference to drive the current. All the energy of the oscillator is stored in the magnetic field through the inductor.

The magnetic field then starts to collapse, delivering its energy to the electrons in the inductor and keeping them moving. At the same time, the capacitor starts to get charged in the opposite polarity, creating a growing potential difference that slows the electrons until all the energy is once again stored in the electric field.

The natural frequency (f_0) of the oscillation of electrons through a resonant circuit is determined by the square root of the inductance (L) and capacitance (C) according to the equation $f_0 = 2\pi\sqrt{(LC)}$. In practice, f_0 is varied by changing the separation of the capacitor plates so as to alter the value of capacitance in the circuit. Just as in the case of a pendulum, the amplitude of oscillation will increase if the circuit is stimulated at its natural frequency.

In tuning circuits for radio applications, signals from antennas stimulate the resonant circuit. A loop attached to the aerial is placed alongside the inductor, so oscillating signals produced by radio waves striking the aerial create an oscillating magnetic field. That field also passes through the inductor of the resonant circuit, providing a means of transferring energy from the aerial to the circuit. The circuit absorbs energy from the aerial only at frequencies at or very near to its natural frequency, and thus, a tuner filters one station from others at similar frequencies.

In an electronic oscillator for producing signals, a resonant circuit forms part of a circuit with a vacuum-tube or transistor amplifier. The base signal for amplification is picked up by an inductor close to that of the tuned circuit. Part of the amplified output signal is then fed back to the tuned circuit to sustain its oscillation.

Other signal generators

The piezoelectric effect of quartz crystals is used to create sinusoidal electrical signals of precise frequencies. The natural frequency of vibration for the compression and expansion of a quartz crystal is accompanied by a varying potential difference across opposite faces of the crystal. That potential difference can be harnessed in a variant of the tuned circuit already described.

Square-wave signals can be generated by arranging transistors so that they switch one another on and off in a regular manner that produces abrupt changes in voltage connected by plateaux of constant voltages. Sawtooth signals are produced by circuits that repeatedly charge capacitors to a threshold value and then discharge them.

Signals at microwave frequencies are produced by magnetrons, tuned cavities in which electromagnetic fields resonate. Electrical circuits are inefficient at such high frequencies.

▲ A resonant circuit based on a quartz crystal. The crystal is the square slab, and it is suspended between contacts that connect it to the rest of the electrical circuit.

SEE ALSO: AMPLIFIER • ELECTRONICS • MICROWAVE OVEN • OSCILLOSCOPE • PENDULUM • PIEZOELECTRIC MATERIAL • RADIO • SYNTHESIZER

Oscilloscope

An oscilloscope is an instrument that displays the variation of one electrical signal against another on a luminous screen. The two variables are plotted against a horizontal x-axis and a vertical y-axis (the terms *x-axis* and *y-axis* originate from the Cartesian coordinate system for defining locations in graphical plots, or graphs).

In many cases, the x-axis variable is time, so the plot displays the evolution of the y-axis value with time. The electrical signal whose voltage is plotted on the y-axis can originate from any of a diverse range of sources—a microphone, a signal-generating circuit, a pressure sensor, the ignition circuit of a car engine, or an electrode on a heart patient's chest, for example. For this reason, oscilloscopes have uses in a wide range of settings, from hospitals through electronics research and teaching laboratories to car workshops.

Working principles

The first oscilloscopes, called Braun tubes, were developed in 1897 by the German physicist Karl Braun. They were developed from cathode-ray tubes—evacuated glass tubes in which electrons are released by a heated cathode, and then accelerated and formed into a beam by a series of anodes (positive electrodes). The cathode ray travels toward a screen at one end of the tube, and chemical compounds called phosphors glow at the point on the screen where the electrons strike.

Without other influences, the electron beam strikes the center of the screen. The beam can be directed to portray the variations of electrical signals by deflecting it between two pairs of metal plates. A potential difference between the vertical pair—the X plates—creates an electrical field that deflects the beam along the x-axis toward the more positive plate; a potential difference between the horizontal plates—the Y plates—deflects the beam along the y-axis.

The phosphors that coat the inside of the screen are so called for their property of phosphorescence—they glow when excited by radiation, such as an electron beam, and continue to glow for some time after irradiation has ceased. This afterglow is useful, since it holds a trace of the path of the beam for an instant after the beam has passed. Coupled with persistence of vision—the eye's natural ability to hold an image for some time after it has passed—phosphorescence is the key to how oscilloscopes make it possible to observe the variation of a signal with time.

▼ The main diagram shows the circuitry of a typical oscilloscope. The input signal first passes through an amplifier that adjusts its amplitude to make it measurable. This signal then passes to the Y plates. Part of the signal also passes to a trigger circuit that emits a pulse when the signal reaches a certain value. The trigger pulse switches on the electron gun and activates the time-base circuit, starting the sweep.

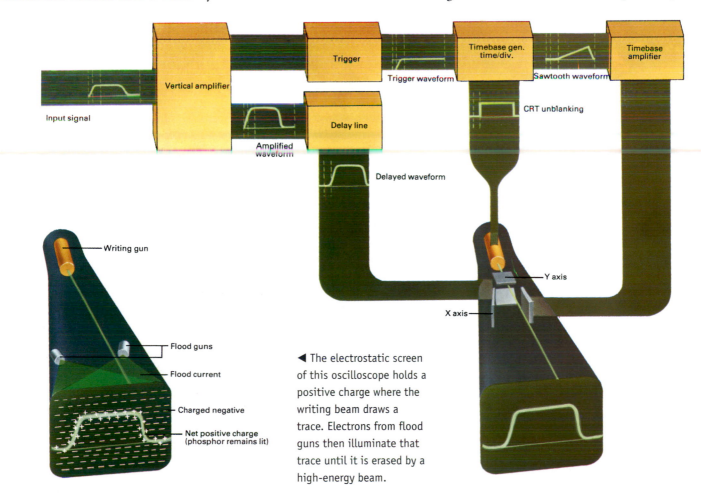

Input signal

Vertical amplifier

Amplified waveform

Trigger

Delay line

Trigger waveform

Delayed waveform

Timebase gen. time/div.

Sawtooth waveform

CRT unblanking

Timebase amplifier

Writing gun

Flood guns

Flood current

Charged negative

Net positive charge (phosphor remains lit)

Y axis

X axis

◄ The electrostatic screen of this oscilloscope holds a positive charge where the writing beam draws a trace. Electrons from flood guns then illuminate that trace until it is erased by a high-energy beam.

Some oscilloscopes store traces on electrostatic screens that become positively charged when irradiated by electron beams. When a display of the stored trace is required, a flood gun in the tube emits a diffuse spray of electrons toward the screen. The positively charged trace attracts electrons, causing the trace to glow again when they strike.

Time-base circuitry

If an input signal is connected to the Y plates, sometimes through an amplifier, variations in the voltage of that signal will deflect the beam up and down as the electrical field along the y-axis varies. Time-base circuitry provides an X-plate signal that makes the beam sweep steadily from left to right across the screen and then jump back, so the beam plots the Y-plate signal against time.

The signal to the X plates must start at a voltage that deflects the beam to the extreme left of the screen, change in a linear manner to a voltage that deflects the beam to the extreme right, and then return to the first voltage in the shortest possible time. Such a signal is provided by a sawtooth oscillator, so called for the shape of a plot of its output voltage against time.

Synchronization

Occasionally, a single sweep is used to record the variation of an irregular signal. In most cases, however, repeated sweeps trace the variation of a periodic signal—one that repeats itself at regular intervals. In this mode, each sweep must start at exactly the same point if a clear trace is to be obtained. The system that ensures this will happen is called the synchronization, or sync, circuit.

The sync circuit generates a trigger pulse when the input signal reaches a threshold value. The trigger pulse initiates the sweep signal from the time-base circuit, and at the end of one sweep, the beam returns to the start position and the time-base circuit then awaits another pulse from the sync circuit. Since the time-base sweep is triggered at the same point in every cycle of the signal, the trace is steady and does not drift.

Multiple traces

It is sometimes desirable to display more than one signal on a single screen at one time, for the purpose of comparing two or more signals or simply for the convenience of viewing two signals on one oscilloscope.

Individual traces are shifted to separate vertical positions on the screen by adding a fixed voltage to the signal. The variations of the signal then appear as oscillations of its trace around a y-axis position that corresponds to the fixed voltage.

In one configuration, the oscilloscope completes the sweep for one signal before starting the sweep for the next signal. A high-persistence screen—one whose phosphor coating glows for a particularly long time—prevents each trace from fading between its consecutive sweeps.

As an alternative, the oscilloscope can switch between signals several times in each sweep. The switching rate must be much greater than the speed at which the signal varies. Otherwise, the details of one signal will be lost if it occurs while the oscilloscope is displaying a different signal.

Some oscilloscopes use multiple beams to display separate traces. The beam from the electron gun is in this case divided into the required number of beams before it reaches the deflector plates. Each beam has its own Y plates, but a single set of X plates produces the sweep for all the beams.

Lissajous patterns

Lissajous patterns are traces that appear when one signal input is connected to the Y plates and another signal feeds to the X plates in place of the signal from the time-base and synchronization circuitry. The oscillator then displays the variation of one signal relative to the other.

Unlike traces in the time-base mode, which start at one side of the screen and track to the other, typical Lissajous patterns are closed loops. For example, the Lissajous pattern for two sinusoidal signals will be a circle or an ellipse if both signals are of the same frequency, but one signal is 90 degrees out of phase with the other. The exact form of the pattern also depends on the amplitude of one signal relative to the other.

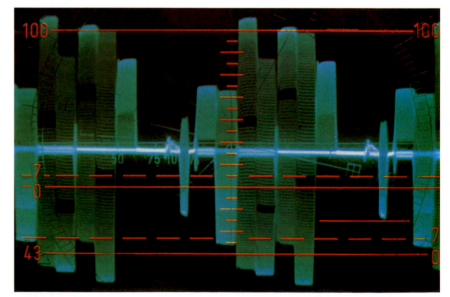

▼ This oscilloscope has illuminated scales that facilitate the measurement of waveforms. The red scale allows measurement of peak heights, while the radial scale is useful for measuring characteristics of Lissajous patterns.

SEE ALSO: AMPLIFIER • CATHODE-RAY TUBE • OSCILLATOR

Osmosis

If two solutions that have different concentrations are separated from each other by a permeable membrane, it is sometimes found that the solvent (the dissolving liquid) molecules will pass through the membrane more quickly than the solute (the dissolved substance) molecules. The result is that the solvent passes from the less concentrated solution to the more concentrated one, tending to equalize the concentrations. This process is called osmosis.

The phenomenon was discovered in 1748 by the French physicist Abbé Jean Antoine Nollet. He covered the wide end of a glass tube with parchment paper and filled the tube with a solution of sucrose (a sugar) in water so that it reached a mark on a glass stem drawn out from the other end of the tube. When the covered end of the tube was immersed in a beaker of water, the level of the solution in the stem rose because the water molecules in the beaker were diffusing through the parchment more rapidly than the sucrose molecules leaving the glass tube by the same route. The rise in the solution level in the glass stem created a hydrostatic pressure, subsequently termed osmotic pressure, which is a measure of the pressure caused by the migration of water through the membrane. Since the parchment membrane was slightly permeable to the sucrose molecules, the osmotic pressure was not permanent.

The word *osmosis* comes from the word *osmose*, introduced in 1854 by the Scottish chemist Thomas Graham, who also discovered the principle of dialysis. Dialysis is the diffusion of solute molecules through a membrane, a process used in artificial kidney machines.

Semipermeable membranes

When a membrane is permeable only to solvent molecules, it is called a semipermeable membrane. In 1877, the German plant biologist Willhelm Pfeffer discovered that a gelatinous precipitate of copper ferrocyanide ($Cu_2Fe(CN)_6$), formed on the walls of a porous clay cell, exhibited semipermeability to cane sugar solutions, and he was able to achieve osmotic pressures four times atmospheric pressure for a 6 percent by weight solution.

The membranes surrounding the cells of animal and vegetable tissue frequently exhibit semipermeability. If the outer cells of a plant such as *Tradescantia discolor* are examined under a microscope, it will be seen that the cells are pressed against the cellulose sheath surrounding them. When the cell is placed in a 7.5 percent sucrose solution, however, the osmotic pressure of the solution is greater than that of the cell sap, and water passes out of the cell, causing it to contract away from the cellulose sheath. This phenomenon is known as plasmolysis, and a similar process occurs in the preservation of jellies.

Reverse osmosis

When a pressure greater than the osmotic pressure is applied to an aqueous solution, water molecules can be driven through a semipermeable membrane. The solution is concentrated, and pure water is obtained on the other side of the membrane. The membranes can be formed by precipitating materials such as zirconium oxide (ZrO_2) on a porcelain support. Two widely used membrane materials are cellulose acetate and Permasep. Cellulose acetate membranes have two

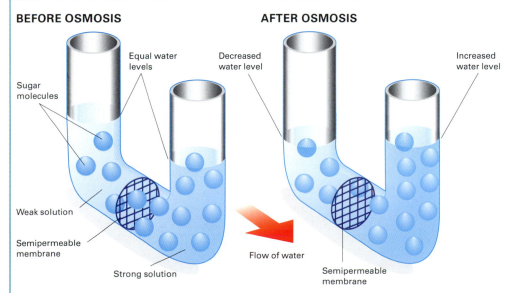

BEFORE OSMOSIS

- Equal water levels
- Sugar molecules
- Weak solution
- Semipermeable membrane
- Strong solution

AFTER OSMOSIS

- Decreased water level
- Increased water level
- Flow of water
- Semipermeable membrane

OSMOSIS

Two solutions, such as sugar in water, separated by a semipermeable membrane will be modified by osmosis to give solutions of intermediate strength. Mixing occurs as water crosses the membrane from the weaker to the stronger solution. The sugar molecules are too large to pass across the membrane, so the concentrations of the two solutions changes. This process continues until either the concentrations are the same or until the pressure of the water prevents further osmosis.

layers, one film and one sponge, that are used in thicknesses of 50 to 135 mm. Permasep is a synthetic polymer that is made of many hollow fibers.

A major application of reverse osmosis is in the desalination of brackish water and seawater. High pressures—200 to 1,000 lbs. per sq. in. (14–70 kg/cm^2) or more, depending on the salinity—are used to extract around 50 percent of brackish input water in purified form—though with seawater, the recovery falls to around half that level. Commercial desalination plants can have very high outputs, with fresh water production rates of tens of millions of gallons per day.

Reverse osmosis is also widely used in food processing, with an important application being the concentration of cheese whey. About 30 percent of the nutritive value of milk is lost in the whey, which contains about 7 percent dissolved solids. These dissolved solids consist mainly of lactose but also contain from 0.5 to 1 percent protein and about 1 percent lactic acid and other salts. The whey is first passed through an open membrane, which retains the protein fraction for subsequent spray drying. The filtrate from this stage then passes to a tight membrane, where mainly lactose is retained. The water and some of the dissolved salts are discharged after passing through the membrane. The process not only recovers valuable food sources but also reduces the polluting effect of cheese whey.

Another application of reverse osmosis is in the treatment of hazardous waste. The metal-plating industry, for example, produces waste water with environmentally harmful concentrations of metals such as cadmium, zinc, and nickel. These metals may be removed using cellulose acetate with an efficiency of between 90 and 95 percent. The resulting concentrated solution of water and metal may then be returned to the plating bath and the cleaned water may be reused for rinsing the plated metal, thus reducing wastage. Similarly, reverse osmosis can be used to clean hazardous waste in landfill sites. Here, the harmful chemicals, known as leachate, can be filtered from the waste to meet more stringent standards of environmental cleanliness.

The techniques of nanofiltration, ultrafiltration, and microfiltration are means of filtering different sizes of molecules and particles. Ultrafiltration is used for separating large molecules from a solvent. In this case, the membrane is formed as a thin film on a supporting base, and a large number of very small channels pass through it. Pressure is applied to the solution and forces the solvent through the pores, with the molecules being retained on the surface of the membrane. Membrane materials are similar to those used in reverse osmosis. Ultrafiltration has been applied to the concentration of a sugar beet extract, skimmed milk, enzymes, and polio vaccines.

The shape and design of the filtering device has a great effect on its overall size and efficiency. Spiral membranes consist of tightly packed filter material that increases the surface area of the semipermeable membrane. These types of filters are widely used for the recovery of sugar. Other shapes include flat sheets and hollow fibers.

Osmotic dehydration

Methods have been developed to preserve fruits by a combination of osmosis and dehydration by fluidized bed, vacuum, or freeze drying. The method has been successfully applied to apple slices that have first been blanched to inactivate the enzymes. The apple slices are immersed in a bath of sucrose syrup at a concentration of about 70 percent by weight and a temperature of 140 to 149°F (60–65°C). The syrup is circulated in the bath by a pump to avoid dilution at the fruit surface and thus maintain the osmotic pressure. After four to six hours, approximately 40 percent of the apple slice weight has been lost by migration of water from the fruit by osmosis, and the apples are then washed to remove sucrose syrup from the fruit surface. Final drying is achieved in a vacuum oven.

◀ The level of the sugar solution in an inverted funnel rises by osmosis as water passes through a membrane at the lower end of the funnel.

SEE ALSO: CELL BIOLOGY • DESALINATION • DIALYSIS MACHINE • SUGAR REFINING

Osteopathy

Osteopathy is a therapy that involves manipulating the bones, joints, muscles, and ligaments. Osteopathy (from the Greek *osteo*, bone, and *pathos*, disease) is founded on the belief that a disturbance in one function of the body can alter the balance and affect another quite separate function. The osteopath claims to be able to treat a wide range of illnesses besides bone or joint disorders. However, osteopaths will not treat some conditions, including fractures, malignancy, acute arthrosis, various disease of the bones, severe cases of disk prolapse that cause neurological problems, and tuberculosis.

Dr. Andrew Taylor Still, the U.S. inventor of osteopathy, founded the first osteopathic training organization in the world, The American School of Osteopathy, in 1892. There are now 19 osteopathic colleges and over 200 osteopathic hospitals in the country, and it is expected that by the year 2020 there will be 80,000 practitioners.

Osteopathic training resembles that for the M.D. degree, including four years of schooling, internship, and residency. Osteopaths are familiar with and use many conventional medical techniques along with manipulative therapy.

Until 1976, the American Medical Association (AMA) forbade its members to refer patients to chiropractors; it is now common practice, but the AMA still argues that there is no scientific evidence that manipulative therapy is appropriate for such ailments as essential hypertension, cancer, heart disease, stroke, and diabetes.

The power of touch

After a conventional physical examination, including an assessment of posture and range of movement of the joints, an osteopath will conduct an examination by touch, seeking to locate such problems as fractionally misaligned vertebrae, and may then massage the muscles or manipulate the spine or other joints.

To treat a fixed or misaligned joint, the osteopath may perform a high-velocity thrust, moving the joint quickly through its normal range of movement. This procedure often produces the clicking noise that people associate with osteopathic treatment, which is the result of a vacuum forming within the joint as it is moved.

Cranial osteopathy is a specialized manipulation of the head and upper neck to reestablish a balanced relationship between the structure of the head and spine. It is used to treat conditions such as visual disturbance, migraine, sinusitis, and sleeplessness.

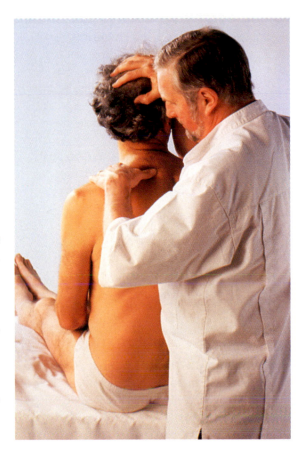

◄ Touch is a key factor in osteopathic diagnosis. Osteopaths conduct examinations by touch in order to identify problems, such as misaligned vertebrae.

Computerized diagnostics

Some osteopaths use a computerized diagnostic machine that is able to identify disorders of the lumbar region of the spine. It also acts as an exercise machine for rehabilitation of injured patients.

The patient is placed in a restraint system that limits movement to the lumbar spine and performs a series of tasks against varying resistances. The machine monitors the patient's force, speed, and range of movement; this information is then summarized on a computer-generated report. When used for rehabilitation, the machine supplies movement exercises that assist in the healing of soft tissue.

Chiropractic

Chiropractic is another form of manipulative therapy. The word chiropractic translates literally as "done by hand." Developed by a Canadian, Dr. Daniel David Palmer, chiropractic is based on the theory that illness causes an imbalance in the structure of the body, and in turn, imbalance can cause illness. Chiropractors concentrate on spinal imbalance and posture.

SEE ALSO: BONES AND FRACTURE TREATMENT • CANCER TREATMENT • MEDICINE • MUSCLE

Otolaryngology

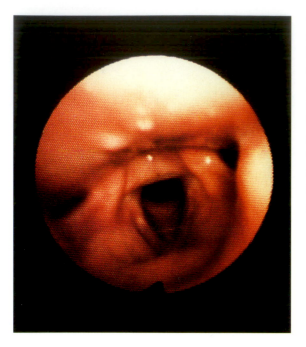

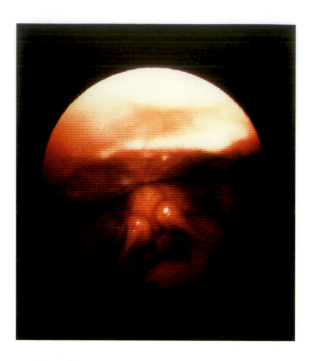

◄ ► Endoscopic views of an open and closed larynx (left and right, respectively). The endoscope is vital to modern ear, nose, and throat surgery, giving surgeons an illuminated view of the area being operated on without the need to make unsightly incisions.

Otolaryngology, or otorhinolaryngology, is the study of the ear, nose, and throat and related structures in the head and neck. Specialists studying this field of medicine are known as otolaryngologists, or ear, nose, and throat (ENT) physicians. Recent advances in medical technology are helping alleviate the suffering of people with problems in these areas.

Common ENT problems

Disorders of the ear include hearing loss, ringing in the ears (tinnitus), balance problems, infections, and congenital defects of the inner and outer ear. Nearly one in ten North Americans will suffer from some form of hearing loss in their lifetime. However, some 35 million Americans are affected by chronic sinusitis every year, making it one of the most common health problems that otolaryngologists have to deal with. Other nasal problems affect the sense of smell and taste or are caused by allergies to pollen, animal hair, dust mites, and certain foods.

Diseases of the larynx and throat can lead to difficulties with speech, singing, and swallowing. Cancers of the voice box or tongue can create particular difficulties, as the patient may find it hard to eat or communicate after surgery. The neck also contains a number of nerves that are essential to the functioning of the ears, nose, and throat. Otolaryngologists are also skilled in treating deformities of the face, such as cleft palates and harelips, and carry out reconstructive and plastic surgery to counteract the effects of cancers and facial traumas.

Help with hearing

One advance that has affected the lives of thousands of people suffering from deafness has been the ability to make smaller and smaller hearing aids with the help of modern microchip technology. Yet the challenge remains to develop a hearing aid that will magnify the sound of speech but not of background noises.

Hearing aids that stimulate the auditory nerve directly—cochlear implants—have successfully helped many deaf people. The deaf person has an operation to insert a sound receiver under the skin behind the ear; it is connected to a wire that stimulates the nerve. He or she also has to wear a microphone connected to a device worn behind the ear to pick up sound. This device transmits the sound to the receiver under the skin.

Cochlear implants are suitable only for people who are totally deaf, even though the auditory nerve functions normally. Only people who remember being able to hear are likely to benefit from having one, as they need to be able to relate to the sound they "hear" via the implant.

Another problem dealt with by the otolaryngologist is that of blocked sinuses. This condition affects millions of people, who can now be helped by a simple operation that involves none of the major incisions in the face that used to be necessary for surgery on the sinuses, with all the bruising and scarring that they caused. The sinuses are a honeycomb of cavities in the bones of the face. They are found between the eyes and behind the nose, within the cheekbones, and within the bones of the skull. These passages are lined with the same kind of membrane that lines the nose. They sometimes become blocked by swelling, by polyps (small outgrowths of tissue), or even by malignant growths. As a result, a person may find it difficult to breathe or have a continually "stuffed up" feeling or a constantly running nose.

Endoscopic surgery

Endoscopic sinus surgery has made it much easier to diagnose and treat such conditions. The surgeon first looks at detailed scans of the head to find out the exact anatomy of the patient's sinuses, as their position and mass vary greatly from patient to patient. The surgeon then inserts a fine optical tube called an endoscope up the nose and into the sinuses. Fiber optics make it possible to see around corners. It provides an excellent illuminated view of the sinuses, making it easy to remove polyps and open up blocked passages.

For the larynx, a major advance has been the removal of growths from vocal cords with a laser. The people to benefit most from this development have been those suffering from persistent hoarseness, which is common and extremely disabling, particularly for those who rely on their voices at work, such as teachers and lawyers.

Hoarseness can have many causes, ranging from polyps, swelling, and benign growths to precancerous growths and malignant tumors. Children may suffer from papillomata of the larynx, a viral infection that causes a rash of growths on the vocal cords. These growths may threaten to block the airway and endanger the child's life.

These conditions can now easily be treated with the help of the carbon dioxide laser. The

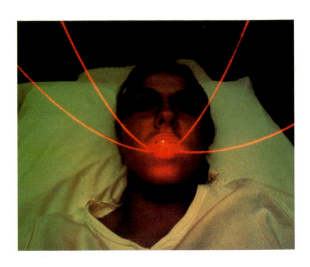

▶ A patient receives laser-activated cancer therapy. The use of lasers has been one of the greatest of recent breakthroughs in the treatment of throat cancers. In this case, a low-powered argon laser beam is being used to activate a drug, hematoporphyrin derivative (HPD), previously injected into the patient. HPD does not affect normal cells but is highly toxic to cancer cells, which strongly absorb it.

properties of this laser allow it to vaporize cells down to a very shallow depth on a structure without affecting the tissues underneath.

Treating cancer

People who have surgery for conditions such as cancer of the nose and sinuses need no longer experience the effects of the severe disfigurement that often followed such operations.

Cancer of the nose and nasal sinuses is very rare; it accounts for less than one percent of all cancers. Without treatment, it causes gross disfigurement, blindness, and severe pain. The sufferer is unable to eat or sleep. The treatment for such cancers used to involve a large incision around the cheek, removal of the cheekbone, and often, removal of the roof of the mouth. The patient had to wear a plate in the roof of the mouth and suffered severe disfigurement with all the associated social and psychological problems.

Two new developments have revolutionized treatment for cancers of the nose and nasal sinuses. One is a new surgical technique. An incision is first made in the mouth. The surgeon removes the tumor and surrounding tissues from the inside, leaving the skin covering the face intact. A prosthesis can be fitted inside the mouth so that the patient looks completely normal.

With extensive cancers of the nose and its associated sinuses, it is not always possible to avoid removal of the nose or sometimes the eye. These patients can be helped by a new generation of extremely lifelike prostheses. The surgeon inserts tiny screws made of titanium into the bone that remains around the area removed. Onto these screws can be fitted a custom-made removable prosthesis that is undetectable except after close examination.

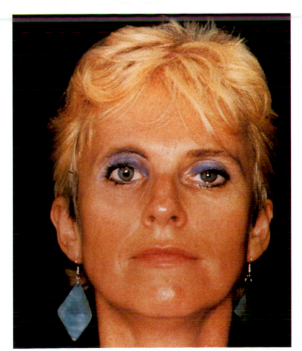

◀ Extensive cancers of the nose and sinuses sometimes necessitate the removal of the nose or even an eye. This woman has had her left eye replaced by a prosthesis.

SEE ALSO: Cancer treatment • Endoscope • Hearing • Microsurgery • Plastic surgery • Smell and taste

Outboard Motor

An outboard motor is basically a self-contained power unit for small boats and dinghies that is clamped to the transom (stern) of the craft. By contrast, inboard motors have their engines mounted permanently in the hull and are connected to the propeller by a drive shaft. The earliest outboard motors appeared at the beginning of this century, the first being a French design, the Motogodille, in 1902. In the mid-1900s, Cameron Waterman in the United States produced a small outboard, but it was Ole Evinrude, a Norwegian-American living in Milwaukee, who produced the first commercially successful design—a one-cylinder engine that produced 1.5 horsepower—which went into production in 1909, after about three years of development.

The powerhead

The unit containing the engine, electric system, and on smaller motors, the fuel tank, is called the powerhead. Almost all outboard motors have two-stroke gasoline engines, although some are four-stroke, and small electric-powered motors are available. The first Wankel-powered outboard motor was the Mac 10, with a single rotor Sachs-Wankel KM48 engine of 160 cc (cubic centimeters) capacity giving 9.5 brake horsepower at 4,800 rpm, and many manufacturers have since developed other rotary-engined outboard motors.

The cylinders are usually horizontal, with the drive being taken from the lower end of the vertical crankshaft by a shaft that drives the propeller via the transmission and propeller shaft, which are housed in the underwater unit. Ignition is by a magneto on the smaller motors, where a starting cord wound around the flywheel provides the necessary motion for the magneto. Most motors above about 5 or 6 brake horsepower, however, have electric starters as standard or optional equipment, often with a starting cord provided for emergency starting.

Most outboards are water cooled, the cooling water being drawn in by an impeller in the lower (underwater) unit and circulated around the engine before being expelled through ports at the rear above the propeller. Engine exhaust is usually discharged underwater through a submerged outlet port, and some types discharge the exhaust through the outboard's propeller hub.

A wide range of power outputs is available, from 1 horsepower to 300 horsepower for standard production outboards and up to 450 horsepower for racing engines.

Lower unit

The lower unit houses the transmission, gearchange mechanism, propeller shaft, and cooling-water impeller, except on the smallest motors, which have no gearchange, reversing being achieved by turning the motor right around so that the propeller acts in the reverse direction. The transmission has forward, neutral, and reverse gears, selected either by a mechanical linkage from the gearshift or on some models by a solenoid unit.

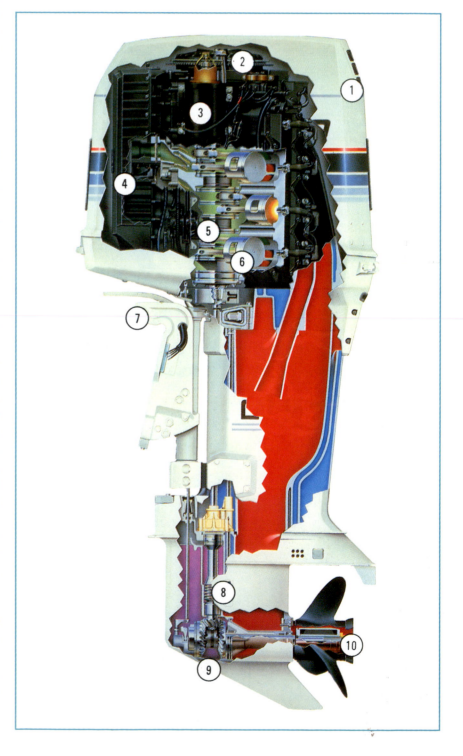

▼ The Johnson 3.6 GT outboard motor. (1) Outer casing, (2) flywheel, (3) starter motor, (4) carburetor, (5) crankshaft, (6) pistons, (7) transom mounting, (8) integral torsional damper, (9) drive bevel gears, (10) exhaust outlet.

The rotation of the propeller tends to turn the boat, that is, if the propeller is turning clockwise (viewed from the rear), it will tend to drive the rear of the boat toward the right, and the boat will self-steer toward the left (port). On many outboards, this tendency is counteracted by a small fixed rudder, the trim rudder, mounted above the propeller. The trim rudder also serves to reduce the amount of electrolytic corrosion of the propeller caused by the action of saltwater on the propeller and adjacent metalwork. If the propeller is made of bronze and the trim rudder of zinc, the electrolytic action will erode the relatively cheap and easily replaceable trim rudder but not the more expensive bronze propeller. On many modern outboards of up to 4 horsepower, the propellers are of plastic material or plastic-coated stainless steel, so electrolytic corrosion of the propeller is not a problem. Larger outboards have aluminum or stainless steel propellers.

Control

Small engines are usually steered by a tiller-type steering handle, and engine speed is controlled by a throttle lever mounted on the steering handle or by a twist-grip control at the end of the handle. Gearchange is by means of a gearshift mounted on the powerhead.

On engines with higher power outputs, this arrangement is unsatisfactory, as it may be almost impossible to steer the craft when the engine is producing about 20 brake horsepower or more. For these motors (and when more than one motor is fitted), the steering is by cables linked to a steering wheel, and the gearchange and throttle are operated by levers connected to the motor by cable links. Some motors use a single lever for both throttle and gears. When the lever is in its midway position, the transmission is in neutral and the engine is idling. As the lever is moved for-

ward, forward gear is selected, and further movement of the lever opens the throttle. To reverse, the lever is moved back through its midway position (so the gears are put in neutral), and further movement backward changes the gears into reverse and then opens the throttle again.

When two levers are used, one for throttle and one for gears, there is usually a safety interlock so that the gears cannot be changed unless the throttle lever is in the idling position. If two or more engines are used to drive a boat, a single cable-linked lever arrangement is used for each engine, with the levers mounted next to each other near the steering wheel so that they can be operated simultaneously with one hand.

Boat types

Outboard motors are used on a variety of leisure and sports craft. They are perhaps most common on runabouts, or motor launches, which are the small open boats commonly used for fishing. Occasionally outboard motors are used on smaller motor cruisers, which contain accommodation for sleeping and cooking.

▲ An Evinrude portable outboard motor. Its electronic ignition and plug-in ignition coils give greater resistance to moisture and corrosion.

◄ Portable outboards are cheap and versatile and can be used with many different kinds of boats.

SEE ALSO: IGNITION SYSTEM, AUTOMOBILE • INTERNAL COMBUSTION ENGINE • PROPELLER • SPEEDBOAT

Oxidation and Reduction

Oxidation and reduction are classes of chemical reactions. Since an oxidation reaction always accompanies a reduction reaction, the combined processes are called redox (from *re*duction and *ox*idation) reactions.

The term *oxidation reaction* was originally restricted to those reactions in which elements combine with oxygen to form oxides; the term *reduction reaction* was restricted to reactions in which oxides lose all or part of their oxygen. As such, oxidation reactions included combustion and some corrosion reactions; reductions included the smelting of metal oxides to extract metals.

The scope of reduction reactions grew to include reactions with hydrogen, because of the explosive reaction that occurs between hydrogen and oxygen to form water: hydrogen was thought to be the chemical "opposite" of oxygen.

▲ The copper-clad roof of the Library of Congress was once reddish-brown. Over time, it acquired a greenish patina of basic copper carbonate by the atmospheric oxidation of copper. The patina protects the underlying metal from further corrosion.

Electronic theory

The modern definition of redox reactions classifies them in terms of electron transfers. Analysis of simple oxidation reactions reveals that the element that becomes oxidized loses electrons, so iron atoms lose electrons to form iron cations when they react with oxygen. Similarly, an element acquires electrons when it reacts with a reducing agent. An aid for remembering this description is the phrase "oil rig"—*oxidation is loss; reduction is gain* (of electrons).

The concepts of oxidation and reduction have therefore been extended to include all reactions in which electrons are transferred between elements. The participation of oxygen is no longer implied by the use of the term oxidation.

Oxidizing and reducing agents

When magnesium (Mg) reacts with chlorine (Cl_2), each magnesium atom loses two electrons as it forms a magnesium ion (Mg^{2+}), and each chlorine molecule accepts two electrons as it forms two chloride ions (Cl^-):

$$Mg \rightarrow Mg^{2+} + 2e^-$$

$$Cl_2 + 2e^- \rightarrow 2Cl^-$$

Viewed in one way, chlorine is reduced, while magnesium is oxidized; viewed in another way, chlorine acts as an oxidizing agent, while magnesium acts as a reducing agent in this reaction.

In general, a good oxidizing agent is an element or compound that readily accepts electrons. The nonmetals toward the right of the periodic table (but not the noble gases) are good oxidizing agents; they include chlorine, fluorine, and oxygen.

A good reducing agent is an element or compound that readily donates electrons. The metals toward the left of the periodic table are good reducing agents; they include calcium, magnesium, potassium, and sodium.

Oxidation numbers

The oxidation number of an element is the real or theoretical number of electrons it must lose as it forms a compound. In sodium chloride (NaCl), for example, sodium is present as sodium ions (Na^+), so each atom of sodium actually loses an electron in the formation of this salt.

In aluminum chloride ($AlCl_3$), which is molecular, no aluminum ions are present. Nevertheless, aluminum is assigned oxidation number +3 in this compound by analogy with ionic compounds.

Some elements—notably transition metals, such as iron (Fe)—can exist in several oxidation states. Manganese, for example, forms compounds in which its oxidation number is +2, +3, +4, +6, or +7. A negative oxidation number indicates an element that has more electrons in a compound than in its uncombined state.

A few elements can have positive and negative oxidation numbers. Sulfur, for example, forms compounds in which its oxidation number is –2 (H_2S), +4 (SO_2), and +6 (SO_3).

Oxidation number 0 (zero) usually refers to uncombined elements; nickel carbonyl, $Ni(CO)_4$, is one of the few compounds where an element—in this case nickel—has oxidation number 0. The oxidation state is often expressed as Roman numerals in the names of compounds, so $FeCl_2$ is iron (II) chloride, for example. Neither negative nor positive signs are used in these names.

Combustion

Combustion is a form of oxidation reaction. The common fuels—petroleum, gas, coal, and wood—are mixtures of carbon-containing compounds. On ignition, these fuels react with oxygen to form oxides of carbon—carbon monoxide (CO) and carbon dioxide (CO_2). Hydrocarbon fuels produce water vapor by the oxidation of hydrogen in the fuel, and fuels that contain sulfur or nitrogen compounds produce oxides of those elements in addition to the carbon oxides and water.

Combustion is not exclusive to carbon-based fuels. Hydrogen burns, as do boron hydrides, which are sometimes used as rocket fuels. Some metals are capable of burning. Magnesium burns with an intense white light when it is ignited in air; iron in the form of wire wool can be ignited and burns vigorously in oxygen.

Smelting

Smelting is an industrial process that extracts metals from their ores by chemical reduction reactions. Many smelting reactions use burning coke as a source of heat and carbon monoxide, which reduces a metal oxide ore.

In blast furnace smelting of iron oxide, the main reactions are partial combustion of coke (practically pure carbon, C), then reduction of iron oxide (Fe_2O_3) by carbon monoxide:

$$2C + O_2 \rightarrow 2CO$$
$$Fe_2O_3 + 3CO \rightarrow 2Fe + 3CO_2$$

Blasts of air for the first of these reactions enter through inlets near the base of the furnace; molten iron produced by the second reaction collects at the bottom of the furnace.

◄ Chemical or electrolytic reduction are two methods that extract metals from their compounds. In steel manufacture, a simple chemical reaction is used to reduce the carbon content of iron.

▶ Rusting is an oxidation process that affects iron and some of its alloys. Rusting and other forms of corrosion are a great burden to the economies of developed countries.

Electrolysis

Electrolytic processes are redox reactions. In an electrolysis reaction, cations gain electrons from the cathode, so cathode processes are reductions; at the same time, anions give up electrons to the anode, so anode processes are oxidations. In the electrolysis of molten sodium chloride, for example, chloride ions are oxidized to chlorine at the anode, while sodium ions are reduced at the cathode to form elemental sodium.

Corrosion

The rusting of iron is an example of corrosion, which is an often destructive oxidation of metals. The rapid rusting of iron occurs through an electrolytic process that has three requirements: a source of oxygen (usually air), surface damage where metallic iron is exposed, and moisture. Metallic iron becomes oxidized to iron (II) ions at the exposed surface, which acts as an anode. The iron (II) ions dissolve in water, where dissolved oxygen oxidizes them to iron (III) ions. Elsewhere on the metal surface, oxygen acquires electrons (is reduced) and reacts with water to form hydroxide ions. Where the iron (III) ions and hydroxide ions meet, they form insoluble hydrated iron (III) oxide ($Fe_2O_3 \cdot 3H_2O$), or rust.

Energy from food

The method by which the human body obtains energy and heat from food is an oxidation reaction. Digestion enables chemicals from food to enter the bloodstream, which acquires oxygen in the lungs. This oxygen combines loosely with hemoglobin in the blood, then oxidizes chemicals from food to form carbon dioxide and water.

SEE ALSO: ▷ CORROSION PREVENTION • ELECTROLYSIS • METABOLISM • METAL • PHOTOSYNTHESIS

Oxygen

◄ The atmosphere contains 20.9 percent by volume of oxygen, but as altitude increases, barometric and oxygen pressures decrease rapidly, and the air becomes difficult to breathe. At a height of 25,000 ft. (7,600 m), it is necessary to breathe in four times the amount of air that one does at sea level to take up the same amount of oxygen. Still, this difficulty can be overcome—these British mountaineers climbed the 25,000 ft. Mount Kongur in China without additional supplies of oxygen.

The discovery of oxygen, chemical symbol O, and the development of the modern theory of combustion were milestones in the history of science. These discoveries established chemistry as a modern science clearly divorced from alchemy. Although the ancient Greek and Arab philosophers were vaguely aware of some connection between air and combustion and life, no major discovery in this field occurred until the late 18th century.

On August 1, 1774, the English chemist Joseph Priestley examined the effect of intense heat on mercuric oxide. He noted that an air or gas was readily expelled from the specimen. To his surprise, a candle burned in this air with a remarkably vigorous flame. He called the new substance dephlogisticated air in terms of the current chemical theory of combustion. On a visit to Paris in 1775, he related his discovery to a French chemist, Antoine Lavoisier. Immediately, Lavoisier checked the results by accurate experiments and found that Priestley's dephlogisticated air combined with metals and other substances. Since some of the compounds he formed produced acids, he regarded the dephlogisticated air as an acidifying principle and called it oxygine, derived from the Greek words for "sour" and "I produce."

About the same time, a Swedish apothecary named Carl Scheele had been carrying out research similar to that of Priestley. He had discovered and identified a gas that he called fire air; it was oxygen. He did not publish his results, however, until 1777, by which time the discovery of oxygen had been attributed to Priestley.

From his experiments, Lavoisier recognized that air was composed of two main constituents: vital air, or oxygen, and azote (Greek for "lifeless"—now called nitrogen), which would not support life or combustion. From these facts, Lavoisier developed the theory of combustion and thus laid the foundation of modern chemistry.

Manufacture

Originally oxygen was prepared on an industrial scale by the Brin process. Barium oxide (BaO) is heated in compressed air to form barium peroxide (BaO_2). The temperature and pressure are reduced and the peroxide reverts to the monoxide. During this process, oxygen is released.

$$2BaO_2 \quad \rightarrow \quad 2BaO \quad \rightarrow \quad O_2$$
barium peroxide   barium oxide   oxygen

Today, a little oxygen is prepared by the electrolytic decomposition of water, but the principal method of production is the liquefaction and fractional distillation of air. In a typical air liquefaction plant, there are three fundamental processes: air purification, partial liquefaction of the air using heat exchangers, and separation into oxygen and nitrogen by fractional distillation. Air is compressed to 150 times atmospheric pressure and passed through a carbon dioxide removal unit and a moisture removal unit. It then enters the heat exchanger, where the temperature is reduced to –274°F (–170°C). The cold nitrogen from the column is used in the heat exchanger. Some of the cold air is fed to an expansion engine, where it is made to do work, thus reducing the temperature of the air as energy is removed. It rejoins the rest of the cold air from the heat exchanger and enters a high-pressure column, where it is fractionated to a stream of almost pure nitrogen and an oxygen-rich stream.

The nitrogen from the high-pressure column is condensed in a condenser (reboiler) and is used as a reflux stream in the low-pressure column. The oxygen-rich air stream is drawn off the high-pressure column and fed into the low-

pressure column, where it is fractionated. Both nitrogen and oxygen are drawn off from the low-pressure column.

Uses

Oxygen is of fundamental importance in the respiration of plants and animals. The most important industrial use, however, is in steelmaking, where hot liquid iron from a blast furnace is metallurgically converted to steel by using oxygen to reduce the level of carbon in the liquid metal. To achieve this result, a large, constant supply of oxygen is required, generally supplied directly from a manufacturing plant in or adjacent to the steelworks. The oxygen is piped directly into the converter vessel and, depending on the type of vessel used, can be fed into the top or the bottom of the vessel. High-pressure oxygen is required to ensure strong agitation to complete conversion from iron to steel.

▼ The liquefaction and distillation of air produces oxygen. After the air has been cooled and compressed in the heat exchanger, it loses pressure driving the expansion engine and partly liquifies. The distillation column then separates it into liquid oxygen and nitrogen.

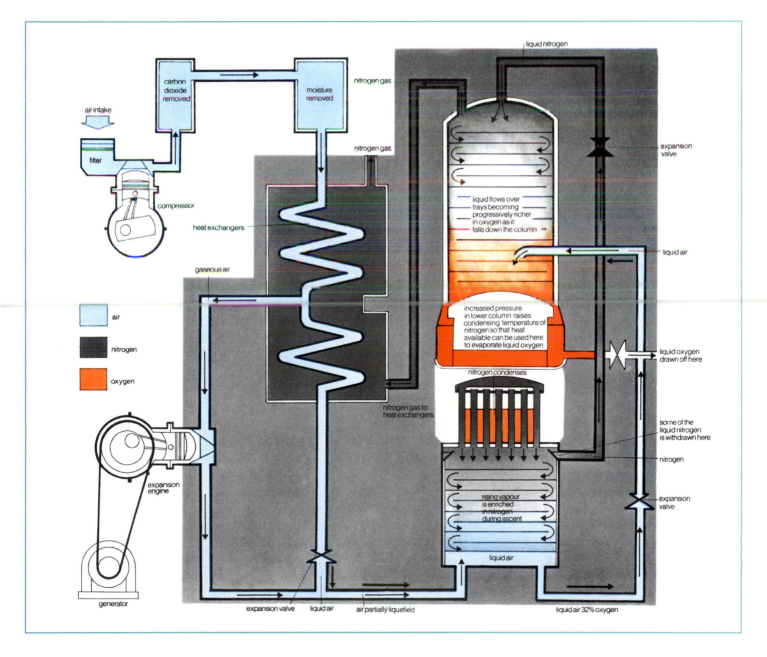

There have been major advances in the use of oxygen in other industrial areas, particularly in those processes where a combustion system is used. Combustion of a fuel requires oxygen, which is only 20.9 percent of the air. The remaining portion, which is mainly nitrogen, serves only to reduce the efficiency of the combustion process. It has been found that increasing the levels of oxygen to the flame greatly improves the combustion efficiency. (Pure, and particularly liquid, oxygen can cause combustible matter to explode.) This trait has practical applications in the melting of nonferrous metals, the production of limestone and cement, the production of glass and fiber glass, and the production of iron in the foundry industry.

The level of oxygen can be increased by the addition of pure oxygen to the combustion air or by the use of 100 percent oxygen in an oxy-fuel burner that is specially designed to cope with the different flame conditions produced in this instance. Oxygen is also used in primary smelting of metallic ores, where the rate of conversion to pure metal is increased by raising the level of oxygen in the air supply to the process.

In the chemical industry, many chemicals are now produced on a large scale using oxidation reactions. Oxygen from an air-separation unit (distillation process) is used to replace conventional air streams to improve the efficiency of these processes. Examples of chemicals produced in this manner are ethylene oxide from ethylene, vinyl chloride from ethylene and chlorine or hydrogen chloride, and vinyl acetate from ethylene and acetic acid. Another important commercial application for oxygen is in the cutting of ferrous metals into shapes for fabrication. In this technique, the metal is heated by means of a fuel-oxygen flame to the point of combustion, and then a high-speed stream of oxygen is fed to the center of the flame. The metal burns and melts leaving a narrow cut. Oxyacetylene welding has been widely used since the beginning of the century. Acetylene in the presence of oxygen produces a high-temperature flame that will melt most metals, allowing them to be welded together.

Up to a height of 14 miles (22 km) above the surface of Earth, the proportion of oxygen in the atmosphere remains constant at 20.9 percent. However, the atmospheric pressure and the partial pressure of oxygen decrease rapidly. Therefore, in high-flying aircraft, although the aircraft is pressurized, an emergency supply of oxygen is provided. In deep-sea diving at depths greater than 250 ft. (76.2 m), compressed air cannot be used because of the formation of nitrogen bubbles in the diver's circulatory system (air contains approximately 78 percent nitrogen). Neither can pure oxygen be used, because prolonged exposure produces toxic effects. Mixtures of oxygen and the noble gas helium, however, have been found to be suitable for respiration at these depths.

Almost all hospitals now have piped installations providing oxygen to wards and operating rooms. Oxygen tents are used frequently for patients with respiratory difficulties, and in anesthesia, oxygen is mixed with the anesthetic gas, for example, nitrous oxide or cyclopropane.

In the aerospace industry, liquid oxygen is the most commonly used oxidant in rocket propulsion. The oxygen and the fuel (usually kerosene) are fed under pressure into the thrust chamber, where they are mixed and burned at high pressures. The gaseous reaction products are accelerated and ejected at high velocities, thus providing the necessary propulsive thrust.

Oxides

Since the atmosphere contains 20.9 percent by volume of oxygen and since it is capable of reacting with most elements other than the noble gases, it is not surprising that oxides are widely distributed in nature. The most common and the one having the most vital importance to life is water (H_2O), which was once thought to be an element. Without it, life on Earth would not exist, because it plays an essential part in the physiological processes of both plants and animals. Pure water, however, does not exist in nature. Its purity varies according to its source; seawater can have dissolved salts at concentrations as high as 3.5 percent. Although its chemical formula is

◄ The NASA space shuttle, being tested here, is fueled by liquid hydrogen, which is oxidized by liquid oxygen.

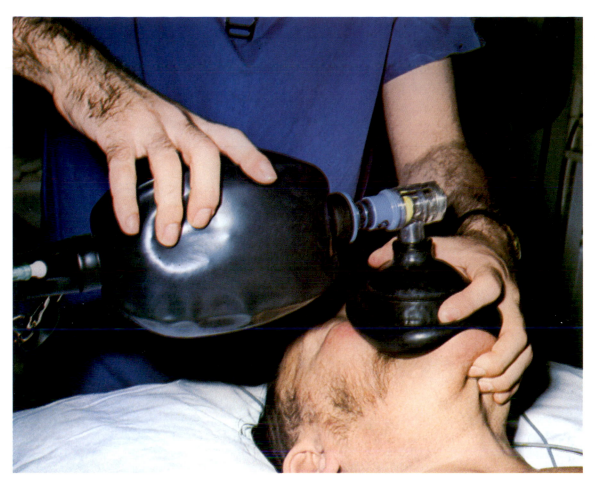

H_2O, pure water is really a polymeric material better represented as $(H_2O)n$, n being a large number, in which the individual molecules are linked together through their hydrogen atoms by chemical bonds called hydrogen bonds. The exact structure of the pure water polymer has been a subject of controversy for many years. Compared with similar chemical compounds, water has unusual physical properties: its boiling point, 212°F (100°C), and melting point, 32°F (0°C), are higher than would be predicted from this comparison. These unusual properties can be explained only in terms of its polymeric structure.

The second oxide of hydrogen, in which two atoms of oxygen are combined with two atoms of hydrogen (H_2O_2), is called hydrogen peroxide. This compound, which has been known for more than 150 years, is not very stable in its pure state and decomposes easily to form water and oxygen. On an industrial scale, it is prepared by the electrolysis of ammonium hydrogen sulfate (NH_4HSO_4), using a platinum anode and a lead cathode. Because of its instability in the pure state, hydrogen peroxide is usually used in dilute aqueous solution. It decomposes to form water and oxygen and is a powerful oxidizing agent that is used for bleaching purposes.

Many of the industrially important metals exist in nature as their oxides. The pure metals are obtained by a process known as reduction. Iron is the second most abundant metal in Earth's crust and is the most important. Even though it is obtainable from oxides, in the presence of air and moisture, it slowly reverts to its oxide (rusting).

Ozone

Ozone (O_3) is an allotrope of oxygen; in other words, it is the same element existing in a different form. Structurally, the difference between the two compounds is that oxygen has two atoms per molecule whereas ozone has three.

Chemically the properties of these two compounds are very different. A simple example of this difference is their effect on human respiration: oxygen is essential for respiration to take place, whereas ozone at concentrations greater than 1 part per million is toxic to humans. Ozone occurs naturally in the atmosphere at very low concentrations (0.03 parts per million). In the stratosphere there is an ozone layer that is formed by the action of short-wavelength radiation from the Sun on oxygen. This ozone layer is vital for life, for it absorbs ultraviolet radiation, too much of which would be fatal to most living creatures.

SEE ALSO: Air • Anesthetic • Distillation and sublimation • Metal cutting and joining • Rocket and space propulsion • Water

Packaging

▲ Drinks packed in bottles made of polyethylene terephthalate (PET), a material that can be molded easily by the stretch-blow method.

The design and operation of packaging machinery involves expertise in chemistry, ergonomic design, computers for automatic control, and many other branches of art and science. A package can be anything from a slender glass ampoule containing a product for injection, filled and sealed in a sterile atmosphere, to a catheter sealed in a plastic bag and sterilized ready for use after the bag is sealed, or it may be a softwood crate in which an automobile is shipped across oceans. Between these extremes are millions of bags, bottles, cartons, tubes, injection molded or thermoformed plastic nests, and so on. As an antipilferage precaution, small items for sale in self-service shops are displayed inside plastic blisters sealed to the surface of large cards. It is now common for the customer to carry away not just a package but a package of packages, such as a carton containing a number of bottles of soft drink.

The slow speed and expense of manual handling, filling, weighing, labeling, and so on, has led to the development of machinery that does the job faster. Today, there are complex automatic packaging systems that take the product and the package from bulk to produce entire pallets of packages, strapped, shrink wrapped or stretch wrapped for shipment. The only limitation on the design of packaging machinery is the fact that some functions, such as weighing, are slower than labeling, for example, which can be undertaken at speeds in excess of 1,000 bottles a minute in the case of glass.

Bottles

Bottles are delivered by slat conveyor to smoothly turning plastic spirals that space them correctly on individual platforms mounted on a turntable or carousel, which as it turns lifts them (by means of cams) and brings the bottle mouth firmly into contact with injecting nozzles. The entire sequence of events is controlled by fail-safe devices so that if a bottle breaks, the line stops, or if a bottle fails to arrive on its platform, the relevant nozzle does not discharge. The amount from the nozzle is measured volumetrically by a piston action and suitable valves or by the turning of an auger in a tube for the handling of semiliquids and those containing solids in suspension. Drip cut-off devices ensure that the outside of the bottle and the surface that will accept the cork, cap, or other closing device is not soiled.

Cartons

Machinery can insert or construct a bag inside a carton, for example a cereal box, seconds before it is filled. The cartons themselves are withdrawn as flat packages by a machine, which selects them individually from a magazine. The suction device that pulls them into the machinery opens them into a three-dimensional form, then the bottom flaps are turned over and tucked in or brushed by a glue wheel and closed. Next, the cartons are placed on conveyor-mounted flights or paddles, carried in line or on a carousel. A similar top-sealing operation takes place after a checkweigher ensures that the fill is present and complete.

Bagging

Bags are made from various plastic films, aluminum foil, and laminates (materials combined in layers) as well as paper. The bags are formed by specialized machinery from a strip of preprinted material called the web: the preprinted web is positioned correctly for cutting by the addition of printed spots or bars, which effectively act as a command to electronic scanning devices above the web that activate the cutting mechanism. Bags used for bulk materials are sealed by quick-set adhesives or by thermal bonding. Where dissimilar materials are used or when paper or board is coated or laminated with polyethylene on one side only, hot melts are used that adhere to any surface and cool to seal in seconds.

Some of the most highly developed packages today are the pouches used for powdered soup and similar products. They are made of paper on the outside for its low cost and ability to take print, aluminum foil on the inside to shield the product from light and to ensure impermeability, and polyethylene inside that to make a heat seal.

The pouches are made from a single printed web of the laminate, sealed around three edges, filled, and closed by applying a heated sealing bar to the pouch mouth. Cans or bottles can also be collected in packs of various numbers on a simple

cardboard tray and covered with polyethylene film, which is then shrunk using heat—but not high enough temperatures to affect the contents—to create a tightly bonded covering for the group of bottles.

Other operations

In many cases, filling accuracy is demanded by legislation, or filling may involve valuable or even dangerous substances. Today weight filling is an integral part of the packing machinery, and the systems frequently include feedback mechanisms that amend the action of the filling device when the packages coming forward are sensed to be slightly over- or underweight.

Bottles and cans are wrapped by the machinery in preerected containers. The machines use die-cut, creased board blanks, wrapping them around a group of cans, bottles, or whatever so tightly that they will not need partitions to prevent the labels from rubbing against each other and so that their mutual support actually reduces damage in transit. In addition, less board is used than in older methods that allowed a size tolerance to permit easy loading.

Machinery can code mark packages with factory location, packing date, sell-by date, and so on—a legal obligation in many countries. A number of sealed cartons, bottles, or bags are collected on a platform from a conveyor and then wrapped, as above, or dropped into a case or a large carton

◀ This machine deposits a measured weight of candy on the packaging material, and then seals it.

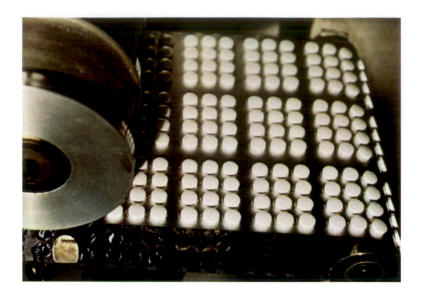

or tray; the sealed units in turn are collected on a pallet. For dispatch, individual items or whole pallets can be automatically wrapped in plastic. Shrink-wrapping involves using a plastic film that is stretched cold around a product; when heat is applied, plastic "memory"—molecules of plastic always try to retain their original form— causes the film to try to return to its original shape. Stretch wrapping is almost the same, except that the product is pushed through a curtain of film so that the film stretches tightly around it, thus avoiding the expense of a heat tunnel. Swedish and British engineers developed methods of stretch wrapping entire pallet loads, keeping the goods cleaner in transit and reducing pilferage and breakages. Packages today are also printed with a bar code, which is used in supermarkets to display the price and description of the article. Coupled to a computer, the bar code assists the store with stock control and also ensures fewer errors for the customer.

▲ Arrays of aspirin pass an optical checking device, and then drop into foil in preparation for final packaging in boxes.

Systems

The trend in packaging is toward systems sold by companies that design, supply, and guarantee the cartons and the machinery. In some cases, they offer complicated double-wall cartons that could not be set up, filled, and sealed manually. The cartons that contain cigarettes, for instance, are made up, as are the cigarettes and the triple-layer packets, on integrated systems that also case the cartons in corrugated fiberboard cases.

One of the most highly developed packaging systems is that designed in Sweden for the packaging of milk in the familiar tetrahedral cartons called Tetra-Paks. The package is made from a continuous roll of preprinted web, which is pulled over forming shoulders onto a metal tube with a small overlap. By applying heat to the overlap, a continuous sealed tube is formed that is pulled

► Packaging cookies. The boxes move along a conveyor and the cookies, which come up on an elevator, are inserted automatically.

down by two pairs of heated jaws at right angles to each other. The milk is fed into the top of the metal tube, and the action of the heated metal jaws presses hard enough on the tube to force the milk away from the sealing point, enabling the creation of a completely full package with the largest possible capacity, made from a paperboard tube. The machinery has been adapted to make automatically formed, filled, and sealed rectangular milk cartons of various sizes.

The next development was to enable this type of package to be rendered sterile. This process is achieved by passing the plastic-coated web through a bath of hydrogen peroxide just before it is formed into a tube. By then applying heat in such a way that the liquid is literally burned off, the resulting carton is sterilized. If the milk itself is sterilized by heat treating and the whole operation is undertaken in an enclosed sterile atmosphere, the end product is a packaged milk product that will keep for long periods without refrigeration.

Automated dairy plants are now able to receive, empty, and return milk churns; check the milk quality; feed it to the correct dispensing machine, depending on what shape and size milk carton is desired; stack the unit packages into automatically erected fiberboard trays or crates; and palletize complete loads and efficiently shrink-wrap them, with only a few trained engineers in attendance. Each pallet holds 72 cases of aseptically formed milk cartons containing in all 456 gals. (1,728 l) of milk.

The next development was the addition of a plastic seal to the top of the carton; turning a cap was an easier means of opening the cartons than the original "pull-apart" top. The plastic inserts are simply added by another element of the

machinery, which cuts a small hole in the top of the carton and punches through the one-piece plastic opener.

The idea of using a continuous heat-sealed tube is also being exploited for other products in tandem with developments in plastics technology that have enabled the production of extremely thin, tough, and flexible plastics. These plastics can be formed into tubes to protect such products as chocolate bars or other small items. The process is called flow wrapping because a continuous flow of items is produced. There are vertical machines that produce bags of weighed-out candy or potato chips, heat-sealing the web to make the packages; with a weldable plastic like polyethylene, a hot wire passed through the web cuts it off and makes a bead seal on each side.

Developments in materials have also led to the production of permeable membranes for such products as coffee, enabling the product to be sealed within the membrane and also an outer layer of plastic or card for instant use once the external packaging is removed.

In another development, the web is heated and stretched by the application of a vacuum into a dish shape that provides a nest for the product. Then a second web is heat sealed to a flange on the dish, completely enclosing the item. A similar technique is used to make the plastic sachets containing shampoo and similar products; two webs or a single V-folded web are thermoformed from PVC and finsealed using high-frequency current to weld the plastic together.

It is not necessary for the packages to be made of similar materials to enable a seal to be achieved. Provided one or both sides of the package are heat sealable, a plastic film can, for instance, be sealed to a printed card to make the familiar blister packs. Alternatively, a thin web of plastic film can be heated and drawn down on a heat-sensitive card by use of a vacuum, a process described as skin wrapping. More complex techniques involve the use of two layers of card, in between which a plastic blister is sandwiched. A hole has to be cut in both card layers and the plastic blister carefully aligned by the machinery to ensure that, as the card layers are glued around it, they overlap the lip of the plastic blister so that it is firmly held in place.

All these packaging techniques, and many that have not yet been discovered, are necessary in a society orientated to consumption and in which the manual filling, sealing, and so on would be too slow, too expensive, and too boring for the people who would have to do it. New permutations on packaging methods are constantly being invented and refined to make the various processes

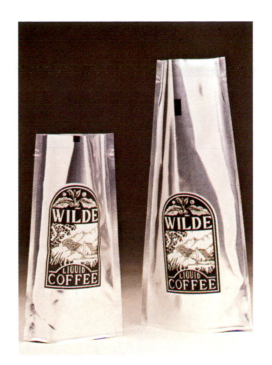

◀ The airtight, sterile containers for this liquid coffee were made from polyester, aluminum, and polyethylene film laminate.

involved less time consuming, more efficient, and even more highly automated. Machinery can fold, cut, insert, perforate, seal and wrap products so that they can be delivered faster and more conveniently to the customer.

Packaging waste

However, there are moves to reverse the trend toward excessive packaging, such as the European Union's Packaging Waste Directive. This directive holds manufacturers responsible for the packaging waste that is used to contain their products and places a levy on any waste material that is left once the product has been used—even on the plant pots that are used to contain flowers and shrubs at nurseries. This measure, although still controversial within Europe, has caused some reductions in the amount of packaging that is used and more significantly has led to coherent moves by manufacturers and product distributors to ensure that packaging is recycled. Many distributors now remove external packaging from "white goods," such as washing machines and refrigerators, on the customer's premises and recycle the waste themselves. Information on the material from which the package is made is often included on the package itself—for instance, plastic bottles are described according to the type of plastic they are made from, thus enabling recyclers to treat the material appropriately and ensure that different types of waste are not mixed.

SEE ALSO: CANNING AND BOTTLING • CONVEYOR • FOOD PRESERVATION AND PACKAGING • PACKAGING-WRAP MANUFACTURE • PAPER MANUFACTURE • PLASTICS • RECYCLING • ROBOTICS

Packaging-Wrap Manufacture

Packaging wraps are materials used for wrapping goods for protection, preservation, and transportation. Early methods of packaging included containing goods in leather or ceramic. In the 20th century, however, with the introduction of plastics, the range of packaging materials available expanded dramatically. Most packaging wraps are supplied as a roll of thin transparent plastic that is then applied to the product either by using a vaccum or by manual or machine wrapping methods.

Cellophane

Cellophane is made from cellulose, a complex carbohydrate found in the cell walls of plants, and was first made in small quantities in Britain in the early 1900s. Cellophane became readily available in 1919 with the invention by the Swiss chemist Dr. J. E. Brandenberger of a machine for continuous production of the film. By the early 1970s, production had reached over 600,000 tons (540,000 tonnes) in 32 different countries. Since then, however, biaxially oriented polypropylene that has been stretched to give it strength has taken over a large part of the cellophane market.

Cellulose arrives at a cellophane factory in the form of sheets of wood pulp. Film manufacture commences by treating these sheets of wood pulp with caustic soda to form alkali cellulose, which is shredded into crumbs and reacted with carbon disulfide to form sodium cellulose xanthate. These bright orange xanthate crumbs are then dissolved in dilute caustic soda to form an orange-brown syrup. This syrup is pumped to the film-casting machine, where it is extruded through a long metal slot into a bath of sulfuric acid, where it coagulates into a continuous web of regenerated cellulose. Rollers carry this web through a series of reagent baths that successively purify and bleach it to a clear transparent film and finally into a bath where chemical softeners are added. The film then enters a drying chamber to reduce its moisture content, and finally it is wound into rolls.

Cling film

Cling film is widely used in domestic and commercial food wrapping. The basic materials used to make cling film are the plastics polyvinyl chloride, (PVC), $(-CH_2CHCl-)_n$ or polyethylene $(-CH_2CH_2-)_n$. The chemicals that cause cling film to cling are called plasticizers, which are usually nonvolatile solvents. The plasticizers are added to the plastic, causing the chains of polymers to separate a little from each other. This

separation allows the chains to slide a little over each other and thus causes the plastic to soften. In addition, the hard solid plastic is made more rubbery by the addition of an alkyl phthalate ester, such as dioctyl phthalate.

Cling film made from PVC came under scrutiny in the late 1980s over fears that some of the plasticizers used to give cling film its clinging properties were able to migrate from the film into fatty foods. After extensive studies, it was decided that although this leaching of additives presented no real health risk, it was still advisable to avoid using cling films with these particular additives for the wrapping of fatty foods. Cling made from polyethylene uses plasticizers that do not migrate into fatty foods. However, these plasticizers also produce less cling than those considered harmful.

Polyethylene is not restricted in its use to cling film, it is also widely used for other retail and industrial packaging requirements. Production techniques permit continuous extrusion coupled with eight-color printing, thus allowing a wide range of flexibility in the range of products to which this material can be applied.

Films that are used to wrap industrial pallets may be made so that their clinging properties are restricted to one side of the film, thus preventing the different pallets from sticking to each other when in close proximity.

▲ Cling film being made using a continuous factory process. The wide sheet of cling film overhead is divided and wound around separate rollers to create large rolls of film.

SEE ALSO: ADHESIVE AND SEALANT • FOOD PRESERVATION AND PACKAGING • PACKAGING • PLASTICS • PLASTICS PROCESSING • POLYMER AND POLYMERIZATION

Paint

A paint is a fluid material formulated to spread on a solid surface and then to dry and harden to form a coherent layer that adheres to that surface. A paint differs from a varnish by being to some extent opaque, so it hides or modifies the color of the underlying surface with its own color.

The oldest examples of the use of paint are cave paintings, such as the depictions of animals on the walls of former dwellings in the Lascaux cave near Montignac, France, and in the Altamira caverns near Santander, Spain. Cave painting probably arose from humans' desire to decorate their homes with images of things they prized.

Cave paintings were probably produced by smearing the rock surfaces with mixtures of colored earth and water or animal fat. These simple constituents—a coloring material and a fluid carrier—are still key ingredients of paints.

While decoration seems to have been the original purpose of paint, the ability of suitably formulated paints to protect the vulnerable surfaces of manufactured objects has since acquired its own importance. The application of paint to houses, ships, vehicles, and furniture, for example, makes them more attractive and more durable. Specialist coatings for containers such as food cans perform an additional protective role: they not only protect the container from its contents but also help prevent degradation of the contents through contact with container materials.

Fundamental components

The color and hiding power, or opacity, of a paint formulation is largely due to finely powdered solids, called pigments. The hiding power and color intensity contributed by a pigment increases with increasing fineness of its particles. The presence of pigment in a paint formulation can also improve the coating's resistance to chemicals.

In a dried coat of paint, pigment particles are held in place by a network of chainlike molecules, called polymers. This network must be strong enough to resist physical damage yet sufficiently flexible to accommodate deformations in the coated surface. The polymer network must be able to resist chemical attack by the environment in which it will serve—sea spray, for example, is a challenging environment—and might have to withstand ultraviolet light in strong daylight.

The building blocks of the polymer network are present in the liquid paint, where they are called film formers or binders, because of their dual function of forming the final paint film and binding the pigment together in that film.

A number of different types of film former systems are in current use, but all are high-molecular-weight polymers or oils. In liquid paint, molecules of film formers wrap themselves around pigment particles, preventing them from coagulating and settling out of the paint during storage. In dry paint, this wrapping effect prevents pigment particles from dropping out of the film.

The high molecular weights of film-forming substances make them viscous or semisolid when pure, because their molecules tangle together, inhibiting fluid motion. The application of paint usually requires low viscosity, however, since the applied paint must be able to "flow out," or spread under the influence of surface tension, so as to eliminate brush marks and other irregularities that arise during application.

In conventional paints, viscosity is reduced by adding thinners, mixtures of low-molecular-weight organic compounds that dissolve and dilute the binder. The thinner must also dissolve catalysts that promote the drying action of the paint and other chemical additives.

Pigments

By far the most important white pigment is now rutile—one of the three crystalline forms of titanium dioxide (TiO_2). Rutile is manufactured by burning titanium chloride ($TiCl_4$), a volatile liquid, in air. The process forms rutile as an extremely fine powder that is then graded by size. The various grades are sold for different applications according to their specific requirements.

▲ The makeup stage of paint manufacture, in which the final additives, color, and tinting are added to the paint and quality control checks are carried out.

For many years, the principal white pigments were white lead (any of a number of basic lead compounds, including lead hydroxy carbonate), zinc oxide (ZnO), and lithopone (a blend of zinc sulfide, ZnS, and barium sulfate, $BaSO_4$). The use of white lead has since been restricted because of the toxicity of lead compounds, while zinc oxide and lithopone have now been largely superseded by titanium dioxide, which has a superior opacity.

The predominant orange, red, and yellow pigments are various forms of iron (III) oxide (Fe_2O_3); whereas chrome (III) oxide (Cr_2O_3) gives a green pigment. Copper phthalocyanine is a blue pigment that can also be used with yellows to achieve shades of green. Black paints are made using carbon black—a finely powdered synthetic soot.

Red lead (Pb_3O_4) and yellow-to-orange chromates of lead and other metals were once widely used but are now restricted or at least avoided because of the toxicity of lead and chromium (VI) compounds, which include the chromates.

Pearlescent coatings—those that have a mother-of-pearl effect—are made by including mica-based pigments with the coloring pigments. Micas are silicate minerals whose laminar structures break down to form flat chips when crushed. The flatness of mica particles is responsible for their unusual optical properties.

Aluminum paste—a dispersion of minute aluminum plates in solvent—can be used to give a metallic sheen to paint. It also provides protection from staining in some internal can coatings for high-sulfur foods, such as meat products. Metallic zinc paste improves corrosion resistance.

Oil paints

Oil paints are essentially dispersions of pigment in a drying oil, such as linseed oil. Drying oils are natural triesters of polyunsaturated fatty acids with glycerol, $CH_2(OH)CH(OH)CH_2(OH)$.

The polyunsaturation of drying oils takes the form of $-CH=CH-CH_2-CH=CH-$ blocks in the fatty acid chains of the oil. Oxygen in air gradually oxidizes the polyunsaturated blocks, removing hydrogen atoms from their central $-CH_2-$

▲ A professional color matcher grinds a blend of pigments together in a liquid medium. This step gives a more accurate impression of the final color of paint than would be obtained by viewing the dry pigments. Once the pigment blend has been matched to a color standard, a batch of paint can be made. Any deviation of color in the finished paint can usually be corrected by adding tinting pastes—highly concentrated pigment dispersions—to the batch. Once approved, the paint batch can be dispensed into cans or drums.

units and replacing them with ether (–O–) linkages, which connect pairs of fatty acid chains. With time, so many ether linkages form that the oil molecules become part of a polymeric network that is mechanically tough and insoluble in solvents. The air oxidation of drying oils is an example of a cross-linking reaction.

Paints based on linseed oil have two major drawbacks: they yellow with aging, and they can become so inflexible that they crack. Yellowing results from an oxidation reaction that discolors polyunsaturated groups. The loss of flexibility occurs because the cross-linking reaction continues long after the paint has dried (become cross-linked) sufficiently to make it resistant. An excess of cross-linking makes the paint film too hard to flex if the substrate swells, shrinks, or deforms, so the paint cracks instead.

Superior results are achieved with oils that have less polyunsaturation, such as soybean oil. The resulting films yellow less on aging and are therefore favored for white and pastel colors. Other nonyellowing oils sometimes used are those extracted from the seeds of plants such as tobacco, safflower, sunflower, and poppy—a favorite for artists' oil colors.

Alkyd paints

Alkyd paints developed from oil paints in the first few decades of the 20th century. Their binders are alkyd resins derived from natural oils in a two-step process. In the first step—alcoholysis—an oil or blend of oils is heated with two molar equivalents of glycerol. Fatty acid groups slowly transfer from the oil molecules to the glycerol molecules until most molecules are monoglycerides with the general formula $RCOO-C_3H_5(OH)_2$, where R is the hydrocarbon chain of a fatty acid.

In the second step—polymerization—the monoglyceride is heated with a dibasic acid, such as phthalic acid ($HOOCC_6H_4COOH$). Water boils out of the mixture as the acid groups form ester linkages with the alcohol groups:

$$-COOH + HO- \quad -COO- + H_2O$$

The product of this reaction is an alkyd, a type of polyester in which glycerol groups alternate with diacid groups. The structure of the molecules resembles a comb, whose teeth are fatty acid chains, although the "teeth" are flexible.

The average molecular weight of an alkyd can be controlled by quenching the reaction with cold solvent as soon as the amount of water distilled corresponds to the desired extent of reaction. The viscosity of the mixture increases as molecular weight builds up, so the reaction can also be stopped when a specified viscosity is reached.

How alkyd paint dries

Alkyd resins are more viscous than oils, so for use in paints, they must be thinned using solvents such as turpentine or hydrocarbon blends from petroleum distillation. When an alkyd paint is applied, the solvents evaporate to leave a touch-dry paint film—entanglement of high-molecular-weight alkyds is sufficient to prevent paint from running. This stage is called physical drying.

The full mechanical and chemical resistance of an alkyd develops slowly as air oxidation creates cross-links between polyunsaturated fatty acid chains, as happens with oil paints. The greater initial molecular weight of alkyds means that they rely less on cross-linking to provide resistance when compared with oil paints. A well-formulated alkyd resin therefore uses oils that have less polyunsaturation than the oils used in oil paints, so the resulting coating is less prone to yellowing and cracking from aging than are oil paints.

The chemical drying of an alkyd can be optimized by including driers—salts of transition metals with fatty acids—in the paint formulation. The appropriate use of driers ensures that alkyd paint develops a reasonable degree of hardness in an acceptably short time for the intended application. Less polyunsaturation is required if driers are used, so the resulting coatings are more flexible than those formulated without driers.

Acrylics

Acrylics are paints whose binders are synthetic resins rather than modified natural oils. Acrylic resins are formed by copolymerizing different esters of propenoic acid (acrylic acid, $CH_2=CHCOOH$) and 2-methylpropenoic acid (methacrylic acid, $CH_2=C(CH_3)COOH$). Other types of unsaturated compounds, such as phenylethene (styrene, $CH_2=CHC_6H_5$), are sometimes used in acrylic polymers.

Since straightforward acrylics have no chemical groups that react in air at ambient temperature, acrylic paints harden by physical drying alone. The resulting films have less mechanical and chemical strength than alkyd paints but are immune to yellowing and cracking. Acrylics are used by artists but have limited use in ambient-drying decorative or protective coatings.

Emulsion (latex) paints

Emulsion paints differ from other types of paints in that their binders are dispersed in water rather than dissolved in solvents. The typical binders are emulsion polymers of ethenyl ethanoate (vinyl acetate, $CH_3COOCH=CH_2$), made by dispersing a water-insoluble blend of monomers as an emulsion in water while polymerization proceeds.

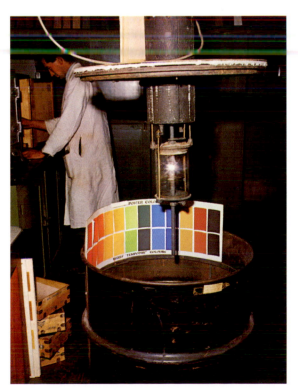

▼ Paint samples are exposed to ultraviolet light for two weeks to test color fastness.

The polymer molecules have little affinity for water, so they curl up into bundles to reduce their contact with water. This behavior allows the mean molecular weights of emulsion polymers to be much greater than those of alkyds and acrylics, because solution polymers unravel in solvent, so adjacent molecules become tangled. This reaction makes solution polymers unworkably viscous at the molecular weights of emulsion polymers.

When an emulsion paint is applied, its water evaporates first, and the coating quickly becomes touch dry. The polymer molecules remain largely separate at first. Gradually, adjacent molecules penetrate each other and get tangled, so the film gradually becomes more cohesive. This process, called coalescence, is assisted by traces of slow-evaporating solvents that swell the polymer.

Stoving enamels

Stoving enamels are paints formulated to be dried and cured—hardened by cross-linking—in heated ovens. As such, they can be used only on items that are sufficiently small and heat resistant to be stoved in ovens after the coating has been applied. In some cases, conveyor ovens are used.

Oven curing accelerates solvent evaporation and cross-linking by air oxidation. It also promotes cross-linking reactions that do not occur at room temperature. The availability of these reactions gives paint formulators more scope for developing coatings that are sufficiently tough, flexible, and resistant for their intended applications.

The film-forming systems of stoving enamels generally consist of one or more binders—acrylic, alkyd, or polyester resins, for example—and one or more cross linkers. The binder resins must have functional groups, usually carboxylic acid (–COOH) or hydroxy (–OH) groups.

Cross-linkers, such as melamine-formaldehyde (MF) and urea-formaldehyde (UF) resins, are low-molecular-weight compounds that have two or more functional sites and can form bridges between the functional groups of binder molecules.

Some compounds, including some phenol-formaldehyde and

epoxy resins, have higher molecular weights than other cross-linkers and can be considered either as binders or as cross-linkers.

The superior properties of stoving enamels make them useful for demanding applications, such as automotive and food-can coatings. Fast-curing stoving enamels may also be applied to long strips of sheet metal delivered and stored as huge coils. The coil is unwound and the strip continuously fed through a roller coater and then cured for a few seconds in a tunnel oven. The coated metal can then be cut, stamped, and formed into sheets for cladding buildings and other uses. This process is called coil coating.

Paint manufacture

Paint manufacture is traditionally a batch process. It usually comprises three stages: pigment dispersion, letdown or reduction, and adjustments.

Pigment dispersion is the most critical stage of paint manufacture, since a good dispersion is essential for paint to have satisfactory gloss (if required) and hiding power. Good pigment dispersion is also necessary for colored pigments to develop their full color intensity.

Pigment dispersions are made by first mixing powdered pigment into a liquid dispersing medium, which is usually a solution of part of the binder resin. The pigment must then be subjected to shear forces that separate agglomerated pigment particles so that they can become surrounded by the dispersing agent.

Easily dispersed pigments, such as titanium dioxide, can be processed using a machine called a high-speed disperser, or HSD. An HSD has a rotating disk whose sawtooth edge separates pigment particles and then mixes them into the vigorously stirred dispersing medium.

Pigments that are more difficult to disperse require the use of a bead mill: a cylinder along whose axis a multidisk impeller rotates and agitates tiny glass or zirconia beads, called ballotini. The ballotini are prevented from leaving the cylinder by fine-mesh filters. A pump forces the premixed pigment and dispersing medium into one end of the mill. The rubbing motion between colliding ballotini disperses the pigment, and a stream of finished dispersion emerges after a few minutes residence within the mill.

A predecessor of the bead mill is the ball mill, a large horizontal rotating cylinder. Around 45 percent of the volume of a ball mill is filled by porcelain balls or flint pebbles and 20 percent by pigment and dispersing medium. As the mill rotates, the tumbling balls crush and grind the pigment into the dispersant. Ball mills take many hours to disperse pigments, but they can run unsupervised. Ball mills are now used to process pigments that are difficult to disperse, such as carbon black, when they can run for a few days.

A widely used unit is the triple-roll mill. In a typical installation, the rolls are 12 in. (31 cm) in diameter and 30 in. (76 cm) long. They rotate at different speeds, the front rolls moving fastest. A typical speed ratio is 1:3:9, the back roll moving at about 30 rpm. A premixed paste of pigment and binder is placed on the nip between the rear and middle rollers and is gradually dragged between them. The speed difference between the rollers subjects the paste to shear that disperses the pigment. The same process acts between the middle and front rollers, then a scraper blade removes the dispersed paste from the front roller.

Once the pigment has been adequately dispersed, it is ready to be made up into paint in a process called reduction, or letdown. The pigment is pumped into a large stirred tank, then the remaining items of the formulation are added, usually in order of decreasing viscosity. The final item is usually solvent, or in the case of an emulsion or water-based paint, it is purified water.

In the final adjustment stage, a sample of paint is taken from the letdown tank and tested for color, viscosity, and solids (the percentage by weight that remains after stoving). These properties are adjusted by adding tinting pastes and solvents. After adjustment, the paint is filtered into reusable "tote" tanks, barrels, or cans.

Solvent reduction

In recent decades, paint formulators have been striving to reduce the solvent content of paints so as to make them safer for those who apply them, kinder to the environment, and cheaper. In one approach, high-solids paints are made by using low-viscosity resins that require little solvent for thinning. In some cases, solvent-free powder coatings have replaced paints.

Emulsion paints are almost free of solvent but have poor gloss. When gloss is needed, water-based solution paints with low levels of glycol-ether solvents offer a compromise.

▼ A high-speed disperser in action. A powerful motor causes the vertical shaft to rotate at great speed. A horizontal disk with a serrated rim stirs the mixture of pigment and dispersing medium. The high rotation speed creates a vortex and regions of high shear where the pigment particles deagglomerate and become dispersed in the liquid medium.

SEE ALSO: CORROSION PREVENTION • POLYMER AND POLYMERIZATION • POWDER COATING • SPRAY GUN • SURFACE TREATMENTS

Paleontology

Paleontology is the scientific study of plant and animal life that lived in prehistoric times and of how the various species developed and the environments in which they survived. In recent years there has been a marked resurgence of interest in the subject so that it now occupies the center stage in discussions of one of the most challenging problems of all—the history of planet Earth and all life on it.

The reason that so much is known about early conditions on Earth is because plant and animal remains have been preserved, or fossilized, by the process of sedimentation, in which dead organisms became buried under layers of mud and sand. Although many of the soft tissues have not survived the process, paleontologists can often build up a picture of how an animal looked from its bone structure or shell. The presence or absence of specific fossils in rock strata has also played a key role in dating rock formations and determining the movement of continents over millions of years.

Major current preoccupations of paleontologists include the nature of the first primitive life on Earth 3.5 billion years ago and the pattern of evolution since life began. The English naturalist Charles Darwin believed that evolution progresses smoothly, but modern authorities suggest its tempo is more uneven.

Paleontologists do steady work for companies searching for new oil fields and mineral deposits and also contribute in important ways to knowledge about environments and climatic changes in the past. They are also concerned with the essential task of cataloging the diverse forms of life that have existed through the ages. Without these reference collections of fossils, paleontologists could not serve science in any meaningful way.

To maintain and enlarge such fossil collections is very expensive. To keep the present momentum going, new fossil localities need to be found and known fossil beds need to be reexamined with the benefit of new techniques and new knowledge. After any discovery, fossils have to be packed up as though they were the finest bone china before being returned to the laboratory for detailed study. Months, perhaps years of work then follow while the specimens are painstakingly cleaned,

▲ A fossil skeleton being conserved in the laboratory. When large fossils are discovered in the field, most of the surrounding rock is carefully chipped away, and the remains are cast in plaster to protect them on the journey to the laboratory. There, the cast and any remaining rock is removed with an almost surgical delicacy using very fine tools or acids. Chemicals may be used to preserve the skeleton. Behind the scientists is the reconstruction of a *Titanosaurus*, a large dinosaur, made from plaster replicas of fossil remains.

◀ Coelacanths were thought to be extinct until one was caught off the South African coast in 1938. This fish had been known in fossil form (below) for a long time, but it was thought that they had died out 65 million years ago in the Cretaceous period. Several live specimens have been caught since then but have never lived long enough when landed to be observed. However, one was captured on film in 2001 and broadcast on the Internet. Since the coelacanth is a primitive fish and the nearest living relative of amphibians, it has provided paleontologists with important information about primitive life forms and their evolution.

prepared, measured, drawn, and then described in print for other paleontologists to see and comment on. Cataloging and classifying fossils may require input from a number of different specialists, such as those who date the rocks in which the fossils were found. Correspondence and exchange of publications are especially crucial in paleontology because a specimen may be unique. If the fossil represents, for example, a new type of ancient fish, interested specialists may be scattered all over the world. Scientific names (in Latin) are, however, universally recognized.

Classification

The principles of the system for naming plants and animals by means of two Latin names, the first indicating the genus and the second the species to which the organism belongs, were established in the 18th century by the Swedish naturalist Carl Linnaeus. Paleontologists follow the same rules of nomenclature as do botanists and zoologists studying living plants and animals.

Although Linnaeus was the father of modern classification, he did not concern himself much with fossils nor was he aware of the evolution of life through time. In his day, paleontology was not yet a recognized science, although its foundations had been firmly laid by the Italian artist and inventor Leonardo da Vinci. Da Vinci was well ahead of his time in recognizing that fossils had an organic nature and in trying to understand

EVOLUTIONARY TIMELINE

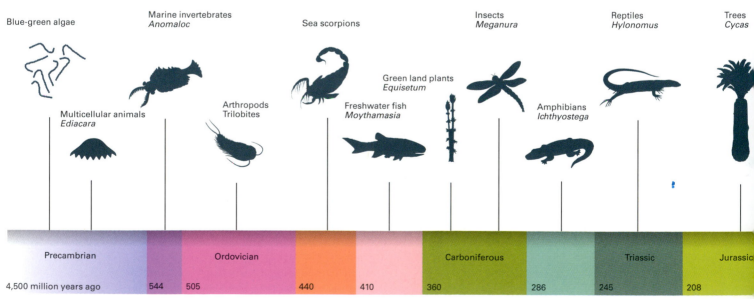

Blue-green algae

Marine invertebrates
Anomaloc

Sea scorpions

Insects
Meganura

Reptiles
Hylonomus

Trees
Cycas

Green land plants
Equisetum

Multicellular animals
Ediacara

Arthropods
Trilobites

Freshwater fish
Moythamasia

Amphibians
Ichthyostega

Precambrian		Ordovician			Carboniferous		Triassic	Jurassic
4,500 million years ago	544	505	440	410	360	286	245	208

Note: geological time periods not to scale

how organisms become fossils. Only in the 18th century was it widely accepted that fossils were the remains of ancient life and were not "sports of nature," "ornaments of the interior of the Earth," or the products of obscure "plastic forces."

These fanciful or mystical notions were slowly dispelled, but there remained the strong belief that fossils were the products of Noah's flood. This view prevailed well into the 18th century despite da Vinci's earlier dismissal of this idea. Even the French naturalist Georges Cuvier, who made some classic studies of the anatomy of extinct mammals and other vertebrates (backboned animals), attributed extinctions of animals to divinely ordered catastrophes. Nevertheless, Cuvier is generally recognized as the father of vertebrate paleontology, and he was the first to present irrefutable evidence for the reality of extinctions of species. Now, more than 200 years later, paleontologists are still preoccupied with finding a satisfactory explanation for the phenomenon of extinction.

The 19th century

In the 1830s, the term *paleontology* was coined from the Greek roots *palaios* (ancient), *on* (being), and *logos* (discourse). By then, the science of biostratigraphy—the systematic study of stratified rocks and their correlation by the use of fossils—had been firmly established by the English engineer and surveyor William Smith and others, and the foundations of evolutionary theory had been laid down by the French naturalists Georges-Louis Leclerc and Jean-Baptiste Lamarck. It was Charles Darwin, though, who was the most suc-

▶ Ammonites are one of the most recognizable fossils, dating from the Mesozoic era. Some species lived for less than half a million years before evolving into another species; the fossils provide a relative time scale for Jurassic and Cretaceous rocks.

▼ It has taken over 3.5 billion years for man to evolve from primitive blue-green algae. As conditions on Earth changed, species evolved to occupy and take advantage of niche environments. Sudden extinctions and species diversifications have been crucial in determining key geological events, such as the splitting up of continents, climate changes, periods of mountain building, and the impact of meteorites.

cessful in welding together knowledge of ancient and modern life, proclaiming in his book *On the Origin of Species* of 1859 that fossils are the true historical records of life and that species have changed over long periods of time. Some paleontologists have tried to find fault with the theory, saying that evolution has not taken place gradually, but it has resisted attack extremely well. The discovery of large numbers of fossils of extinct species in North America in the 19th century by, among others, the rival U.S. paleontologists Othniel Charles Marsh and Edward Drinker Cope helped make Darwin's theory of evolution acceptable. By the 1870s, paleontologists had become professionals, aided in their work by societies, conferences, periodicals, museums, and government-sponsored geological surveys.

It is now believed that life originated on Earth around 4 billion years ago, although undisputed living things (bacteria and primitive single-celled

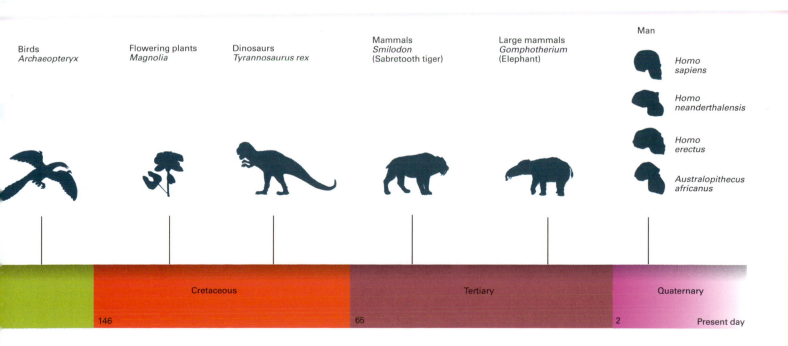

Birds
Archaeopteryx

Flowering plants
Magnolia

Dinosaurs
Tyrannosaurus rex

Mammals
Smilodon
(Sabretooth tiger)

Large mammals
Gomphotherium
(Elephant)

Man

Homo
sapiens

Homo
neanderthalensis

Homo
erectus

Australopithecus
africanus

Cretaceous	Tertiary	Quaternary
146	65	2	Present day

algae) are not known from the fossil record until around 3.5 billion years ago. With so much time and so many fossils, no one paleontologist can hope to master more than a small percentage of the subject, even with the help of computers.

Micropaleontology

Micropaleontologists study microfossils. These are fossils so small that their detailed structure is visible only with a microscope. They include minute parts of animals such as fish scales or mammalian ear bones, plant spores and pollen, bacteria and algae, and important from the economic point of view, shell-bearing single-celled animals called foraminiferans and radiolarians and shell-bearing single-celled plants called coccolithophores and diatoms. Vast numbers of these tiny plants and animals occur in sediments at the bottom of the oceans and are useful indicators of the possibilities of stores of oil and gas in the rocks. More than half of all professional paleontologists are believed to be engaged in the field of micropaleontology and are employed mostly by oil companies and geological surveys.

A subspecialty of micropaleontology, palynology, is growing in popularity. This study is restricted to fossil spores and pollen of plants and includes a varied group of hollow-walled, single-celled structures of uncertain affinity called acritarchs. Some acritarchs are as much as one billion years old and thus of special interest. Fossil pollen and spores are important in coal and oil exploration and in determining the stages of evo-

lution of land plants and the changes in vegetation during the past three million years in prehistoric human times.

Evolution

Paleontologists who study fossil plants or their vegetative parts, rather than just their pollen and spores, call themselves paleobotanists. This specialty is attracting increasing interest because of the light it can throw on such subjects as the evolution of adaptations for life on land and of associations between insects and plants.

Invertebrate paleontologists study all animals without backbones, such as corals, brachiopods, mollusks, and arthropods. This speciality is probably the oldest subdivision of paleontology. Its origins date back to ancient Greek times, when such writers as Herodotus observed marine sea shells far inland in Egypt. The Chinese also took an early interest in fossil sea shells and fish. The Frenchman Lamarck, though, was the founder of modern studies. His seven-volume *Natural History of Invertebrate Animals* was published between 1815 and 1822.

Although invertebrate fossils do not have the general appeal of many other fossils, they are the most abundant of all fossils, and they contribute in many ways to knowledge, such as the disposition of the land and seas in past geological periods. They also shed light on plant and animal associations, and they help identify centers of evolution. Some invertebrates, such as extinct marine arthropods called trilobites and a group of mol-

◀ Dinosaurs are always popular exhibits in museums. This specimen in the Royal Tyrrell Museum in Alberta, Canada, is a member of the ceratopian group of horned dinosaurs, which are characterized by a neck frill. Despite their great size, these dinosaurs were herbivores. These frills were a protective device against attack from two-legged carnivorous dinosaurs.

lusks with ornamental shells called ammonites, are used to correlate rocks in different parts of the world and provide evidence of plate movement.

Dinosaurs

The comparatively few paleontologists who study dinosaurs and other backboned animals are vertebrate paleontologists. Vertebrate fossils are mostly found in sediments laid down on land, and they can be useful for correlating deposits where other land fossils are rare. In Africa, fossil pigs and antelopes have played an important part in dating some of the earliest known humans.

The reptilelike bird *Archaeopteryx* was first found in Bavaria in 1861, two years after the first publication of Darwin's classic book. It provided the first fossil evidence of the possibility of evolutionary links between separate animal classes, in this case birds and reptiles. This animal, believed to be the earliest bird, lived about 140 million years ago. It clearly had feathers, but scientists still cannot agree whether it flew and, if it did so, how. They also cannot agree about its ancestry. Many but not all researchers assume that *Archaeopteryx* is most closely related to bipedal meat-eating dinosaurs called theropods.

The dinosaurs (Greek for "terrible lizards") were so named as a new group of reptiles by the English anatomist Richard Owen in 1841. More than 150 years after the first specimens were found in England in the early 1800s, scientists are still discovering new types of dinosaurs and interesting new facets of their behavior, and they are extending the fossil record.

Since the 1990s, for example, paleontologists working in South America have discovered the skeletons of some of the biggest dinosaurs ever to have roamed the planet. Specimens of the plant eating *Argentinosaurus* have been found measuring 127 ft. (42 m) in length. They in turn were preyed upon by the *Gigantosaurus*, at 47 ft. (14 m) an even bigger cousin of *Tyrannosaurus rex*.

To many people, dinosaurs represent what paleontology is all about. Certainly these strange reptiles encapsulate some of the most interesting problems in paleontology at present, such as their origin about 230 million years ago in what geologists call the Triassic period, their relationships to other reptiles and to birds and mammals, and their seemingly dramatic demise, along with various other animal groups, about 65 million years ago at the end of the Cretaceous period.

This event was one of several so-called mass extinctions of species that may or may not have occurred at regular intervals in the past. That at the end of the Cretaceous period was not the largest of such events, but it has attracted the greatest attention, not just from paleontologists but from scientists from many other disciplines, even astronomy. The debate hinges on whether there was a sudden natural catastrophe of some sort or whether dinosaurs died out gradually over several million years. If they and other species were wiped out by a sudden event, was it caused by an extraterrestrial body colliding with Earth? Some scientists claim to have evidence for such a happening, but no one explanation is generally accepted, and the controversy seems likely to continue for some time.

Homo sapiens

Paleoanthropologists—paleontologists who study human fossils—are perhaps under more pressure to make such finds than members of other paleontological disciplines. Although humans are a comparatively recent species, the origins of modern man and his predecessors attracts a great deal of controversy. The key debate centers on whether modern man originated in a small region in east Africa (the "out of Africa" hypothesis) or over a much broader area of Africa and Eurasia (the multiregional hypothesis). Research on mitochondrial DNA samples from humanoid skeletons supports the out of Africa theory in that the DNA of African specimens shows a greater genetic diversity than that of non-African populations. As a result, some scientists believe that mankind originated in Africa and spread outward.

However, the multiregional theory is indicated by the continuity of physical characteristics in skulls from eastern Asia and Europe. If these traits were influenced by genetic inheritance, then it is a strong possibility that modern man evolved directly from local ancestors in some regions or interbred with migrant modern-looking humans. Many paleoanthropologists are now combining elements of both theories into a proposal that modern man first emerged in Africa and then replaced archaic humans elsewhere, interbreeding providing distinctive regional characteristics.

▲ The fossil of a trilobite found in Coal County, Oklahoma. These arthropods dominated the seas some 500 million years ago. Their continually evolving forms have proved useful in dating rocks from the early Paleozoic era.

SEE ALSO:	EVOLUTION • GENETICS • GEOLOGY • LIFE

Paper Manufacture

Papyrus, a water reed, was used as a writing material more than 5,000 years ago by the Egyptians and later by Greek and Roman writers. Animal parchment has been known since Egyptian times and was much favored by the Romans for permanent records. To make papyrus, layers of reeds are set across each other and pressed and dried; parchment manufacture, similar to leather manufacture, involves the scraping and treatment of animal skins (except that today certain grades of paper are vegetable parchment). Neither of the ancient processes in any way changed the structure of the basic materials.

The word *paper* comes from the word *papyrus*, but true paper was invented in China less than 2,000 years ago. The Chinese collected old fishing nets, rags, and bits of plants, boiled the materials well, and beat them and stirred them with large amounts of water to make a pulp. A sieve was dipped in the pulp and removed horizontally with a layer of pulp on it, the water draining away through the mesh. The layer of pulp was then dried and pressed. The difference between papyrus and paper is that in papermaking the materials are reduced to their fiber structure, and the fibers are realigned.

The technique spread to the West when some Chinese papermakers were captured by the Arabs. It reached Europe in the late medieval period, and the first English paper factory was established in Hertfordshire in 1490. Paper made literacy attainable, and as literacy spread, there was increased demand for paper. In the 20th century, the latest advances in papermaking were exported from the United States to Japan, so the technology has made a complete circuit of the globe, but the basic principles have not changed.

Materials

Rags are used for the highest quality paper, especially handmade varieties. At the other end of the scale, seed fibers—jute, flax, grasses, and other plants—may be the source of raw material for papermaking; straw was used extensively in Britain during World War II. The majority of paper today, however, is made from wood pulp.

Synthetic and animal fibers have also been tried, but these techniques have remained experimental or too expensive for wide application; papermaking means almost exclusively the use of cellulose vegetable fibers. The fibers vary in size and shape but are hollow tubes closed at the ends

PAPERMAKING PROCESS

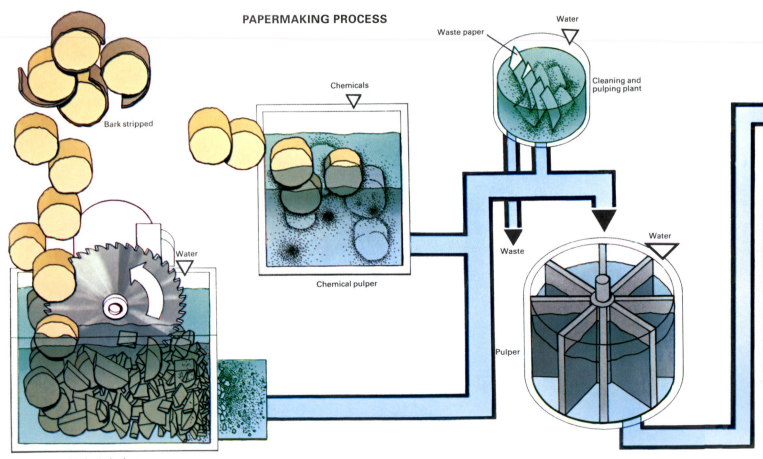

Bark stripped

Water

Mechanical pulper

Chemicals

Chemical pulper

Waste paper

Water

Cleaning and pulping plant

Waste

Water

Pulper

that are often tapered. They are held together in their natural state by substances, principally lignin, that must usually be dissolved and removed, a task accomplished by chemical treatment and washing of the pulp. The wide variety of methods used in papermaking can be seen by comparing blotting and greaseproof wrapping papers: the one is soft and absorbent, while the other is hard, smooth, and dense. The difference is in the choice of fibers, the way they are prepared, and the way they are processed on the papermaking machine. There are basically two methods: mechanical and chemical (cooking).

Pulp manufacture

Mechanical pulping is used chiefly for coniferous woods. It aims at a high yield rather than a pure pulp; the result is a cheap paper, of which newsprint is a good example, that is not expected to last. The logs are trimmed, debarked, and then ground, usually by rotating grindstones, and the fibers are flushed away from the stone using water. If the water supply is reduced, more heat is generated and longer fibers are obtained; in general, shorter fibers (up to a point) result in better paper. The pulp is screened several times, and the larger lumps are retreated or burned.

Depending on whether the pulp is to be processed on the spot or shipped, the excess water is removed in a concentrator or on a machine resembling a simple papermaking machine. The result is either air-dry pulp (10 percent moisture) or pulp with 45 percent moisture. A hundred tons (90 tonnes) of dry cut logs can yield more than 90 tons (81 tonnes) of air-dry pulp, but the strength

of the resultant fibers is not high, and mechanical pulp must be mixed with 15 to 50 percent chemical pulp before it is ready to be used to make paper.

Chemical, or cooking, methods remove more of the unwanted materials from the basic wood pulp, resulting in a lower yield but a higher quality pulp. The processes are divided generally into two categories: acid liquor and alkaline liquor.

The acid-liquor process is used mostly for spruce, which is the largest commercially profitable tree crop in the United States. The liquor is essentially an acid bisulfate with some free sulfur dioxide gas. It can be made by letting water trickle down through a tower containing limestone and blowing in sulfur dioxide gas at the bottom. The liquor is highly corrosive, and thus the equipment must be made of acid-resistant materials. The logs are sliced and the slices broken up into chips, which are then screened. Chips from one-quarter to three-quarters of an inch (6–19 mm) in length are pressure-cooked in a steam-heated digester. The quality is controlled by regulating chip size, liquor strength, pressure (75 to 110 psi, 520–760 kN/m^2) and cooking time (usually 7 to 12 hours). The unused sulfur dioxide and some of the heat can be recovered when cooking is over, but the spent liquor is highly polluting. It can be used in leather manufacture as a tanning agent, to lay the dust on roads, and in several other ways, but so much of it is produced that it remains a serious pollution problem.

Alkaline-liquor processes are similar, but the cooking agents are naturally not acidic and therefore are less polluting. These processes are used for non-woody fibers such as grasses and rags, for

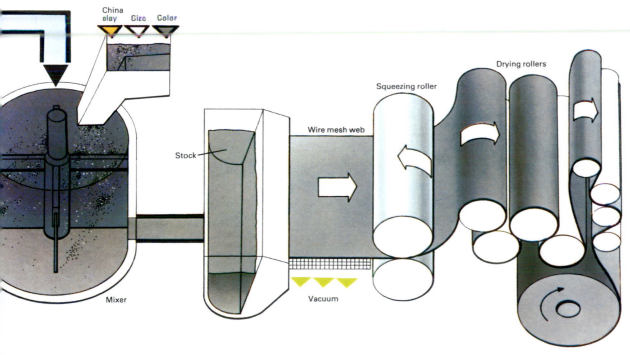

◀ The logs are reduced to a pulp by a mechanical or chemical process; then the additives are mixed in. The resulting mixture is first shaken on a wire belt to align the fibers, then pressed and dried on a series of rollers.

China clay   Size   Color

Drying rollers

Squeezing roller

Wire mesh web

Stock

Mixer

Vacuum

Reel of finished paper

◄ Wood chips are emptied into a digester, where they will be pressure-cooked with chemicals to form a pulp.

deciduous woods (hardwoods), and for coniferous woods with a high resin content, such as pine, because the alkali dissolves the resin. The wood is prepared in the same manner as for acidic cooking; other materials are prepared according to their properties. For example, rags must be sorted and straw must be chopped and the dust removed in a cyclone extractor.

The soda process uses caustic soda (sodium hydroxide). The amount of soda, cooking time, and pressure all vary according to the materials being cooked. With wood, up to 85 percent of the soda can be recovered from the waste liquor; with other materials, less is recovered because of the difficulty of washing it out of the fibers and because the amount of soda used is smaller to begin with.

The kraft, or sulfate, process results in a stronger fiber (*kraft* is the German word for strength). Sodium sulfate is added to the digester; it has no effect on digestion but is converted to sodium sulfide during the burning of the recovery process. When this in turn is added to the digester, it is automatically converted in controlled amounts to sodium hydroxide; this aids in digestion but conserves strength. The process generates objectionable smells and is not used near towns; it results in a scum on the waste liquor, which is called tall oil and can be used to make soap and lubricants. Sodium monosulfite, also called the neutral sulfite process, is one of the newer cooking methods. It depends on sulfur

dioxide and caustic soda and results in a high yield. It can be used to treat hardwoods that were not previously considered suitable for papermaking. A recovery process is being developed.

Continuous digestion is also under development, and there are combined mechanical and chemical methods in use that do not need pressure but lend themselves to continuous operation. For example, straw can be treated in an appropriate vessel with an impeller and a solution of hot soda, resulting in a high yield of straw pulp suitable for use in making packaging grades of paper.

Pulp preparation

After digestion, the pulp must be washed and often bleached. Washing is necessary to get rid of impurities; some pulps can be washed while still in the digester, and this is part of the waste recovery. The first wash results in a strong liquor that can in some cases be recovered; the next wash will result in a weaker liquor that can be used for the first wash of the next batch, and so on.

With wood pulps and in high-capacity operations, the digester is emptied immediately so it can be used again. Screens in series, both flat metal tray types and rotating devices, are used to remove impurities, but centrifugal, or vortex, cleaners are now so efficient that they can replace screens altogether. In a vortex cleaner, as the pulp is rapidly rotated, heavier impurities fall to the bottom while pure pulp passes through outlets near the top. One widely used centrifugal machine is called a rotary vacuum filter; it comprises a wire drum revolving in a vat. Suction from inside the drum draws a layer of pulp onto the wire, sucking the liquor out. The pulp is then washed with hot water sprays and scraped off the wire by a doctor blade.

Next follows, if required, some type of bleaching process, depending on the type of pulp and its intended use. Methods vary from the simple addition of bleaching liquor to a series of chemical steps that must be carefully monitored to avoid damaging the fibers. Increasingly, the bleaching is an extension of the digestion process, the exact process being a combination of methods chosen to accomplish maximum yield, strength of fibers, and degree of whiteness. Multistage bleaching systems are now common, in which various chemical treatment sequences are used, depending on the type of pulp and its end use.

Beating

In most cases, the pulp arrives at the paper mill in sheet form and must be broken up again. For this purpose, a machine called a hydrapulper may be used, a cask-shaped vessel with an impeller that disintegrates the pulp in water. Similar treatment is applied to recycled paper, an increasingly important raw material, particularly in view of increases in the price of pulp.

Next comes the beating. Prolonged beating with traditional machinery is still practiced, especially for handmade papers, but highly developed quality control followed by treatment in machines called refiners increasingly fulfills the beating function. In any case, the quality of the finished product is determined more at this point than at any other. The physical action of beating affects the length of the fibers, their plasticity, and their capacity for bonding together in the paper machine; therefore, beating also determines such characteristics as bulk, opacity, and strength.

The most common type of beating machine is the hollander, developed in Holland in the 18th century. It is an oval-shaped tub with a low wall, called a midfeather, running across the center but stopping short on each side so that the pulp can circulate around it. On one side of the midfeather, the beater roll is mounted on a shaft; the beater roll may weigh as much as 10 tons (9 tonnes), and the capacity of the tub may vary from about 200 lbs. (90 kg) of rags to about 1½ tons of wood pulp, with perhaps 5 parts pulp to 95 parts water. The roll has bars on its circumference parallel with the shaft; the pulp, now called the stock or the stuff, is ground against stationary bars on the floor of the tub beneath the roll. The clearance between the roll and the stationary bars is small but adjustable. The refiner, which has completely superseded the beater in the making of newsprint, for example, is a cone-shaped beater roll in a similarly shaped housing, also equipped with bars and adjustable clearance; the bars in the refiner run at a speed of 3,000 ft. (over 900 m) per minute. The stock goes through the refiner only once, and the refiners are connected in series if further beating capacity

▶ Papermaking the traditional way in Thailand. A sieve is dipped into the tub, then removed horizontally; after the water has drained away, the layer of pulp that is left is dried and pressed.

is needed. There are also disk refiners, with one rotating disk and one stationary, and combination cone and disk models.

Loading (fillers), pigments or dyes if required, and most sizing agents may be added to the stuff during beating. Loading materials are added to give improved opacity, and they also help to make the paper stable dimensionally and assist in obtaining a good finish. They are white materials, of which the most common are china clay, titanium oxide, and precipitated chalk. Chalk, for example, is added to cigarette paper to make it burn more evenly. Sizing agents, of which resin is the most common, render the paper resistant to penetration by water (but do not make it waterproof) so that it can accept water-based writing ink. Printing inks are oil or spirit based, and so papers for printing do not need to be sized, but completely unsized paper, called waterleaf, is not common. Wrapping papers may have to be written upon, for example, and certainly papers used in lithography need some water resistance.

Papermaking machines

The actual papermaking process is a continuous one. The most common type of machine is the Fourdrinier, named after two brothers, stationers, who built the first one in Hertfordshire, Britain, in 1803. Their machine deposited paper onto pieces of felt, after which it was finished by hand. The modern machine starts with the dilute stock at the wet end and finishes with reels of paper at the dry end. The additives can be mixed into the stock at the wet end of the machine instead of in the beating, if desired.

The stock is continuously delivered onto an endless belt, called the cloth, which is made of a wire or plastic mesh. A short sideways shake is applied to the cloth where the stock first meets it,

◀ The dry end of a continuous-process papermaking machine. The paper has just gone through the drying train and the calender rollers.

to improve the way the fibers mesh together. Drainage of water begins immediately through the mesh of the cloth, bringing the fibers closer together until the stock becomes a cohesive web. Then suction is introduced by means of vacuum boxes underneath the web. At this point, a light wire-covered roll, called the dandy roll, rides on the upper surface of the web, usually turned by the traveling web (but sometimes turning under power) and gently pressing it. A wire design can be wired or soldered to the dandy roll to impress the watermark, which identifies the manufacturer, onto the web.

The web is now separated from the cloth by a pair of rollers or, on the latest machines, by a single suction roller. They are called couch rolls. The volume of water removed up to this point is rich in fiber, chemicals, and so forth, much of which is recovered. The web is deposited on a felt and carried between pairs of pressure rolls that remove more of the water—the felt frequently becomes clogged and must be cleaned.

The water content of the web has now been reduced to about 65 percent, and the web moves to the dry end of the machine, where it passes around a series of pairs of steam-heated iron cylinders. At the end of the drying train, the paper has no finish and has been overdried to about 3 to 4 percent moisture content. The paper passes through several calender stacks, pairs of highly polished, chilled, iron pressure rolls that smooth the surface. Finally the paper passes over cooled sweat rolls, which adjust the moisture content and reduce the static electricity, and is wound onto large reels. To avoid dimensional instability, many printing papers are conditioned on the reel by passing through a hot, wet atmosphere that adjusts moisture content to 6 or 8 percent, normal for this type of paper when mature.

The paper is slit to the width and reel diameter required if it is to be used from the reel; paper for use in sheet form is taken to a cutting machine, where it is slit and crosscut in the same operation. For greater accuracy and clean edges, some papers are guillotine trimmed. Sheet papers are inspected, torn or faulty sheets removed, and counted for packing; today this processing can be done electronically at the cutting stage.

Other machines

The MG (machine glazed) machine produces paper highly glazed on one side and rough on the other. It is used for posters, wrapping paper, and shopping bags; the glaze is imparted by a large, highly polished drying cylinder. The paper is stuck to the face of the cylinder, and the surface in contact takes on the polish of the metal.

Cardboard for cartons, packaging, and so on is made by a different method of sheet formation on a cylinder-mold machine. A wire-covered roll rotates in a vat of dilute stock. Water filters through to the inside of the roll, and a layer of fibers is left on the surface, which is transferred to a felt. The process makes only a thin layer; to make up the greater thickness of cardboard, several such molds are placed in series, so a multi-layer structure is built up on the underside of a making felt, which is then reversed and carried through the rest of the machine. The advantage of this type of machine is that the center layers of this cardboard can be made of cheaper materials.

Today suction devices are becoming more common to assist the couch and other rollers on paper-making machinery. Some machines have the dry end entirely covered by a hood, within which fans and pipes remove moisture-laden air, enabling the machine to run faster. A modern fast newsprint manufacturing machine will run at around 3,280 ft. per minute (1,000 m/min).

◀ The wet end of a continuous-process papermaking machine. The pulp is poured onto a moving belt of plastic or wire mesh; its shaking action causes the fibers to align. Meanwhile, water is sucked out from below by means of vacuum boxes placed under the web.

SEE ALSO:	ACID AND ALKALI • CHINA AND PORCELAIN • DYEING PROCESS • INK • LUMBER • NEWSPAPER PRODUCTION • PRINTING

Parachute

A parachute is a device, usually shaped like an umbrella or a rectangle, that is used to produce drag when it is pulled through a medium, normally air or water. When a parachute is strongly constructed and is to be used underwater or at high speed in the air, it is usually called a drogue. As its name implies, the parachute was intended to prevent an object from falling too rapidly. Many early experiments were made using animals dropped from cliffs or high buildings, but it was not until the advent of the free balloon that an unaided descent could be made.

In 1797, André-Jacques Garnerin made the first jump with a linen parachute; it was 48 ft. (14.6 m) across when laid out as a flat disk, and despite a violent descent, he demonstrated his parachute in Europe for several years. Many other experiments were tried, but the parachute did not achieve more than entertainment value until World War I, when British army balloonists and German aircrews used similar devices to jump safely from crashing craft. In 1926, parachutes were produced for aircrews using the flat disk design but with panels cut on the bias (diagonally across the fabric) to give greater flexibility and strength. This basic design is still in use.

A typical parachute assembly comprises a harness for the parachutist to which is attached a pack containing the folded canopy. The harness is designed to fit the parachutist in such a way that the violent deceleration when the parachute opens will not cause injury and that it can be quickly released if the parachutist comes down in water or in a high wind that might drag him or her across the ground. The rip cord is pulled by the parachutist a few seconds after leaving the aircraft so that the opening chute will be clear of the superstructure. Pulling the rip cord removes a pin that holds shut the flaps on the pack; a small pilot chute, folded between the flaps, is ejected by a spring and, entering the slipstream, pulls the main parachute out of the pack. For paratroopers, the rip cord is attached to a static line in the aircraft so that it opens automatically. In high-speed aircraft, the crew member is ejected from the aircraft, seat and all, and the descent is automatic.

A safe rate of descent is considered to be about 20 ft. (6.6 m) per second. A larger parachute is provided for paratroopers to maintain this rate, because they are more heavily laden than an ejecting pilot or a sport parachutist. Sky divers will free fall for thousands of feet, altering the rate of descent and direction by spreading or arching their bodies. Parachuting for sport is carefully controlled for safety, and sky divers are required to open their parachutes at not less than 2,200 ft. (670 m). The force with which a parachutist strikes the ground is about the same as that of jumping from a height of 8 ft. (2.6 m).

Design

The rate of inflation, the stability, and the general performance of the canopy depend on its porosity. A parachute inflates when the air entering the mouth is arrested by the fabric at the crown so that the pressure created there spreads to the outer panels. If the permeability (also called porosity) of the fabric is excessive, the pressure will be sufficient only to spread the outer panels, and the parachute will only partly inflate. When the porosity of the fabric is insufficient, the parachute will inflate rapidly, but air will spill around the edge of the advancing periphery, forcing the parachute to swing sideways.

A parachute made with concentric ribbon rings must have further narrow ribbons running from the crown outward at right angles across the concentric rings in addition to the load-carrying webbings. During inflation, all the ribbons flutter until the air pressure spreading outward from the crown tensions the radial ribbons, thus restraining the fluttering of each successive ring.

▲ A parachute with open gores, which allow it to be steered by pulling on the nylon cords. The pulling action distorts the gores and moves the chute according to the pull.

In 1942, it was noticed that if a complete fabric parachute suffered a split in one gore during inflation, it did not swing but maintained a steady glide in a direction away from the split. Gores are the triangular-shaped panels that, sewn together, make up the canopy. A parachute with an open gore was fitted with two handles connected to the bottom corners of this gore, and it was found that a light pull would distort either side of the gore and that a reasonable degree of control was achieved.

After this design had been entered for the Second World Parachuting Championships in 1953, the principle was developed by parachutists in many countries until today a parachutist can control his or her parachute so as to touch a target a few inches across. Important features in these advanced designs are the center cord, which holds the crown down to force the rapid opening of the canopy; the set of control slots, which allow a quick change of direction or speed; and the extension panels, which aid rapid turns.

The principle of inducing lift over the front surface of a gliding parachute led inevitably to the construction of fabric wings. One successful design has a neatly triangular shape, with internal rigging to maintain its form and slots to extend the lift over the upper surface. Inflation of this type is rapid and has to be carefully controlled to avoid injury to the parachutist. The rectangular type of parachute with its ram air-inflatable front section and rear edge flaps has to be flown as a winged glider. It cannot be turned about an axis as a circular parachute can but must be aimed at the target and stalled to reduce the speed; the action is similar to that of a bird when it is landing. Rates of turn of rectangular-shaped parachutes generally exceed those of circular canopies. These wing designs are effective but complicated to make, and this problem has led to the development of basic umbrella shapes that have good gliding qualities. A virtually nonporous fabric is used to make a conical shape whose half section is the upper surface of an airfoil at a declination of about 45 degrees to the axis of the cone. Two large open panels, covered with fine netting, are positioned apart at the back of the cone to give the control necessary to glide and turn.

Manufacture

Most parachutes are made up from triangular gores that are constructed by sewing together panels cut from layers (as many as 200) of fabric. The panel patterns that determine the shape of the parachute are marked out on the layers and cut through with an electrically powered knife. Each panel has to be calculated to give the parachute its correct size and shape, and because cost is important, the simplest design to meet the performance specification has to be chosen, ranging between the specially shaped parachute with a great variety of panels and the flat disk with a few bias-cut panels. The construction must also permit a steady flow of work through the sewing machines with a minimum of handling of the large bulk of fabric. Automatic pattern and sewing machines are used wherever possible to facilitate a high degree of manufacturing integrity.

When supply-dropping parachutes became very large—as much as 66 ft. (20 m) when inflated—it was decided that they should be made in five pieces: a strong crown to withstand the initial air forces of the inflation and four lighter-weight side segments to spread and give the full drag. This method allowed the workshop facilities for making human-carrying parachutes to be used, and the pieces could be stored separately until required for rigging into a complete assembly.

An extension of this manufacturing method was the move towards the production of squares of fabric, which can be assembled into three different parachute sizes as required. Each square measures 13 ft. (4 m) across, and they are tied together in regular cross-shaped patterns; five squares to carry 500 lbs. (230 kg), twelve for 1,500 lbs. (690 kg) and 20 for 2,500 lbs. (1,150 kg); the rigging lines and webbing straps are all made separately, ready for assembly as required. Parachutes of this type have been flown at velocities of more than twice the speed of sound.

When German engineers designed parachutes, they made a ribbon foundation from which the gore shapes were cut after the main load-bearing webbings had been stitched into place. This stitching required the use of specially designed traveling sewing machines. Without such machines, the ribbons have to be laid out on a jig and tacked, usually with a hot needle, before being stitched together. To avoid this complexity,

◀ The brake parachute on a Mirage fighter trainer of the French Air Force is a drogue and is used to reduce the landing distance on short runways.

the ring slot parachute was devised, in which fabric rings much wider than the ribbons were used. These rings were reinforced along their edges and then assembled with the techniques normally used for making human-carrying parachutes. Ribbon designs are still essential where great strength is required.

Materials

Until World War II, parachutes were made from either natural fibers such as flax, cotton, and silk or from modified cellulose fibers such as viscose and acetate rayon. Designs were limited by the bulkiness of the cotton and flax or the cost of the silk and fine rayons until the discovery of nylon in 1939 in both the United States and Germany. This continuous synthetic fiber was so superior in strength and extendibility that fine fabrics, equivalent to silk but more capable of sustaining parachute inflation shocks, became widely available. Automatic finishing and heat setting ensured that large quantities of parachutes could be manufactured to extremely tight specifications.

The main disadvantage with nylon parachute fabric is that, being a thermoplastic, if it experiences sudden friction (rubbing) under pressure, it can suffer local melting, which can lead to extensive damage. This problem can be avoided by the application of a light coating of silicone, but the most important preventative is careful packing to achieve the correct sequence of deployment phases. The fabric can also be calendered (pressed by rollers) to spread the yarns and reduce the porosity drastically, thus ensuring that the lifting

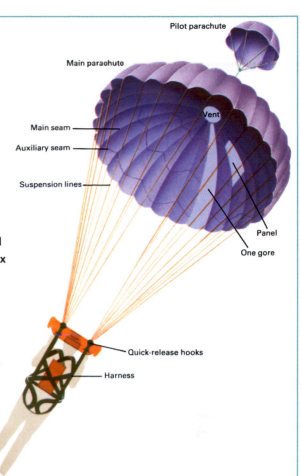

PARACHUTING

When a sky diver deploys a parachute, the pilot chute at the top opens first and pulls the main chute out of the pack. The harness has quick-release hooks so that parachutists can release themselves in a hurry if they land in high winds. An apex vent in the top of the parachute allows compressed air to escape and permits a steady descent. Without the vent, the air would spill from the periphery of the parachute, causing it to swing violently from side-to-side.

Pilot parachute
Main parachute
Main seam
Auxiliary seam
Vent
Suspension lines
Panel
One gore
Quick-release hooks
Harness

surfaces of steerable parachutes can be kept to a minimum bulk and yet retain their strength. In addition, the tearing strength of a fabric can be reduced if a thin coating of silicone is applied to reduce the porosity.

Drogue parachutes

Drogue parachutes are durable, normally conical devices deployed at the rear of high-speed vehicles—usually aircraft or submersibles, but on occasion high-speed land vehicles—to assist with the braking process. Jet fighters and NASA's space shuttle both use such parachutes.

Another recent development is the whole-plane, or airframe, parachute. In 1999, the first plane to be fitted with such a parachute went into production. The airframe parachute had previously been used widely in ultralight and experimental aviation and is credited with having saved lives in a number of loss-of-control accidents.

Airframe parachutes work in the same way as personal parachutes except, because of the weight of the aircraft, they have to be considerably larger and are deployed by rocket motors.

FACT FILE

■ In 1785, a Frenchman, François Blanchard, dropped a dog by parachute from a hot-air balloon. In the late 18th century and throughout the 19th century, primitive canvas parachutes of the type used by Blanchard were employed by performers making exhibition descents from balloons. Blanchard's own first parachute jump, in 1793, ended with a broken leg.

■ The Paraplane is a microlight aircraft using a sports parachute as its wing. This parachute is attached to a lightweight alloy tricycle T-frame. The nylon ram-air parachute wing is controlled by feet pedals and lines. Power comes from twin two-stroke engines, for a cruising speed of 26 mph (41 km/h).

SEE ALSO: AERODYNAMICS • BALLOON • EJECTION SEAT • GLIDER • HANG GLIDER • SPACE SHUTTLE • ULTRALIGHT AIRCRAFT

Parasitology

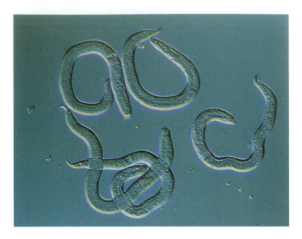

Parasitology is the scientific study of parasites and their way of life. Parasites are plants and animals that spend part or all of their lives living on or within and at the expense of another animal or plant, called a host. Because parasites harm their hosts, it is important to study them. When the hosts are ourselves or our food, parasites can cause immense suffering and damage.

Often, different plants or animals will live in close association with each other where one benefits from the relationship without harming the other (commensalism) or even with some mutual benefit from the association (mutualism). These relationships are termed *symbiotic*. Parasitism is also a form of symbiosis, but in this case, the host always suffers, although the actual damage may sometimes be very slight—a parasite that severely damages, or worse, actually kills its host has deprived itself of a living and created prematurely the problem of finding its next host. This situation does occur in certain flies, wasps, and butterflies and is referred to as parasitoidism.

Different kinds of parasite

Parasites that live on the skin of the host, such as fleas and leeches, are called ectoparasites, while those that live within a host are known as endoparasites. Endoparasites are further divided into intracellular, those that live in the cells of the host's body, such as viruses and bacteria, and intercellular, those that live within spaces in the host's body, such as tapeworms, which live in animal intestines.

Parasites that are completely dependent on their host for survival, such as tapeworms and viruses, are known as obligate. Those that can survive without a host, such as leeches, are known as facultative. Parasites that live their entire adult lives in a host are called permanent parasites, while those that attach temporarily to their hosts,

◄ The nematode *Heligosomoides polygrus,* which is a parasite on rodents but does not affect humans.

▼ A mosquito is one of the worst of human parasites. While feeding on human blood, it transmits potentially fatal diseases, such as malaria and yellow fever. In this picture, blood from a human arm can be seen flowing up the proboscis of a female yellow fever mosquito.

such as fleas and ticks, are called temporary. Hyperparasitism describes species that are parasites of parasites. For example, protozoa live in fleas that in turn live on cats.

Brood parasitism occurs in birds, such as cuckoos, that do not build their own nests or rear their own young. Instead, the female deposits her eggs in nests belonging to other bird species. The females of some cuckoo species eject any eggs already in the nest; alternatively, when the cuckoo hatches in the host nest, it may eject any eggs or hatchlings of the host, thus ensuring that it does not have to compete for food.

Several ant species use other ant species as slaves, stealing ant larvae and rearing them in the parasite ants' nest. The larvae hatch and work for the parasite ants as slaves.

Plant and fungal parasites

Some plant species, including the world's largest flower, *Rafflesia arnoldi*, are parasites. *Rafflesia arnoldi* lives in Malaysia on the roots of the species *Tetrastigma*, a large vine belonging to the grape family. Mistletoe, also a parasitic plant, lives on a variety of host trees. Some species of mistletoe are hyperparasites: one species of mistletoe lives on another species of mistletoe, which in turn lives on the host tree.

All fungi are either parasitic or saprophytic, meaning that they feed from dead tissue. Most fungi have a mass of rootlike threads called hyphae that absorb food and water. In parasitic fungi, the hyphae penetrate host plant cells and

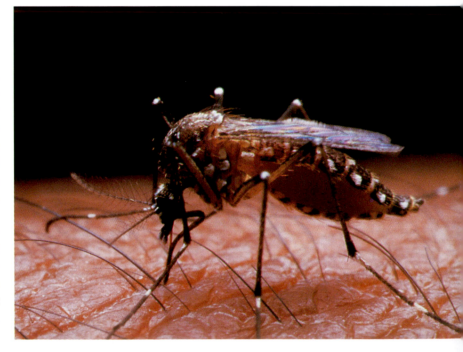

absorb the cell contents. Many fungal parasites do not cause much damage, but some, such as the honey or bootlace fungus *Armillaria*, can kill even huge trees. Others, such as *Pythium*, are devastating to seedlings, while the mildews and rusts are harmful and unsightly on ornamental plants and very damaging to crops.

Fungal parasitism tends to be most damaging in crops grown in monoculture, as in the U.S. corn belt. Where both parasite and host are native and in natural surroundings, evolutionary processes have resulted in a reasonable balance between parasite and host. Where humans have intervened to modify the situation by introducing monocultures of specialized crop plants, often alien in origin and lacking the natural defense mechanisms evolved by native wild plants, pests can be devastating.

Researchers are seeking to identify other fungi that inhabit the plant surface without doing the plant any harm. The hope is that encouraging the harmless fungus will crowd out the parasite. *Armillaria* may be successfully combated by another nonparasitic, root-inhabiting fungus called *Trichoderma*.

Parasites in pest control

Some parasites are now being employed as pesticides. The fungus *Verticillium lecanii* can be applied in water just like a chemical spray to control a range of pests, such as aphids. Parasitic nematodes are being used to control soil pests such as weevil larvae. Pesticide treatment of soil is difficult, expensive, and uncertain; there is no guarantee the chemical will reach the depth at which the pest lives. Nematodes sprayed onto the soil, however, move through it under their own power to find their prey.

On their own, the nematode parasites would slowly incapacitate their weevil larva host, but it takes many weeks. Many parasitic nematodes carry symbiotic bacteria in their guts that enter the host and kill its cells, making them easier for the nematode to digest. Careful selection has provided a nematode-plus-bacterium combination that is lethal in a couple of days. Genetic engineering has the potential to enhance the speed of killing the bacteria still further.

Not all nematodes are so helpful. The appropriately named root knot nematodes attack many tropical crops, some of great commercial value, such as cotton, citrus, corn, and tobacco. As they feed, they inject the roots with saliva containing biochemicals that drastically alter cell growth. Around the embedded head of the feeding nematode, the cells enlarge dramatically, causing the crumpled knotlike root swellings that give

◄ A close-up of the nematode *Toxocara vitalorum*. Most nematodes are parasitic, affecting either plants or animals. Among the nematode diseases found in humans are hookworm, threadworm, maw-worm, and toxocariasis.

the nematode its name. Researchers have now found soil-dwelling fungi that naturally attack the nutrition egg masses of the nematodes and are seeking to enhance their effectiveness as biological control agents. Unlike the broad spectrum toxic effect of most chemical pesticides, such biological agents can be precisely targeted at only harmful pathogens.

Animals as parasites

In the animal kingdom, most parasites are so-called lower animals with comparatively simple anatomy. Parasitism is commonplace among insects, flatworms (or flukes), tapeworms, and roundworms (or nematodes). Most parasitic insects, such as ticks and mites, live on the outer surface or skin of their host, while most flatworms, tapeworms, and nematodes live within their host. Most animal parasites are small, many microscopic, but a few can grow to a substantial size; tapeworms, for example, occasionally growing as long as 10 ft. (3 m).

Some species of parasitic fish, such as lampreys and hagfish, grow to around 3 ft. (90 cm) in length. These species attach to their fish hosts using their mouths and then suck out blood and nutrients from the host fish. In the Great Lakes of the United States and Canada, the sea lamprey has caused great damage to the trout industry by living off the trout and in the process reducing the health of the fish stocks.

Parasites need a method of getting from one host to another. In many cases, it is passive—the eggs or larvae are left in places where they stand a chance of being picked up by the host. For example, chickens pick up the eggs of a nematode worm, *Ascaridia galli*, when feeding and pass on the next generation of eggs in their droppings. Other parasites travel to their host or need vectors—that is, other agents that unwittingly transport the parasite from one host to the next.

A classic example of a vector at work is the mosquito, which carries the tiny protozoans that cause malaria. For many years, the disease has been well controlled both by use of antimalarial drugs and by killing the vector—the mosquito—with insecticides. Now, however, malaria is on the increase again. The protozoan parasite has developed resistance to the drugs, and pesticides, such as DDT, that initially controlled the mosquitoes are now considered to be too persistent and too environmentally damaging to be used.

One novel approach to the problem aims to interrupt the life cycle of the protozoan when it is actually within the mosquito. A vaccine has been developed for this purpose, but it will not protect the person bitten by a mosquito. Instead, a mosquito that bites a vaccinated person will not then transmit the protozoan to other people that it bites. Although it will still be necessary to protect the human carrying the vaccine using conventional methods, the hope is that the protection will gradually spread throughout the community.

The advantage of blocking the transmission of the disease at an early stage in the parasite's development is that there is less risk of particularly robust parasites surviving to pass on their successful genes and so create a resistant strain.

Multihost parasites

The life cycles of parasites can be fascinatingly complex. Gall wasps that attack oak trees begin their cycle in late summer when fertilized females lay their eggs on the undersides of leaves. Injected with the egg are biochemicals that manipulate the leaf tissue to produce characteristic galls. One causes pale spanglelike outgrowths, another, golden galls resembling microscopic silk buttons. Within the gall, which in fall drops to the forest floor, the egg develops into a larva by feeding on the plant tissue. The larva pupates, and in spring, an asexual wasp emerges, quite different in appearance from its parent. Without mating, it flies to the newly opening tassels of oak flowers and there lays its eggs. Again these are accompanied by chemical secretions, but in this case, the gall that forms is fleshy and spherical, closely resembling a red currant fruit. From these eggs hatch the males and females, which will mate on the wing before the female lays her eggs in a leaf for the cycle to start again.

An understanding of the mode of action of the biochemicals injected by the gall wasp could be of great value in manipulating the rate of tree growth, and research is being actively directed to this goal both in orchard fruits and in hardwood timber trees.

▲ A close-up of part of an oak tree. A gall, caused by an unidentified parasite, can be seen near the center of the frame.

Schistosomiasis, a disease that afflicts 200 million people worldwide, is caused by worms that begin life as tiny larvae swimming in fresh water. The larvae first infect snails and multiply in them, then escape again into the water. If a person steps in the water, they burrow through the skin and enter the bloodstream. After growing for a few weeks in the lungs, they travel to veins that drain the intestine or bladder and remain there for around 20 to 30 years, constantly laying eggs. Some of the eggs are excreted from the intestine or bladder and, if they reach fresh water, hatch and start the cycle again.

Recent research at the University of California at San Francisco has revealed that at least one species of the worms has evolved to respond to a human hormone that calls immune system cells to the site of bacterial infections. The hormone is always present in veins that drain the intestine, because these veins contain waste products from intestinal bacteria. The presence of the hormone tells the worms they are in the right place to lay their eggs.

In many cases, parasitism is extremely damaging to us and our crops and may even be life-threatening. A detailed understanding of its modes of action will help resolve the problems caused and should also lead to a steadily increasing range of environmentally friendly pest- and disease-control strategies.

SEE ALSO: AGRICULTURE, ORGANIC • BIOCHEMISTRY • GENETIC ENGINEERING • PEST CONTROL • ZOOLOGY

Particle Accelerator

Particle accelerators are machines used to give energy to beams of electrically charged subatomic particles. They make it possible to have high energies concentrated in a tiny volume at predetermined positions and in a controlled fashion. This ability has been used for a variety of experimental and practical purposes in the field of nuclear physics.

Accelerators of many types have been developed in an effort to achieve higher and higher energies. Yet in all the different types, there are some basic features in common. The essential ingredients are a source of charged particles and electric and magnetic fields that are used to accelerate and guide them. Many kinds of particles can be accelerated—not only the basic protons and electrons but also composite ones, such as alpha particles, which consist of two protons and two neutrons and are therefore helium ions.

Basic features

A familiar object that uses all the principles of a particle accelerator is the cathode-ray tube of a television set, in which a narrow beam of electrons is fired at a fluorescent screen and made to travel across it rapidly. Where the beam strikes the screen, it makes the fluorescent material glow to produce a picture. The electrons are produced by heating a filament so that they gain enough energy to break away from the atoms in the filament wire and boil off. Each electron carries with it a single negative charge. When they boil off, they find themselves in an electric field that is set up by applying a voltage between the filament (which becomes the electrically negative cathode) and another electrode (the anode) nearer to the screen.

The electrons fly away from the cathode toward the anode, gaining energy as they do so. Just as with the attractions and repulsions between north and south poles of magnets, so a negative electron is repelled by a negative electrode and attracted by a positive electrode. Exactly the opposite would happen with a particle carrying a positive charge, such as a proton. It is accelerated away from the positive electrode toward the negative.

Magnetic fields have the property of curving the paths of charged particles. Therefore, magnets can be used in televisions to bend the elec-

▼ A linear accelerator. Particles are accelerated by waves of electric field along the walls of the cylinder. The polarity is shielded by various drift tubes that increase in length along the cylinder.

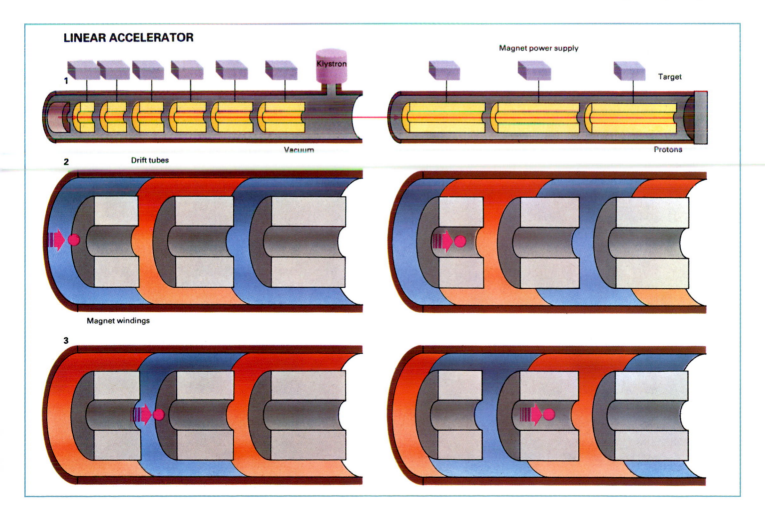

LINEAR ACCELERATOR

Klystron

Magnet power supply

Target

1

Vacuum

Protons

2   Drift tubes

Magnet windings

3

tron paths so that they finish up in a narrow beam in spite of emerging from the filament as a spray of electrons moving in all directions. The bending power of the magnet focuses the electron beam in a way comparable to the effect of a lens on a beam of light.

These principles underlie even the most advanced accelerator techniques. What is needed is a source of charged particles where electrons, protons, or other ions are broken away from atoms. The particles are then exposed in one way or another to an electric field that accelerates them (this concept is known more correctly as an electric potential gradient—the electrons in the television tube roll down an electric hill). Magnetic fields are also employed to bend their paths to focus them or to control their direction.

One more feature is usually necessary: a good vacuum in the region where the particles are accelerated prevents them from being scattered on air molecules, thus making it more difficult to hold them in a beam.

The expression *electron volt* is used to describe the energy a particle receives, since this provides a simple relationship to the accelerating voltage. For example, a television will have its anode at something like 10,000 volts (usually expressed as 10 kV) positive compared with the cathode. Each electron reaching the television screen has been accelerated to an energy of 10,000 electron volts (written 10 keV).

The other common energy units are MeV for million electron volts and GeV for billion (giga) electron volts. Accelerators are described as a 10 GeV machine, and so on. The Tevatron particle accelerator at Fermilab in Illinois is capable of producing over 1 TeV (1,000 GeV) and is currently the most powerful accelerator in the world. By 2007, however, the Large Hadron Collider at CERN (Europe's center for nuclear research) in Switzerland will have been completed and will be seven times more powerful than the Tevatron.

Uses of accelerators

The most powerful particle accelerators are used in research to discover the fundamental components of matter and to study their behavior. As accelerators have been developed to give higher and higher energies, they have uncovered an incredibly complex world on a smaller scale than the atomic nucleus involving hundreds of previously unknown particles. Studying these particles has revealed phenomena that overthrow many commonsense ideas about how nature works.

At GeV energies, accelerated particles can penetrate not just the cluster of particles in a nucleus but other individual particles leading to

▲ An electrostatic generator. The energy particle beams produced initiate nuclear reactions.

spectacular transformations. At the instant a collision takes place, the energy can be sufficiently high to create completely new particles (in accordance with Einstein's famous $E = mc^2$ relationship, which specifies that mass and energy are interchangeable). It is accelerators of GeV energies that are used in the most advanced research into the nature of matter.

However, only a very small proportion of particle accelerators, and these the most powerful ones, are used in research of this type. The vast majority are used in industry and medicine. Quite apart from television tubes, there are X-ray machines used in hospitals and for nondestructive testing in industry. Other accelerators produce radioisotopes (forms of elements with unstable nuclei, which throw off particles after a time and can thus be traced in medical, industrial, or agricultural systems by using particle detectors). There are also radiation therapy machines for the treatment of cancer and a long list of other practical applications.

Types of accelerators

The simple types of accelerators are linear—they move particles in straight lines. A television tube is a linear accelerator in this sense (except for the deflections in the beam needed to produce the picture). So is the Van de Graaff generator, a high-voltage generator often used in the laboratory.

There are also more specialized linear accelerators. A common type was invented by the U.S. physicist Luis Walter Alvarez. It has a long cylindrical tank along which hollow tubes are set up in a straight line with gaps in between them. The tank is fed with electric power at high frequency, having the effect of swinging the electric field backward and forward between the tubes. Charged particles are fed in at one end in a beam directed through the hollow tubes. The timing of the swing of the electric field and the length of the tubes is arranged so that when the field is in the right direction to accelerate the particles, they emerge into the gaps between the tubes. In effect, if they are positively charged particles (protons), when the tube behind them becomes positive, the tube in front becomes negative, and they are accelerated across the gap. The electric field then swings in the opposite direction. Ordinarily, changing the field would decelerate the protons, but they are safely hidden inside the next tube, and the decelerating field does not reach them.

This process is repeated many times along the tank, and the protons emerge with an accumulated energy of perhaps 20 MeV. They will be traveling faster as they approach the end of the tank, and the tubes have to be made longer than at the input end so that they hide the faster protons for sufficient time while the field swings around. Magnetic fields play an important role in keeping the beam focused as it travels along the axis of the tank; a magnet is usually built into each tube.

Cyclotrons

A limitation of the linear accelerator is that each of its components is used just once in the acceleration process. To reach very high energies, linear accelerators become prohibitively long, and circular machines hold an advantage. If particles can be made to come around again to pass through the same acceleration station many times, there are obvious gains.

The first accelerator of this type was invented by the U.S. physicist E. O. Lawrence and is known as the cyclotron. The charged particles are fed into the center of a vacuum chamber shaped like a large shoe polish tin containing a slightly smaller one divided into two D-shaped halves called dees. The halves have a small gap between

them, and the accelerating electric field is applied across the gap. A circular magnet covers the chamber and gives a constant field throughout the whole chamber volume where the particles travel, thus having the effect of curving the paths of the particles as they shoot from one dee to another. The radius of the curve that a particular particle follows depends on its speed—the higher the speed is, the shallower the curve.

Particles are fed in at the center. They cross the gap, and the field accelerates them. They then swing around a small semicircle inside one of the dees because of the magnetic field. Meanwhile, the electric field across the gap is reversed, and when they emerge into it again, they are accelerated a second time. In the other dee, they swing around a slightly larger semicircle (since they are moving faster), and when they come out again into the gap, the electric field has again been reversed to give them a further kick. This process continues, and the particles follow a spiral path increasing in energy all the time until they fly out at the rim of the vacuum chamber.

Synchrocyclotrons

The cyclotrons are excellent and comparatively simple machines to provide particles up to energies of about 20 MeV. Above that energy, however, they run into a phenomenon explained in Einstein's relativity theory and they no longer work. In the cyclotron, the electric field across the gap is swung from one direction to another at a fixed frequency. It is therefore important that

◀ The tunnel of the antiproton source at Fermilab—the Fermi National Accelerator Laboratory in Batavia, Illinois. Magnets at the right make up the debuncher ring, where antiprotons emerging from a target are compacted and passed to the ring at the left, the accumulator ring. When sufficient antiprotons have been collected, they are injected into the Tevatron—a two-story building—to collide with protons traveling in the opposite direction.

the particles spend the same amount of time describing the semicircles no matter what their energy so that they always emerge into the gap at the right time to receive their next kick. But when they have been accelerated to speeds close to the speed of light, the particles begin to increase in mass rather than speed.

At 20 MeV a proton has increased in mass by about 2 percent, and it then takes 2 percent longer to get around its semicircle in the cyclotron than when it has low energy at the center of the machine. It begins to get out of step with the accelerating field in the gap.

The solution, which has made higher energies possible, is gradually to reduce the frequency at which the field across the gap is swung around so as to keep in step with the orbiting speed of the particles as their increasing mass slows this speed down. This variant of the cyclotron is called the synchrocyclotron, since its electric field is sychronized with the orbiting speed of the particles. One of the largest machines of this type is at the Joffe Physico-technical Institute at Gatchina near St. Petersburg in Russia. It accelerates protons to a peak energy of 1 GeV.

Synchrotrons

For energies beyond 1 GeV, a cyclotron type of accelerator becomes a technically unwieldy monster. The magnet, for example, weighs many thousands of tons and is about 30 ft. (10 m) in diameter. Above this size, the most advanced type of accelerator to date—the synchrotron—comes into action. It uses the same idea of accelerating particles back around a circle so that the same accelerating stations can be used to increase their energy further.

The difference is that, instead of using a constant magnetic field that allows the particles to spiral outward while their speed grows, the synchrotron increases its magnetic field in step so as

to hold the particles on exactly the same circle no matter what their speed. This allows a hollow central ring of smaller magnets to be used instead of one huge one and a narrow tube instead of a wide chamber.

Charged particles are usually fed into the circular vacuum tube of the synchrotron from a linear accelerator so that they are already at an energy of several tens of MeV. They then move around the synchrotron ring with the magnets powered to give a low field. On moving round the ring, they encounter several accelerating stations where electric fields give them an energy kick. The particles would then tend to move on to a wider circle, but the magnetic field is nudged higher to hold them in the ring. Again, the frequency at which the accelerating stations give their kicks has to be progressively adjusted to take account of the orbiting speed and the effects of the growing mass of the particles. (A proton traveling along with an energy of 30 GeV is about 30 times heavier than when it is at rest.)

More energetic collisions may be achieved with storage ring colliders, which use two intersecting synchrotron loops that accelerate subatomic particles in opposing directions and then cause them to slam together, thus increasing the overall velocity of the collision.

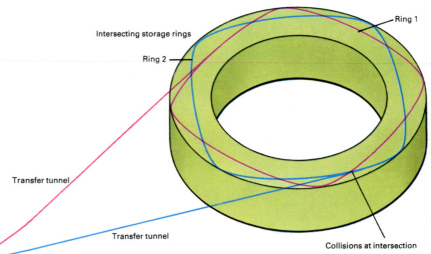

Intersecting storage rings

Ring 1

Ring 2

Transfer tunnel

Transfer tunnel

Collisions at intersection

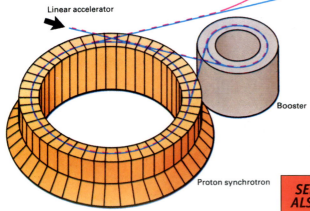

Linear accelerator

Booster

Proton synchrotron

◀ To obtain protons at a high enough energy level for the intersecting storage rings, they are first accelerated to 50 MeV in a linear accelerator; passed to a booster, where they are raised to 800 MeV; and then transferred to the proton synchrotron, where they are taken to the required energy level for the storage rings. Particles travel in opposite directions in the storage rings so that when they collide, the overall energy of the collision is much greater than that of a particle crashing into a stationary target.

SEE ALSO: ATOMIC STRUCTURE • ELEMENTARY PARTICLE • ENERGY, MASS, AND WEIGHT • PARTICLE DETECTOR • QUANTUM THEORY

Particle Detector

Particle detectors are devices that enable the smallest components of matter, such as electrons or protons, to be observed. Since these particles are extremely small, less than a trillionth of an inch across, they cannot be seen directly with the eye, even using the most powerful microscopes. Thus, they have to be observed indirectly by observing the effects that particles produce when passing through a detector, which they can activate in various ways.

The majority of particle detectors use the effect of ionization. When a particle with an electric charge travels at high energy through a solid, liquid, or gas, it can knock electrons out of the atoms that are in its path. This phenomenon is known as ionization, and it is the liberated elec-

trons or ionized atom that can then be picked out in some way to see where the particle traveled.

The scientists who study the behavior of the basic particles of matter like to know several things. For each particle involved, they like to know where it is and when it passed, how fast it is traveling, and what type of particle it is. The particle detectors are therefore designed to give this sort of information as precisely as possible. As an example of the accuracies that can be achieved, different detectors can indicate where particles have passed to within a few thousandths of an inch and indicate when they passed to within a few billionths of a second.

Traditionally, most detectors have given their information in visual form—such as the particles

▲ Technicians performing maintenance work on the central section of the collider detector at Fermilab in Illinois. The Fermi National Accelerator Laboratory is the home of the world's most powerful particle accelerator—the Tevatron.

◄ Setting up the complex equipment for a particle collision experiment at CERN (the European center for nuclear research).

producing tracks in emulsions and bubble chambers. This method has particular advantages in that the particular interactions can be seen and the information is available as a permanent record on film. It involves, however, the time-consuming process of developing the film, looking to see if anything of interest has happened, and if so, measuring the track positions before sending the information to a computer for calculations on some aspect of particle behavior. Today, the tendency is toward detectors that give their information as electric pulses. These pulses can be passed directly to the computer without any intervening stage (a situation known as having a detector online). Information can then be collected much more quickly and easily. There are various types of detectors, the earlier ones still depending on photographic analysis.

Nuclear emulsions

One of the first detection techniques was the use of special photographic emulsions, known as nuclear emulsions because they were used in studies of nuclear particles. Thick layers of emulsion, with a silver bromide content about ten times higher than that in normal film, record the passage of individual charged particles, which damage the silver bromide molecules in their path. Tracks appear when the emulsion is developed.

This technique can pinpoint with very high accuracy (a few thousandths of an inch) where particles pass, but it does not give useful information about when the particle traveled into the emulsion. Also, the emulsion contains a variety of atoms, and it can often be difficult to decipher which particles are involved in producing the tracks. Nuclear emulsions are now used less often,

but in the late 1940s, they were the most popular particle detectors. They were, for example, flown in balloons or stacked on mountain tops to detect particles, called cosmic rays, that hurtle into Earth's atmosphere from outer space. This technique led to the discovery of pions, particles that play a crucial role in the nucleus.

Cloud and bubble chambers

Cloud and bubble chambers also record tracks of particles visually by taking photographs either of the trail of liquid droplets in a cloud chamber or the trail of vapor bubbles in a bubble chamber. They are used in experiments at particle accelerators, where they make it possible to take pictures of all the charged particles emerging from a collision between an accelerated particle and a particle in the chamber. They give good accuracy in measuring positions but again demand the time-consuming process of developing, scanning, and measuring film.

Bubble chambers first came into use around 1955 and consist of a superheated liquid under pressure that is suddenly allowed to expand, with the result that the passage of charged particles causes atoms in the liquid to ionize and boil, thus leaving a trail of tiny bubbles where the particle has passed. This technique was used widely until the 1970s, when it was largely superseded by highly accurate detectors with electronic data recording. Large bubble chambers, however, may still be employed in experiments at accelerators, and the technique has been used in discovering most of the 200 particles that are now known.

Spark chamber

The spark chamber is a particle detector that collects information on the whereabouts of charged particles in the form of electric pulses.

A typical spark chamber consists of two planes of thin parallel stretched wires with a gap of about 0.4 in. (10 mm) between them, which is filled with a gas such as argon. A pulse of about 15,000 volts is applied across the gap when other detectors indicate that a particle is on its way. This pulse is almost enough for electric breakdown to occur so that a spark passes between the planes.

When a charged particle passes through the gap, it causes ionization in the gas and disturbs the electric condition enough for a spark to cross between the gap at the position of the ionization. The spark produces an electric pulse on the wire where it hits, and thus, the particle position is known to be somewhere along the length of a particular wire. Normally, several such chambers are set up back to back with the parallel wires aligned in different directions in each plane. The path of the particle is then known to be where the wires that fire cross one another.

The accuracy to which the particle position can be determined is not very high, since the wires are usually about 0.04 in. (1 mm) apart. Better accuracy can be obtained by photographing the sparks between planes of aluminum foil, called optical spark chambers, instead of wires. A development of this method avoids the intermediary of film by using a television camera to look at the sparks. The camera converts the position of the light produced by the spark directly into electric pulses, operating in much the same way as it does when communicating normal television pictures.

Geiger-Müller tube

The Geiger-Müller tube is another detector that was very useful in the early days of nuclear physics but which has now been replaced almost entirely by more advanced detectors. It uses the ionization produced in a gas by the passage of a charged particle to give an electric pulse on a wire. The voltages that are applied are high, and the liberated electrons and ions are accelerated enough to cause ionization themselves. Thus, the particle initiates an avalanche of electrons, giving a large pulse on the wire.

If the voltage is not set so high, the full avalanche does not occur. Instead, the number of electrons reaching the wire depends only on the number liberated by the particle. The pulse on the wire is proportional to the initial ionization, and the detector is called a proportional counter.

Multiwire proportional chamber

The two latest forms of particle detector use this phenomenon. The first is called a multiwire proportional chamber (MPC). Like the spark chamber, it consists of planes of parallel wires that collect electric signals when they are closest to the path of the particle. Lower voltages are applied, however, and the wires do not receive a full spark but the more moderate number of electrons proportional to the ionization that has been caused. Amplifiers attached to each wire increase the signal before passing it to the computer.

The MPC is continuously receptive to the passage of a particle, since, unlike the spark chamber, it does not need a high-voltage pulse. When a spark chamber fires, its voltage drops and it takes a hundredth of a second before it has recovered enough to give another spark—this delay is a long dead time if a spray of particles is arriving from an accelerator. The MPC can also record several particles at once with signals arriving on different wires and can say when a particle arrives to an accuracy of much better than a tenth of a millionth of a second (over ten times better than the spark chamber).

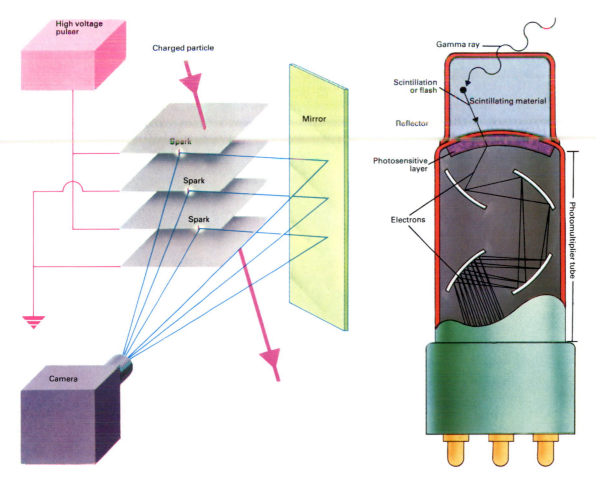

◀ Far left: A diagram of a spark chamber. Sparks form along the path of a charged particle when a high-voltage pulse is applied after it has passed. A camera converts the light into electrical signals. Left: A scintillation counter, which is very fast at detecting particles. The light flash caused by a particle is conveyed via light pipes to a photomultiplier tube then to a computer.

ticle. In a scintillation counter, a block of plastic is wrapped up light-tight, and the light flash due to the passage of a particle is conveyed via light pipes to a photomultiplier tube. The light falls on an electrode, releasing electrons, and thus gives an electric pulse that can be passed to a computer or can alert other detectors that a particle is on its way. The timing accuracy can be up to a billionth of a second.

Cerenkov counter

The Cerenkov counter is often used to tell particles apart. It is based on the principle that a high-energy particle can exceed the local speed of light, for example, in a block of Lucite (similar to Plexiglas). At such a time, the atoms in the path of the particle are so disturbed that they emit light, which comes off at an angle in the wake of the particle, like the bow wave of a ship or like the sonic wave generated by a plane exceeding the speed of sound. By measuring this angle, the velocity of the particle may be found.

If the particle passes through a sufficiently strong magnetic field before it reaches the counter, its path will be curved to an extent, depending on its mass multiplied by its velocity. The Cerenkov counter then measures the velocity, and the particle can be identified from its mass.

Drift chamber

The most recent detector is the drift chamber, a further development of the MPC. The gap between the wire planes is made larger, and instead of determining the particle position simply by detecting a signal on the nearest wire, it picks up signals on several wires, and the time taken by electrons to drift to wires under the influence of the electric field is measured. This detector shows where the particle has passed with great accuracy in position (some hundredths of an inch) and in timing (a few billionths of a second).

Scintillation counters

Even faster timing, but without good information about position, can be obtained from scintillation counters, which use the property of some materials, for example, types of plastic, to give a flash of light when crossed by a high-energy charged par-

▲ The trails left in a bubble chamber by subatomic particles.

▶ Spark chamber detectors being used for the study of the very weak currents produced by the interaction of leptons. The two mirrors reflect the track images to a camera.

Pathology

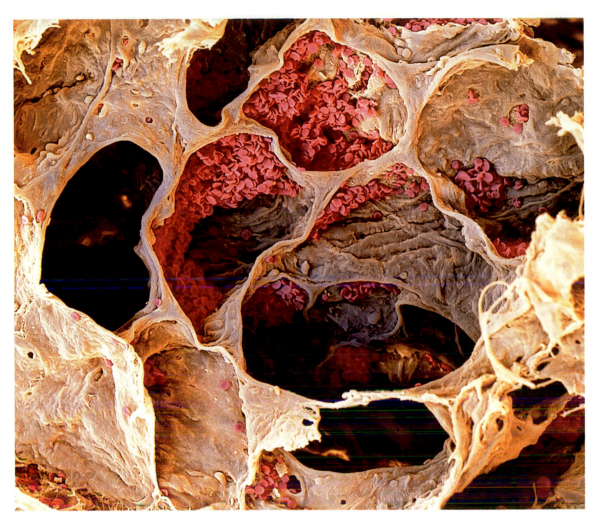

◄ New technologies have revolutionized histopathology. One advance was the development of the electron microscope, which allows much greater magnification of the sample. This scanning electron micrograph of the alveoli (air sacs) of a human lung has been artificially colored to show the red blood cells that have hemorraged into the alveoli as a result of the damage done to the lung walls by cancer. The patient was a heavy smoker and the affected lung had to be surgically removed.

The study of disease and injuries with the aim of understanding their characteristics, causes, and effects is a major branch of medical science known as pathology. Application of laboratory techniques to the diagnosis and treatment of disease is clinical pathology, while analysis to determine the cause of violent death or injury is the practice of forensic pathology, often used in criminal investigations.

Generally, the practice of pathology involves the examination of body tissues and organs for alterations, such as inflammation or abnormal growth. However, the effects of disease can vary considerably with no two cases being the same. Further, the same sort of changes can be produced by several diseases—for example, lung damage due to pneumonia, cancer, and tuberculosis can be similar on initial examination. In such cases, the assistance of the clinical pathologist is often essential in arriving at a final diagnosis.

Various other specialized branches of pathology have been developed along with the growth of the corresponding areas of medicine, such as surgical pathology and chemical pathology, while experimental pathology involves the study of disease under controlled conditions. In addition to human pathology, there are veterinary pathology, which deals with animals, and plant pathology.

The study of the causes of disease, etiology, is a major division of pathology, although in many cases, the causes can be so complex that their study becomes a further specialist branch; for example, toxicology studies the effects of chemical poisons, and bacteriology studies disease-causing bacteria.

Comparative pathology

An important technique for the investigation of the effects of disease and injury in humans is the comparative study of similar diseases and injuries in animals. With some diseases, the animal forms are sufficiently similar to those of humans to allow direct comparison of their progress and response to treatment. With other diseases, such as rabies and bubonic plague, the disease is transferred to humans from an infected animal. The safety testing of products such as foodstuffs, medicines, and even cosmetics is generally based on the use of animals as experimental subjects.

Animal subjects are often used in experimental investigations so that, for example, the progress of a disease can be investigated by infecting a large number of experimental animals (often specially bred with identical genetic characteristics). As the disease progresses, sample animals can be killed and subjected to detailed autopsies (dissection and examination) with the results from the series of animals providing a continuous record of the progress of the disease. Where the cause of a disease is not clear, attempts may be made to infect an animal subject where the symptoms will be more obvious and so easier to diagnose. Similarly, the effectiveness of a course of treatment may be tested using infected animals, as may the efficiency of various means of disease prevention, such as inoculation.

Clinical pathology

Considerable information about the causes and progress of a disease can be obtained by the examination and analysis of specimens obtained from the patient, and this study is clinical pathology. Normally, the tests to be made are chosen on the basis of the other symptoms, since the number of tests that could be made is very large and a lot of time could be wasted without providing any clear clinical guidance. With properly chosen tests, though, a negative reaction showing that the suspected organism is not present can be as important in diagnosis as a positive one. Increasing use is being made of automated test equipment, which allows a wide range of tests to be made as routine practice to help build up a general picture

▶ A scientist uses a special microtome to cut superfine sections of tissue for microscopic analysis in order to assess the effects of a new drug. The sections are placed on a microscope slide and stained in order to show the structure of the different cells, which are visible when viewed through a microscope.

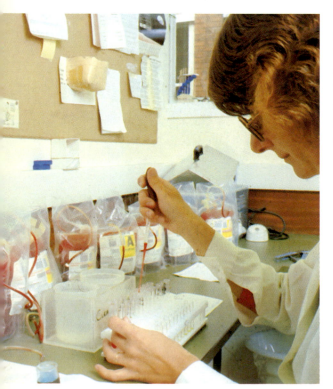

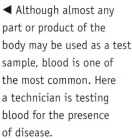

◀ Although almost any part or product of the body may be used as a test sample, blood is one of the most common. Here a technician is testing blood for the presence of disease.

of a patient's condition. Such tests may also be carried out on a regular basis on apparently healthy patients as part of a health maintenance program, with the intention being to identify any potential problems as early as possible, often allowing treatment to start before any symptoms have actually become apparent.

Although virtually any part or product of the body may be used as a test sample, one of the most common is blood, whose study and analysis is known as hematology. There are two main causes of abnormalities in the blood; those directly affecting the blood itself and the blood-producing tissues are termed primary blood diseases. Where the abnormality is due to some other disease, the blood condition is known as a secondary disease. A complex series of tests exists for the investigation of blood condition, with one important group involving the constituents of the blood. For example, blood counts are undertaken to check on the numbers and condition of the red blood cells (erythrocytes), the white blood cells (leucocytes), and the platelets, with the presence of damaged cells or a reduced count providing an indication of possible diseases. Similarly, the fluid part of the blood (the plasma) may be analyzed to check on such factors as the concentration of fats (lipids) and the protein levels.

High levels of blood glucose (hyperglycemia) can be due to a number of causes, the most common being diabetes mellitus, in which the production of insulin is insufficient to break down glucose. If diabetes is suspected, a glucose tolerance test may be carried out with the patient being given a measured amount of glucose after which blood samples are taken at regular intervals for analysis. The rate at which the glucose level in the blood changes provides an indication of the presence or otherwise of diabetes. Tests can also be made for the presence of foreign agents, such as bacteria, alcohol, or drugs.

Another body fluid that is commonly subjected to analysis is urine. In fact, urinalysis is one of the oldest medical practices. Although the older practices of making diagnosis on the basis of the obvious characteristics, such as color and smell, are still used, it is also realized that these characteristics are commonly affected by dietary habits, so diagnosis needs to be supplemented by laboratory techniques. Both physical and chemical tests are employed along with microscopic examination of the solid constituents, which can be separated by centrifuging.

The role of genes

One advance has come from new techniques that allow histopathologists to study the way in which individual genes make proteins in various tissues of the body. The genetic information needed to make a protein is held in the nucleic acid, DNA, which is found in the nucleus of the cell. The cell transcribes this blueprint into messenger RNA (mRNA), which then acts as a template for the structure of the protein. This information can be helpful, because a cell may produce a particular protein only if disease is present. It is thus possible to identify which protein a cell is making by detecting the mRNA for the protein: in nucleic acid hybridization, chemists synthesize short lengths of DNA, which because they are the same as the DNA template from which the mRNA is made, bind or hybridize to the mRNA.

The short lengths of DNA are called DNA probes. Pathologists can tell when the probes have hybridized because they carry a chemical or radioactive label. A probe can be synthesized for any protein as long as its genetic sequence is known. A computer will take just a few seconds to check that the probe selected is unique to the protein being investigated.

External diagnostic techniques

Modern medical techniques allow the pathologist to examine the internal structure and organs of the body without the need for surgery. The use of X rays for this purpose is well established, with computerized techniques allowing a picture to be built up by scanning a series of slices through the body. Magnetic resonance imaging (MRI) is similarly used for scanning purposes and has the special advantage of not causing damage to body tissues, as can happen with excessive use of X rays. Ultrasound techniques are particularly suitable for scanning internal organs, giving real-time pictures that allow observation of the working of certain organs such as the heart. As a further aid to diagnosis, various types of tracer may be injected in the bloodstream or swallowed by the patient to allow, for example, the passage of food through the digestive system to be studied. In a biopsy, small samples of tissue are removed, often using a hollow sampling needle, for examination.

Examinations are also made of tissue removed from the body during surgery. In some cases, the examinations are made while surgery is still in progress to confirm diagnosis and indicate if further action is required, but often the analysis is not completed until after surgery is finished.

◀ Measuring cyanide levels in blood. Cyanide gas eliminated from the blood and acid mixture at the bottom of the flask is trapped for a dye-forming process in the cup. The quantity of cyanide in the blood is directly related to the purple color developing in the cup.

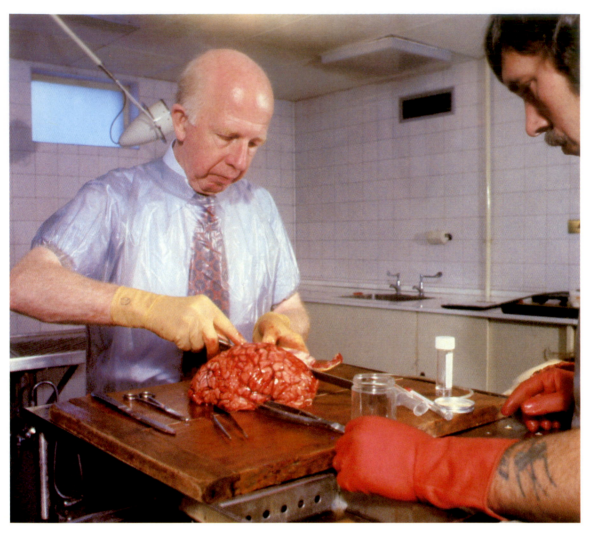

◀ Pathologists perform postmortems on people who die in suspicious circumstances, as well as examining the parts removed by surgeons during operations, thus aiding police in the detection of crime and doctors in the successful treatment of patients. Professor Keith Simpson, shown here working in the City of London mortuary, was an influential figure in the development of forensic pathology to investigate crimes and played a key part in many famous British murder trials of the 1960s and 1970s.

Examination of samples can establish, for example, if a growth is benign or cancerous. In the United States, tissue removed during surgery is subjected to pathological examination as a matter of course. Where death has occurred unexpectedly or under suspicious circumstances, a postmortem, or autopsy, is generally carried out to determine the cause of death, with the internal organs being examined for disease and damage. It may reveal poisoning, for example.

Forensic pathology

Many of the specialized branches of pathology are combined in forensic pathology, which is mainly concerned with the provision of evidence for legal proceedings. Normally it involves investigation of the causes of injury or death, and the pathologist will also try and provide additional information to help other authorities—such as the police—investigating the incident. For example, in a case of a violent death, the pathologist may have to try and establish the time of death in addition to the cause in order to assist the investigation.

Provided that the victim is discovered reasonably soon after death occurs, one means of estimating the elapsed time lies in the gradual

cooling of the body. The cooling rate depends on a number of factors, including the state of dress, physical condition before death, and ambient temperature. All of these factors have to be taken into account to modify the average value for heat loss, which is around 1.5°F per hour. As the time after death increases, the rate of cooling slows down, but after around 12 hours, the body feels cold to the touch while the internal organs remain warm for another 6 to 12 hours. If the body is still warm, the accuracy of such time of death estimates can be increased by taking a series of temperature measurements as the body continues to cool. These measurements are plotted to give a cooling curve from which can be extrapolated the approximate time of death.

Rigor mortis, a stiffening of the body tissues due to changes in muscle protein, normally starts to occur in the face about 5 hours after death, spreading gradually to the rest of the body after around 12 hours. The stiffness remains for around 12 hours and then gradually fades so that after some 36 hours or so it has disappeared. The onset of rigor mortis can be affected by factors similar to the cooling of a body, and they have to be taken into account in determining the probable time of death. In cases where some time has elapsed following death, the degree of decomposition can give an indication of the time; the first signs of decomposition normally appear after 48 hours or so, while under normal conditions, the corpse starts to liquefy after some four weeks or so. The internal organs are known to decompose at different rates, so some evidence of the time of death can be recovered even from badly decomposed bodies.

Following death, the blood drains to the lower parts of the body and after some hours starts to congeal, giving the skin a characteristic staining known as lividity. The lividity occurs in those areas that are not under pressure from the weight of the body or from tight clothing and has characteristic patterns depending on the position of the body. If the lividity patterns do not correspond to the body position, it is a strong indication that the body has been moved after death.

When injuries are involved, the pathologist has to take account of precise details to assist in identification of possible weapons. In addition to determining the possible cause of injuries, where no weapon is apparent, the pathologist also tries to identify the sequence of injuries and the physi-

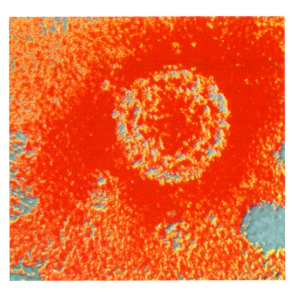

◄ Hepatitis B virus magnified by about a million times. This virus, seen through a transmission electron microscope, has been artificially colored by a technique called posterization.

cal condition of the victim before death. This information can be important in determining the actions that a victim would be able to undertake, for example, in self-defense, again providing valuable information for the investigating authorities.

Plant pathology

Human and animal pathology have many similarities, and the same basic approach can be applied to plant pathology, although the types, causes, and effects of disease are somewhat different. The outbreak of disease among intensively farmed commercial crops can have an immense economic effect, while in undernourished countries, the loss of a crop can lead to widespread starvation.

Treatment of such diseases requires a thorough understanding of the causes, and the investigation starts with the obvious symptoms. These symptoms fall into three main categories: the stunting of plant growth; destruction of growing tissues; and the development of unwanted growths. Lack of growth may be simply due to the lack of essential nutrients but can also be caused by diseases that prevent the plant from making use of the available foods.

Unwanted growths, such as galls, are normally the plant's reaction to some form of attack, while damage to growing tissue takes the form of blight or rot. The main infective organisms include bacteria, viruses, and fungi, which can be freely transferred between plants at different locations to spread the infection, while deficiency diseases and chemical poisoning are noninfectious.

FACT FILE

- *The cause of the French emperor Napoleon Bonaparte's death, which occurred in 1821, was not confirmed until the 1960s, when pathologists using the newly available neutron activation analysis on hair clippings discovered thirteen times the usual concentration of arsenic. Napoleon had ingested arsenic, by accident or design, at least 40 times in the months before his death.*

- *In 1953, the Russian czar Ivan the Terrible, who had died in 1584, was disinterred from his Kremlin tomb. Chemical analysis showed mercury concentrations in his bones from ointment used to alleviate chronic polyarthritis. Adult teeth that emerged very late in life might also have influenced his character by causing excruciating pain that he tried to deaden with alcohol.*

- *British forensic scientists have developed analysis techniques that can be used to identify drugs or poisons from samples no bigger than 1 x 10⁻¹² gram.*

SEE ALSO: BIOCHEMISTRY • BIOTECHNOLOGY • BLOOD • CELL BIOLOGY • CHEMISTRY, ANALYTICAL • ELECTRONICS IN MEDICINE • FORENSIC SCIENCE • GENETIC ENGINEERING • MICROSCOPE, ELECTRON • MICROSCOPE, OPTICAL • POISON • PROTEIN • SURGERY • VETERINARY SCIENCE AND MEDICINE

Pediatrics

The first few years of a person's life can be the most dangerous. Children are particularly prone to many diseases that an older person would shrug off. The science of pediatrics deals with the care of children and, in particular, the diseases from which they suffer. The days when infectious diseases such as smallpox, poliomyelitis, and whooping cough used to kill many children before they reached adulthood are over—in developed countries, at least. Effective vaccines and antibiotics have eliminated some diseases and greatly reduced the threat of others.

But as the menace of many infectious diseases has subsided, other conditions have assumed greater importance in determining the health of children. They include congenital abnormalities, inherited diseases, and childhood cancers.

There are many different congenital abnormalities, that is, defects with which a child can be born. Those affecting the spinal cord include neural tube defects such as spina bifida (in which the spinal cord may protrude from the spine), hydrocephalus (excess fluid on the brain), and anencephaly (absence of the brain, a condition that is incompatible with life). In most developed countries, prenatal screening for neural tube defects has resulted in a drop in the number of children born with these conditions. Where the fetus is found to be affected, the pregnant woman and her partner are offered the option to terminate the pregnancy.

In the case of congenital heart disease, in which the child is born with a deformed heart, new surgical techniques may now make it possible to correct the abnormality. Alternatively, if the defect is very severe, it may be possible to carry out a heart transplant. Such operations have been carried out on infants just a few days old, with donor hearts the size of plums. In one case, in 1987, the abnormality was diagnosed by ultrasound while the baby was still in his mother's uterus. When a suitable donor heart became available, doctors at the Loma Linda Transplant Center in California immediately carried out a cesarean section, and the transplant operation was performed within three hours of baby Paul Holc's birth. Since then, a number of corrective operations have been performed while the baby remained in the mother's uterus.

Inherited diseases

The most common inherited disease among Caucasians is cystic fibrosis. The disease makes the body produce unusually thick and sticky mucus. This mucus clogs up the lungs, making the sufferer prone to chest infections, and blocks the duct leading from the pancreas, and thus, food is not digested properly.

As recently as the 1970s, many children with cystic fibrosis died before they reached their teens. Modern treatment involves antibiotics to prevent and treat infections, chest physiotherapy to drain the sticky secretions, and enzyme supplements to assist digestion. As a result, many cystic fibrosis sufferers now live into their mid-20s. Heart-lung transplants have also helped some teenagers and young adults suffering with cystic fibrosis, although it is too early to say what the overall effect of these operations will be on long-term survival.

The discovery in 1989 by researchers at the universities of Toronto and Michigan of the gene for cystic fibrosis, which codes for a protein that controls the excretion of salt and water from cells, led to more effective drugs being developed to treat this disease. In the future, gene therapy may be able to offer better solutions. Such a therapy may well be available in time to affect the survival of children being born with cystic fibrosis today. Meanwhile, the practice of screening for carriers of the gene, together with prenatal diagnosis and the option of termination of affected pregnancies, may mean that fewer children will be born with cystic fibrosis in the future.

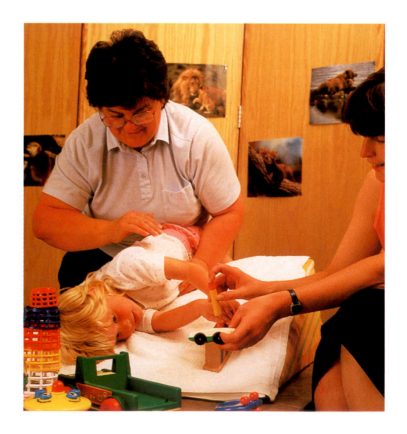

▼ A physiotherapist giving percussion treatment to a three-year-old cystic fibrosis patient. This treatment loosens the mucus, which is coughed up.

1660

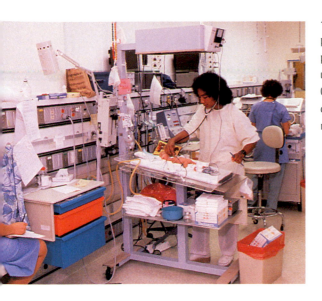

◀ Nurse attending a premature baby in a pediatric intensive care unit at Stamford Hospital, Connecticut. The baby's condition is constantly monitored.

Childhood cancers are relatively rare, affecting about one in 600 children below the age of 15. In children, leukemias are the most common cancers, followed by brain tumors, then lymphomas (including Hodgkin's disease).

More effective combinations of anticancer drugs, developed with the help of large-scale clinical trials comparing the effects of similar treatments, now mean that well over half of all new cases of childhood cancer diagnosed each year can be cured. Such children are likely to have a normal life expectancy.

Some of the most striking advances have been made in the treatment of leukemia. In the 1960s, leukemia in children was almost always fatal, usually within 6 to 12 months. Under one percent of affected children survived long term. Nowadays, thanks to new medical discoveries, three out of four children who develop the most common form of childhood leukemia can be cured.

Saving premature babies

Better intensive care of premature babies means that such a baby born today has a much better chance of surviving than he or she would have had in the 1970s. The main improvement has been in methods of mechanical ventilation to help the baby's breathing. In addition, miniaturization of equipment has made it much easier to insert intravenous drips into a newborn's tiny veins to deliver food and medicines. Equipment designed to monitor the concentrations of gases in the baby's blood through his or her skin (without using needles to sample the blood) has made it easier to deliver the correct amount of oxygen.

Babies born 12 weeks early now have an approximately 80 percent chance of survival, rising to 90 percent for those 11 weeks early. Babies born 16 or 17 weeks also survive, but the more premature the baby, the greater the risk of its suf-

fering disability. Around 40 percent of those who arrive 16 or 17 weeks early suffer some disability.

Apart from advances in mechanical ventilation, two other treatments have also helped many premature babies to survive. Researchers discovered that giving a pregnant woman steroids for 48 hours before a preterm delivery greatly reduces the respiratory problems that the baby will experience once born. This treatment is possible in cases where babies have to be delivered prematurely for their safety, the safety of the mother, or both. It cannot be used, however, if delivery is sudden or unexpected.

A substance called a surfactant can also be given to the premature infant. Because it reduces the surface tension of water, it helps to keep the lungs inflated. Without it, the air pockets in the lungs tend to collapse.

Crib deaths

With modern improvements in health care, infant mortality has declined over the years. But some infant deaths remain unexplained and are attributed to sudden infant death syndrome (SIDS). Less than 2 percent of babies die in this way, mostly before the age of six months, but medical research has failed to find any single cause for this distressing problem. Experts now recommend that babies be placed on their back to sleep, that parents not smoke, that no baby be allowed to get too hot, and that the doctor be called if danger signs appear.

Many parents buy devices that monitor their baby's breathing and movement, but there is no concrete evidence that they reduce the incidence of cot death. There has been a significant decline in the SIDS rate because parents are heeding advice on sleeping positions for infants. Research continues into this baffling condition.

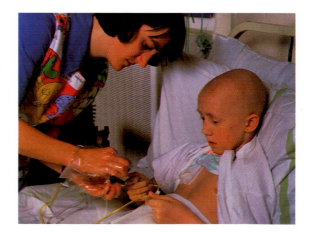

▶ A pediatric nurse adjusting an intravenous line being used to deliver chemotherapy to a young boy with leukemia.

SEE ALSO: BONES AND FRACTURE TREATMENT • CANCER TREATMENT • IMMUNOLOGY • MEDICINE • SURGERY • TRANSPLANT

Pen

A fountain pen is a writing implement that consists of a reservoir to hold the ink, a nib (writing tip) made of gold or stainless steel, and a system of air holes and flow tubes for delivering the ink to the nib. The ink supply system takes advantage of the natural phenomena of capillary action and surface tension.

The earliest fountain pens, patented in Britain more than 150 years ago, did not use capillary action but had a plunger device that had to be frequently operated by the user to keep the ink flowing. The tubes and air holes in modern pens are called the feed, and the first practical designs were made by a U.S. insurance agent, L. E. Waterman, in the 1880s.

The flow tube in a fountain pen must be exactly the right size. If the tube is too small, no ink will flow at all; if the tube is too big, the ink will flow rapidly out of the pen and make a mess. Capillary action is the result of surface tension of a fluid inside a tube: it will cling to the walls of the tube, not flowing until some of it is removed from the bottom of the feed system, in this case by writing. The ink flows onto the nib, which has a vertical slit in the end of it. The surface tension of the ink causes it to seek the slit but prevents it from running off the nib until the slight pressure of the nib on the paper causes the slit to widen.

Surface tension is the property of a fluid that causes it to seek a spherical shape, like a free-falling raindrop. The molecules of a fluid attract each other in such a way that a single drop of the fluid behaves like an elasticized container.

There are a number of ways of filling the reservoir in a fountain pen. Some reservoirs are made of rubber or other elastic material and are compressed by means of a lever; then the tip of the pen is inserted in the ink and the lever released. The reservoir sucks up the ink in reverting to its natural shape. Other pens have a piston suction device or a snorkel (a tube that is extended from the tip and drinks up the ink as suction is applied by a piston). A cartridge pen uses a replaceable plastic container of ink; the cartridge itself is the reservoir. The body of the pen unscrews, the cartridge is inserted, and when the pen is screwed back together, the mechanism opens one end of the cartridge.

Most fountain pens need an air hole to allow air to flow into the reservoir behind the ink, equalizing the air pressure; otherwise the ink would not flow at all. A variety of interchangeable nibs are available with tips of different width to suit the requirement of the user.

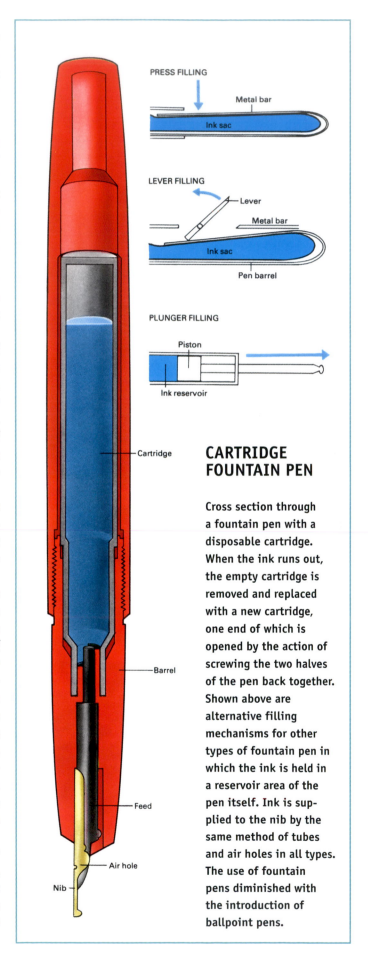

PRESS FILLING

Metal bar

Ink sac

LEVER FILLING

Lever

Metal bar

Ink sac

Pen barrel

PLUNGER FILLING

Piston

Ink reservoir

Cartridge

Barrel

Feed

Air hole

Nib

CARTRIDGE FOUNTAIN PEN

Cross section through a fountain pen with a disposable cartridge. When the ink runs out, the empty cartridge is removed and replaced with a new cartridge, one end of which is opened by the action of screwing the two halves of the pen back together. Shown above are alternative filling mechanisms for other types of fountain pen in which the ink is held in a reservoir area of the pen itself. Ink is supplied to the nib by the same method of tubes and air holes in all types. The use of fountain pens diminished with the introduction of ballpoint pens.

Ballpoint pen

The ballpoint pen became the universal writing instrument of the 20th century. When the tiny metal ball at the writing tip is drawn across a sheet of paper, it rotates within a housing at the end of an ink reservoir and is coated with the ink, which it transfers to the paper.

The first ballpoint pen was invented by an American leather tanner, John Loud, in 1888. Loud had been working on a design for a non-leaking pen to mark leather and fabrics. Although his cumbersome design was similar in essence to the modern item, it was never manufactured in large quantities, and the patent was allowed to expire. The first workable design was patented by a pair of Hungarian brothers, Lazlo and Georg Biro, in 1938.

The ball of the pen is usually made of tungsten carbide and is normally one millimeter in diameter. It is fitted into a socket so that it rotates freely. A number of internal ducts in the socket feed ink to the ball, which therefore effectively rests on several metal ridges. The other end of the socket is drilled and fitted onto a metal or plastic tube that contains the ink. When the ball is pressed on paper and moved, the capillary action draws the ink from the reservoir, and impressions are made as the ink flows down the ducts. In effect, the ball functions as a valve to prevent overflow, and on rotation, it acts as a suction pump drawing out the ink.

One problem with this design was that, as some of the ink ran out, a partial vacuum was formed between the back of the ball and the ink reservoir, having the effect of cutting off the ink supply. This problem was solved by making a small hole at the far end of the reservoir. As the ink at the tip is sucked out, more ink from the tube is drawn into the socket to fill its place, thus avoiding a vacuum.

This method of inking the ballpoint pen depended on finding an ink that was susceptible to capillary action but that would not leak from the vent. At first, printer's ink was used, but it was soon discovered that it was not viscous enough to prevent leakage. Therefore the principal research into making an efficient ballpoint pen was concerned with developing a suitable ink. The earliest ballpoint inks were of a heavy gelatinous type, but now there are two main kinds. The first, containing a dye soluble in oil, dries on the writing surface by absorption. The viscosity of the ink is high, but the impressions formed tend to be less sharp than those created by spirit-soluble inks that dry on the writing surface by evaporation.

The capacity of the ballpoint reservoir varies from 0.5 to 1.5 milliliters (ml). In the smaller

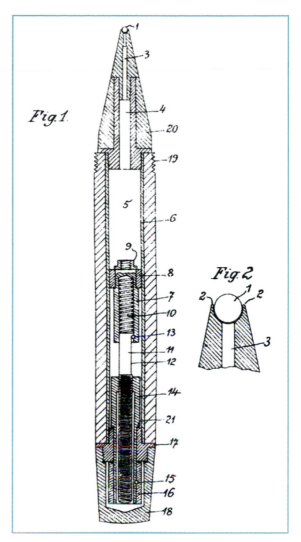

◄ A drawing from the original patent specification for Lazlo and Georg Biro's ballpoint pen. The impetus for wide American acceptance for the ballpoint pen came in 1942, when the U.S. Army demanded a pen that would not leak in high-flying aircraft.

reservoirs, the tube is open at the far end as the viscosity of the ink is sufficient to prevent leakage, but 1.5 ml reservoirs need a vented plug and the use of an even more viscous liquid known as a follower. The follower is solid enough not to leak but liquid enough to follow the ink as it is used up.

Further developments of the ballpoint pen include pens that write at any angle, even upside down, and pens with fiber-ball nibs.

Fiber and felt tips

In the 1960s, a new type of pen was developed by Yukio Horie of the Tokyo Stationery Company. This type of pen uses a nib made of synthetic fibers, which uses dye rather than ink. The dye passes to the nib by a complex system of capillaries. Felt-tip pens use a nib and reservoir that is made of a single length of dense artificial fiber. This reservoir is impregnated with dye and may be cut into a variety of different thicknesses and nib shapes.

 SEE ALSO: INK • SURFACE TENSION • VISCOSITY

Pendulum

A pendulum is a suspended object that is free to swing. The term may also be applied to an object suspended on a spring and free to oscillate vertically and to one suspended on a wire and free to twist to and fro. Pendulums have a property that makes them useful as timepieces: the time taken for a pendulum to swing back and forth is almost independent of the size of the swing, or amplitude of the motion, as long as the amplitude is small.

The physicist speaks of a simple pendulum. An ideal pendulum would be a point mass, the bob, suspended on a fine cord. Contrast this with a compound pendulum, one whose weight cannot be regarded as concentrated at a single point. An example would be a rod free to swing about one end. Spherical pendulums are able to swing in an infinite number of vertical planes and consequently have more complex motion than that of a simple pendulum.

The period of a pendulum is its time of swing from, say, its extreme left-hand position back to the same point. A pendulum that is close to 3 ft. (1 m) in length, for example, will have a period of a second. The period of a simple pendulum that was completely free of frictional resistance would be independent of the weight of the bob. The period is proportional to the square root of the length. Thus, a doubling of the period is brought about by lengthening the pendulum by a factor of four. Clock pendulums are regulated by raising or lowering the bob by tiny amounts.

The pendulum's period also depends on the effective strength of gravity. A pendulum at the equator beats very slightly more slowly than it would at the poles. Gravity is weaker at the equator, because the radius of Earth is greater there. In addition, points on the equator travel at 1,000 miles per hour (1,600 km/h), because of the daily rotation of Earth giving rise to an outward centrifugal force that effectively reduces the pull of gravity. Because the period of a pendulum changes with gravity, pendulums can be used to measure the local acceleration of gravity.

The best-known application of the pendulum is in regulating clocks. This use was suggested by the Italian inventor Leonardo da Vinci and by the Italian astronomer Galileo, but the first practical pendulum clock was made by the Dutch astronomer Christiaan Huygens in 1656. In a pendulum clock, a slowly descending weight drives the hands, and the pendulum controls the rate at which the hands advance. Some of the energy released by the weight is used to give the pendulum an impulse on each swing and so keep it moving.

▲ An integral trembler, or pendulum, car alarm system. It detects movement of the car body, such as when someone gets in.

The metal rod of a clock pendulum will expand when the temperature rises and contract when it falls, causing the clock to run slower and faster, respectively. Some kinds of pendulums have been constructed to overcome this problem, such as the gridiron pendulum, made of alternating rods of brass and steel. Brass changes its length proportionately more than does steel for a given temperature change. Upward expansion of the brass rods in the grid compensates for downward expansion of the steel.

Another kind of temperature-compensating pendulum uses mercury in a jar as a bob. The upward expansion of the mercury compensates for the downward expansion of the pendulum rod. Today, pendulum rods are likely to be made of the nickel–steel alloy invar, which shows little length change with temperature.

Another use of the pendulum is in the musician's metronome. This instrument uses a compound pendulum, having a weight mounted below the center of gravity and another mounted above. The center of gravity, and hence effective length of the pendulum, can be altered by moving the top weight up and down. Hence, the metronome can be made to tick with a varying beat.

A heavy weight hanging from a pivot about which it is free to swing will tend to remain stationary if the support is abruptly moved. This principle is used in many kinds of seismographs (earthquake recorders). Two suspended weights, free to swing north–south and east–west, respectively, record ground tremors in those directions. Vertical tremors are recorded by means of a weight hanging on a spring. The tiny relative movements of the pendulums and the ground can be amplified mechanically, optically, or electronically.

A moving pendulum tends to keep swinging in the same direction even if its support is turned. The French physicist Jean Bernard Léon Foucault exploited this fact in his demonstration of Earth's rotation. A pendulum 197 ft. (60 m) long suspended from the roof of the Pantheon in Paris slowly changed its apparent direction of swing during 24 hours. In reality, the pendulum was keeping the same orientation in space while Earth turned beneath it.

Torsion pendulums consist of a thin wire that oscillates by twisting and untwisting. This kind of pendulum is not strictly a pendulum, since it does not rely on gravity for its motion. The laws governing its movement, however, are similar to those governing a simple pendulum.

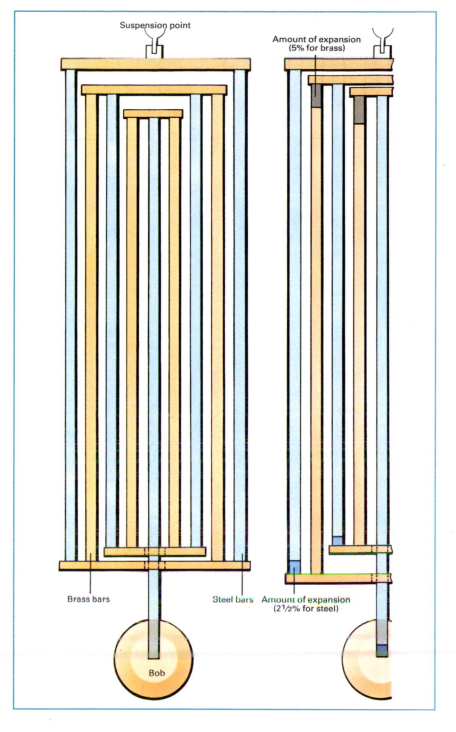

▲ The principle of the gridiron pendulum is shown here in a much exaggerated form for clarity. Brass expands abut twice as much as steel: the expansions that are given here are impossible in practice, as the metals would melt. The amount of expansion of each at the higher temperature is shown shaded in the right diagram. The pendulum stays the same overall length.

◄ Grandfather clocks possess the best-known examples of pendulums. The weight on the upper right slowly descends and in doing so provides the energy to move the hands and keep the pendulum oscillating. The regular oscillations of the pendulum control the rate at which the hands move.

 SEE ALSO: BALANCE • CLOCK • ENERGY, MASS, AND WEIGHT • FRICTION • GRAVITY • METRONOME • SEISMOLOGY

Pen Recorder

When a continuous and permanent record of the way some quantity—such as pressure, temperature, or strain—varies with time is required, it is often made using a pen recorder. In many cases, the parameter to be measured is converted to an analog electric signal by means of a transducer, with the electric signal being used to drive the recording mechanism, although sometimes a direct connection is used.

There are two main types of pen, or chart, recorder design, the main difference being in the format of the recording. In the circular chart recorder, the recording surface is a disk rotated at a steady speed, often so that a complete revolution takes 12 or 24 hours or 7 days in some cases. The size of the chart varies with the application, but a common type is 12 in. (30 cm) in diameter with a (radial) writing track about 4½ in. (12 cm) wide. With the other main design, the recording paper is in the form of a continuous roll that is moved under the pen at a steady speed and can usually be adjusted through a series of standard values to suit the application. Available chart widths range from 2 in. (5 cm) to 12 in. (30 cm) wide, with the wider charts generally being used where more than one recording is to be made across the chart width. Graduations on both types of chart allow easy reading of the timescale and the recorded quantity.

With some designs, the recording pen is directly coupled to the sensing unit; a typical example is the aneroid barometer. Where a transducer is used to make the measurement, the resulting electric signal may be used to drive a moving-coil galvanometer that carries the recording pen on the end of an indicator arm. Movement of the arm carries the pen across the paper (which moves at right angles to the pen motion) to give traces with an arc shape. Linear traces are obtained by the use of a servomechanism to drive a pen carrier from side to side across the paper in response to the applied signal.

Pen recorders are often classified according to their speed of response, that is, the speed at which they respond to changes in the value of the physical quantity being measured. Instruments intended to record information normally shown by conventional instruments have a typical

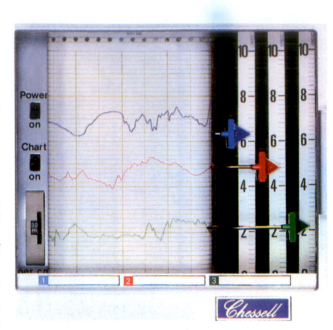

▲ This early version of a Chessell pen recorder clearly shows the arrangement of pens moving at right angles to the paper.

response time, from zero to full-scale deflection, of several seconds. A pen recorder with a moving-coil movement can, however, be made to have a response time of about one-tenth of a second. Here, the moving parts must be as light as possible and the driving power must be increased.

Intermittent recorder

A variation of the normal pen recorder is the intermittent type, where the pen is not kept in continuous contact with the chart but pressed against it at intervals by a chopper bar mechanism. The trace appears as a series of dots as opposed to a line or graph and is satisfactory for recording comparatively slow changes of the recorded quantity.

Intermittent recorders often use a typewriter ribbon in place of liquid ink, since it permits a much longer unattended operating period and a greater range of ambient working temperatures.

Other designs

While many recorders use pens to mark paper charts, there are also a number of other recording systems in use. For example, heat-sensitive paper may be used with a heated stylus, or an electric spark from the indicating pointer may be used to burn marks into some material that has a specially treated surface.

A very sensitive form of chart recorder used in such applications as electrocardiograph (EKG) machines deflects a spot of light onto a light-sensitive chart. The movement is based on a silver-plated quartz filament suspended in a magnetic field. The minute electric currents produced by the contractions of the heart muscles are picked up by electrodes attached to the patient's body and passed through the filament. The filament then undergoes a deflection whose direction and magnitude will depend on both the direction and strength of the current. The movement of the filament is projected by means of an optical system as a spot of light onto a moving strip of paper that is coated with a light-sensitive compound.

SEE ALSO: BAROMETER • ELECTRONICS IN MEDICINE • METEOROLOGY • METER, ELECTRICAL • OPTICAL SCANNER • PRESSURE GAUGE • SEISMOLOGY • SERVOMECHANISM

Percussion Instrument

▲ A women's percussion orchestra playing at a celebration in Rio Hondo in the Philippines.

Traditionally, percussion instruments have been divided into two groups: membranophones and idiophones. Membranophones, such as drums, have skins that are struck, and idiophones, such as bells, castanets, and xylophones, are made of hard, dense materials that vibrate when struck. Both groups may be struck directly with a stick or the hand, or they may be struck using a mechanism such as a drum pedal. Some idiophones are shaken so that pellets either inside or outside vibrate, while others are scraped or plucked. Shaken idiophones, such as rattles, are among the earliest known instruments.

The function of percussion instruments is primarily to produce rhythmic sounds, though many percussion instruments, such as timpani and xylophones, are also tuned and are therefore used to produce melody.

Idiophones

Modern concussion sticks, such as claves, are much the same as those used by Neolithic musicians, while metal concussion instruments, such as cymbals, have altered greatly over the centuries. Over 3,000 years ago, people in countries such as Assyria and Egypt were using cymbals for ritual purposes. By the medieval period in Europe, cymbals had developed into small, thick, high-domed instruments producing a bell-like sound. European cymbals of the 18th and early 19th centuries were based on those used by Turkish military bands and were larger and thinner than those in use today. In parts of East Asia, cymbals are still used to ward off evil spirits.

Modern cymbals are forged from a compound of roughly four parts copper to one part tin and a small amount of silver. The cymbals are spun and hammered under such exact control that they can be produced with long or short vibration periods, according to whether they are to be crash, ride, high-hat, or orchestral cymbals. Cymbals may be played in a variety of ways, including brushing or crashing them together, hitting them with a stick or brush, and operating them with a pedal mechanism, as in the high hat.

Sets of wooden bars of differing musical pitches have been used in Southeast Asia and in Africa since prehistoric times and have diffused from there to the rest of the world. The pitch of a bar depends upon density and thickness; the pitch can be flattened by filing the center of the bar's underside and sharpened by filing the ends. A simple form of xylophone was used in Europe from the 15th to the early 20th centuries, until the modern instrument, with its rosewood notes and metal resonating tubes, was imported from Latin America, where it had been developed from the Mexican and Guatemalan marimbas, which were copies of instruments built in the New World by African slaves. Instruments of similar shape but with metal bars are also used, and they include the glockenspiel (orchestral bells) with small steel bars and the vibraphone. The vibraphone has wider and thinner bars than the glockenspiel, and in the tops of each of the resonating tubes, which hang below the bars, revolving fans open and close the resonators, producing the throbbing vibration that is so characteristic of the instrument. Another type of xylophone is the *gambang kayu*, an instrument used in the gamelan music of Java and Bali.

Other metal instruments in common use include the triangle, a steel bar bent into a triangular shape, the gong, and the bells. The gong is a great dish of forged bronze that originated in western Asia. Orchestral gongs were imported from China, where the best were made, until within the last 50 years, a European firm discovered the necessary technology. Large bells have been cast in Europe since medieval times, often by itinerant bell founders working in the churchyard, but so great a mass of bronze is impracticable in the orchestra; steel plates or brass tubes are used instead.

Membranophones

The sound produced by a membranophone is made by the vibration of a taut membrane. The pitch of the drum is dependent on the drum's diameter and the tightness of its membrane. Drums with larger diameters produce a lower pitch than those with smaller diameters, and a

▶ A selection of membranophones: (1) The tambourine has a shallow wooden frame within which may be pairs of small cymbal-like disks of metal that jingle when shaken. (2, 3) The snare, or side, drum has several strings, made of gut, wire, or nylon, positioned under the membrane. These strings vibrate when the upper membrane is struck. (4) The bass drum was originally a Turkish military instrument and is played using felt-headed beaters. (5) The tenor drum is a descendant of the medieval tabor and may be tensioned using metal rods or ropes. (6, 7) The timpani, or kettle drum, is usually tuned by using a pedal or hand mechanisms.

◄ The modern orchestra has a wide range of percussion instruments. In the 20th century, composers developed the use of percussion to produce innovative new music. Instruments such as the cymbals (1) make a dramatic contribution to the sound of an orchestra. Tubular bells (2) are used mostly to simulate church bells, while the gong (3) can produce sound of great resonance. Made of steel, triangles (4) of different sizes produce different tones. Offering a greater range, the xylophone (5) is a keyboard percussion instrument with bars of rosewood or synthetic resins over resonating tubes. The glockenspiel (6) makes a bell-like sound.

During the 19th century, quicker methods of tuning were invented, ranging from a single handle, the tension of which was transmitted by cables equally around the head, to a foot pedal that controlled a set of tensioning rods. The pedal timpani, on which the drummer can play and tune simultaneously, are now in almost universal use and are played in sets of from two to four drums, occasionally more. Soft-headed beaters are normally used; their manipulation requires considerable skill, for the longer the beater remains in contact with the head, the less sound is produced. Total relaxation of the wrists and very fast reactions are necessary to develop skill.

The side drum, or snare drum, was also introduced in the 15th century but differs from the timpani in that it has a cylindrical body, or shell, with a head at each end and is not intended to produce a note of definite pitch. It is played with wooden sticks and has a set of snares, strands of wire or gut, running below the lower head that give it a dry, rattling sound. The sound is so short that it is impossible to produce a continuous roll with single strokes, and in order to do so, the player must double the striking speed by forcing each stroke to rebound.

Other sizes of drums are also used: the tenor drum, a larger version of the side drum but with-

higher tension produces a higher pitch than does a lower tension. The drum membrane can be made to vibrate using a variety of different techniques. Most simply, the drum may be struck by hand or with a stick or beater or a combination of the two. The membrane may also be made to vibrate by rubbing, and in this case, the drums are known as friction drums.

The earliest of the membranophones was probably the kettledrum, originally, as the name implies, a cooking vessel covered with a skin. The orchestral kettledrums, the timpani, were adopted from the cavalry of the Turkish armies in the 15th century. Timpani are tuned to definite pitches, their pitch ascertained by the tension of the skin, and the range of available notes is determined by the diameters of the drums. The heads of the Turkish drums were tensioned with a network of thongs, but in Europe, tensioning by screwing metal rods into brackets soon became general and is still the method used today.

out snares, and the bass drum, which is larger still, from 3 to 6 ft. (about 1–2 m) in diameter. In popular and dance music, a smaller bass drum, struck by a foot pedal, is employed and is accompanied by several sizes of tom-tom, smaller two-headed drums also without snares. A single-headed drum with a cylindrical frame is the tambourine, which has small metal cymbals let into the frame to provide an added jingle when the head is beaten.

Electronic drum kits

Electronic drum kits are aimed at those who can already play a conventional drum kit. Traditional wood and skin drums—or their modern synthetic equivalents—are replaced by pads—thin electronic triggering devices. Sometimes drummers choose to replace their conventional kit with one that is wholly electronic, but most often, a set of pads is used as an addition to conventional drums.

Electronic drum pads are played in exactly the same way as conventional drums, by being hit with a drumstick, but the sound is generated by a synthesizer device to which the pads are connected. Each drum will trigger a particular drum sound from the synthesizer.

Early electronic drums produced a very characteristic "ping" sound, which can be heard on many rock records from the early 1980s. More realistic sounds are now available, but the role of electronic drums is really to expand the range of sounds that a drummer can make.

Drum machines

Drum machines are designed to be used by people who cannot play conventional drums. They are synthesizers that allow anyone to set up rhythms step by step and then play them back.

Drum machines normally have a range of pre-programmed sounds corresponding to parts of the conventional drum kit—snare drum, tom-toms, cymbals, high-hat, bass drum, and so on—as well as perhaps handclaps and other kinds of percussion. By pressing buttons, these sounds can be stored in the drum machine's memory and can be edited and strung together into rhythm tracks.

Drum machines have many uses and provide some advantages over using a drummer. A drum machine can play in very strict tempo, never tiring and never speeding up or slowing down, but it has the disadvantage of lacking the feel of a human drummer. A machine also cannot react to changes in the music and will carry on exactly as programmed.

Early drum machines had a very characteristic sound that for some kinds of music is still desired and is actually aimed for. The current generation of drum machines offers completely realistic drum sounds and at their best should be indistinguishable from real drums. First-generation drum machines used electronics to generate sounds that resembled those from drums, not always successfully, but drum machines currently contain digital recordings—samples—of real drums being played.

◄ The invention of the drum machine has allowed musicians with little knowledge of drumming to create a broad range of drum sounds and rhythms.

SEE ALSO: BRASS INSTRUMENTS • MUSICAL SCALE • ORGAN, MUSICAL • STRINGED INSTRUMENT • SYNTHESIZER

Periodic Table

An element is a substance that cannot be resolved into a simpler substance by ordinary chemical reactions. Elements were once thought of as materials that can neither be created nor destroyed, an idea first proposed by the Irish chemist Robert Boyle in 1661. Now, however, we know that atoms of each element are themselves made up of smaller particles and may under certain conditions be changed into atoms of other elements. The direct relationship between elements and atoms was not understood until the start of the 19th century, when the English chemist John Dalton proposed his atomic theory. Dalton's assertion that "all the atoms of the same element are identical in all aspects, especially in weight" led naturally to the experimental determination of the relative masses, or atomic weights, of different types of atoms.

In 1865, the English chemist J. A. R. Newlands observed that, on arranging elements in order of increasing atomic weight, "the eighth element, starting from a given one, is a kind of repetition of the first, like the eight notes in an octave of music." Newlands had discovered the essence of the periodic law of the elements, and it is ironic that the London Chemical Society refused to publish his work. Six years later, a Russian chemist, Dmitri Mendeleyev, proposed his periodic law; he demonstrated convincingly that a periodic relationship existed between the properties of an element and its atomic weight, and he showed this relationship in the form of a table. He also predicted the existence and properties of three hitherto unknown elements—scandium, gallium, and germanium—all of which were later discovered by other scientists. Since then, the periodic table has undergone many revisions, and the current system divides the elements into 7 horizontal periods and 18 vertical groups.

Periodic nature of atomic properties

The vast majority of an atom's mass is accounted for by the protons and neutrons, which form the nucleus. On moving along the periodic table, each successively heavier atom has one more positively charged proton in its nucleus and one more negatively charged electron surrounding it. The number of neutrons also increases, there usually being a few more neutrons than protons in any nucleus. Every atom of a particular element will have the same number of protons in its nucleus; this number is called the atomic number and characterizes the element. The number of neutrons in the nucleus may vary slightly, accounting for the various isotopes of an element, which have

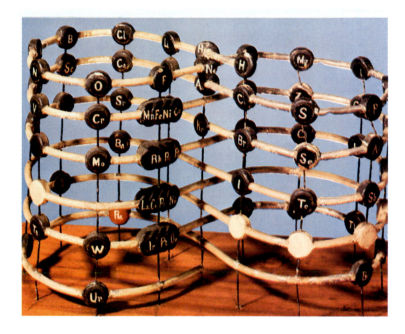

almost identical physical and chemical properties and occupy the same position in the periodic table. Elements normally consist of several isotopes in fairly constant proportions, accounting for the fact that atomic weights are not usually whole numbers and also for the anomaly that argon, Ar, has an atomic weight slightly greater than potassium, K, which immediately succeeds it in the periodic table.

The chemical properties of an atom depend on the organization of the electrons surrounding the nucleus. The number of electrons in a neutral atom will equal the number of protons and therefore the atomic number of the element. The electrons of a free atom are arranged in a series of shells, or quantum energy levels, at increasing distances from the nucleus. The number of electrons permitted on each shell may be calculated using the equation $2n^2$, where n is the number of the shell. Thus, the first shell from the nucleus can contain 2×1^2, or 2, electrons, and the second shell can contain 2×2^2, or 8, electrons. However, the energy levels of the electrons are further subdivided into s, p, d, and f states. For the first principal shell, only s states are possible, for the second s and p states, for the third s, p, and d states, and so on. The various states can accept only a certain number of electrons; s states have a maximum capacity of two electrons, p states have a maximum capacity of six electrons, d states have a maximum capacity of ten electrons, and f states have a maximum capacity of 14. A given state (or electron occupying that state) is described by writing first the principal quantum number followed by the state type, for example, 3s. One can

Group 1

1 **H** Hydrogen 1.0079								

Group 2

3 **Li** Lithium 6.941	4 **Be** Beryllium 9.0122
11 **Na** Sodium 22.990	12 **Mg** Magnesium 24.305

Group 3	Group 4	Group 5	Group 6	Group 7	Group 8	Group 9

Group 1	Group 2	Group 3	Group 4	Group 5	Group 6	Group 7	Group 8	Group 9
19 **K** Potassium 39.098	20 **Ca** Calcium 40.078	21 **Sc** Scandium 44.956	22 **Ti** Titanium 47.867	23 **V** Vanadium 50.942	24 **Cr** Chromium 51.996	25 **Mn** Manganese 54.938	26 **Fe** Iron 55.845	27 **Co** Cobalt 58.933
37 **Rb** Rubidium 85.468	38 **Sr** Strontium 87.62	39 **Y** Yttrium 88.906	40 **Zr** Zirconium 91.224	41 **Nb** Niobium 92.906	42 **Mo** Molybdenum 95.94	43 **Tc** Technetium [97.907]	44 **Ru** Ruthenium 101.07	45 **Rh** Rhodium 102.91
55 **Cs** Cesium 132.91	56 **Ba** Barium 137.33	71 **Lu** Lutetium 174.97	72 **Hf** Hafnium 178.49	73 **Ta** Tantalum 180.95	74 **W** Tungsten 183.84	75 **Re** Rhenium 186.21	76 **Os** Osmium 190.23	77 **Ir** Iridium 192.22
87 **Fr** Francium [223.02]	88 **Ra** Radium [226.03]	103 **Lr** Lawrencium [262.11]	104 **Rf** Rutherfordium [263.11]	105 **Db** Dubnium [262.11]	106 **Sg** Seaborgium [266.12]	107 **Bh** Bohrium [264.12]	108 **Hs** Hassium [269.13]	109 **Mt** Meitnerium [268.14]

Lanthanide elements

57 **La** Lanthanum 138.91	58 **Ce** Cerium 140.12	59 **Pr** Praseodymium 140.91	60 **Nd** Neodymium 144.24	61 **Pm** Promethium [144.91]

Actinide elements

89 **Ac** Actinium [227.03]	90 **Th** Thorium 232.04	91 **Pa** Protactinium 231.04	92 **U** Uranium 238.03	93 **Np** Neptunium [237.05]

think of an atom as being surrounded by a large number of available electron states that are filled by the electrons roughly in order of increasing quantum number.

In terms of electrons, the periodic table represents the progressive filling of electron shells, and the similarity in properties between two elements that lie one above the other in the table can be seen as a similarity in their electron configuration. The similarity in the properties of elements that have the same number of p states occupied by outer electrons is most marked. Compare for example, lithium, sodium, and potassium; beryllium, magnesium, and calcium; carbon, silicon, and germanium; the halogens; and the noble gases. In noble gas atoms, the outer electrons exactly fill a p state (or s state in the case of helium) and are strongly bound to the nucleus. It is therefore difficult for any to be removed for the purpose of chemical bonding, and also the atom is not predisposed to accept any electrons from an adjacent atom no matter how readily available.

Periodic arrangement of the elements

One proton with one 1s electron surrounding it forms a hydrogen atom. The addition of a further electron, proton, and two neutrons gives a helium atom, which has a complete electron shell (the 1s shell) and is therefore a noble gas. Hydrogen and helium together form the first period of the periodic table. The next atom, lithium, Li, has (in addition to the two 1s electrons) one 2s electron, and beryllium, Be, has two 2s electrons. The six elements from boron, B, to neon, Ne, correspond to the progressive filling of the six 2p states. The third period is similar to the second in that it involves the filling of s and p states; the two 3s states corresponding to sodium, Na, and magnesium, Mg, and the six 2p states corresponding to the series from aluminum, Al, to argon, Ar, which completes the third period. The next atom after argon is potassium, K, which starts the fourth period. At first sight, one might expect potassium to start the filling of the 3d states, but instead, its outer electron joins one of the 4s states, and as a result, the element is a typical alkali metal. Calcium, Ca, has two 4s electrons, and it is with the next element, scandium, Sc, that the filling of the 3d states commences. At nickel, Ni, eight out of ten available 3d states are occupied in addition to the two 4s ones. The next element, copper, Cu, however, has all of its ten 3d states occupied, the extra electron having come from one of the 4s states, which is itself filled again on moving to

Group 18

				Group 13	Group 14	Group 15	Group 16	Group 17	2 **He** Helium 4.0026

Key:
13
Al
Aluminum
27

- 13 — Atomic (proton) number
- Al — Symbol
- Aluminum — Name
- 27 — Atomic mass

Group 10	Group 11	Group 12	Group 13	Group 14	Group 15	Group 16	Group 17	Group 18
			5 **B** Boron 10.811	6 **C** Carbon 12.011	7 **N** Nitrogen 14.007	8 **O** Oxygen 15.999	9 **F** Fluorine 18.998	10 **Ne** Neon 20.180
			13 **Al** Aluminum 26.982	14 **Si** Silicon 28.086	15 **P** Phosphorus 30.974	16 **S** Sulfur 32.066	17 **Cl** Chlorine 35.453	18 **Ar** Argon 39.948
28 **Ni** Nickel 58.693	29 **Cu** Copper 63.546	30 **Zn** Zinc 65.39	31 **Ga** Gallium 69.723	32 **Ge** Germanium 72.61	33 **As** Arsenic 74.922	34 **Se** Selenium 78.96	35 **Br** Bromine 79.904	36 **Kr** Krypton 83.80
46 **Pd** Palladium 106.42	47 **Ag** Silver 107.87	48 **Cd** Cadmium 112.41	49 **In** Indium 114.82	50 **Sn** Tin 118.71	51 **Sb** Antimony 121.76	52 **Te** Tellurium 127.60	53 **I** Iodine 126.90	54 **Xe** Xenon 131.29
78 **Pt** Platinum 195.08	79 **Au** Gold 196.97	80 **Hg** Mercury 200.59	81 **Tl** Thallium 204.38	82 **Pb** Lead 207.2	83 **Bi** Bismuth 208.98	84 **Po** Polonium [208.98]	85 **At** Astatine [209.99]	86 **Rn** Radon [222.02]
110 **Uun** Ununnilium [272.15]	111 **Uuu** Unununium [272.15]	112 **Uub** Ununbium [277]		114 **Uuq** Ununquadium [289]		116 **Uuh** Ununhexium [289]		118 **Uuo** Ununoctium [293]

62 **Sm** Samarium 150.36	63 **Eu** Europium 151.96	64 **Gd** Gadolinium 157.25	65 **Tb** Terbium 158.93	66 **Dy** Dysprosium 162.50	67 **Ho** Holmium 164.93	68 **Er** Erbium 167.26	69 **Tm** Thulium 168.93	70 **Yb** Ytterbium 173.04
94 **Pu** Plutonium [244.06]	95 **Am** Americium [243.06]	96 **Cm** Curium [247.07]	97 **Bk** Berkelium [247.07]	98 **Cf** Californium [251.08]	99 **Es** Einsteinium [252.08]	100 **Fm** Fermium [257.10]	101 **Md** Mendelevium [258.10]	102 **No** Nobelium [259.10]

zinc, Zn. Elements that have incomplete d states are called transition elements. The next six electrons fill the 4p states to give the series from gallium, Ga, to krypton, Kr, completing the fourth period. The fifth period is very similar to the fourth, with the 5s states being filled first, followed by the 4d and 5p. The fourteen 4f states are not filled until after the two 6s and one of the 5d states in the next period. The elements corresponding to the filling of the 4f states are known as the rare earths. After the rare earth series, the remainder of the 5d states become occupied, and finally, the sixth period is completed with the filling of the 6p states in the series thallium, Tl, to radon, Rn. The seventh period is only partially complete, but new elements are added to it as they are discovered, or rather as they are made artificially.

The marked similarity in the properties of elements occurring at similar positions in the various periods is emphasized by ordering the table vertically into groups. Groups 1 and 2 and groups 13 to 18 are together called the main group elements, and these groups are further defined by individual names. Group 1 elements are known as the alkali metals. These soft metals react easily and sometimes violently with oxygen and water and for this reason are stored in inert liquids.

Group 2 elements, the alkaline earth metals, are harder and less reactive than those in group 1. Group 18 constitutes the noble gases. Groups 3 to 11 are known as the transition metals. The shielding effect of the inner electrons on these metals results in reactions that do not follow predictable patterns. Other groups include group 17, the halogens, and group 16, the chalcogens. Two special series of elements occur after the transition elements, the lanthanides and actinides. This arrangement was first proposed in the 1950s by the U.S. nuclear chemist Glen Seaborg and was found to predict the behavior of several newly discovered elements that had been synthesized by scientists.

In general, the metallic properties and the atomic radius of an element increase moving downward in a group and toward the left of a period. In contrast, the energy needed to ionize an element and the electronegativity of an element increases moving up a group and toward the right of a period.

▲ This table gives basic information about all the known chemical elements. The elements are grouped according to the number of electrons in their outer shells and by common chemical properties. Hydrogen is shown without color because it does not clearly belong to any one class.

SEE ALSO: ATOMIC STRUCTURE • CHEMICAL BONDING AND VALENCY • ELEMENT, CHEMICAL • GOLD • HALOGEN • HYDROGEN • ION AND IONIZATION • MERCURY • NITROGEN • NOBLE GAS • OXYGEN • SILVER • SULFUR • TRANSITION ELEMENT • URANIUM

Periscope

Periscopes are optical devices that enable the viewer to make observations from a protected or concealed place or to make observations of places and things that are not easily accessible, such as examining the bores of small-diameter tubes. Periscopes are usually associated with submarines, but they have many other uses, for example, observing the amount of smoke passing through a funnel or chimney, bridge observations in destroyers, remote viewing of test rocket and guided missile motors, viewing aircraft models in wind tunnels, making observations in atomic reactors, looking out of army tanks, and looking over trees for forest fires. There is even a periscope in the House of Commons in London, enabling the heating engineer to adjust conditions to suit the number of people present.

The simplest type of periscope, which was used in the trenches in World War I, has a tube with a mirror at the top and a viewing mirror at the bottom. To have a reasonable field of view, the mirrors have to be close together.

Submarine periscopes

The periscope was invented in 1902 by the U.S. engineer Simon Lake and perfected by the Irish telescope maker Sir Howard Grubb. In a submarine periscope, the top window is sometimes 50 ft. (15 m) above the eye lens and the tube less than 10 in. (25 cm) in diameter, so a number of telescope lens systems are fitted to maintain the field of view. Two types of periscope, are fitted in submarines, a monocular type with a small-diameter top tube, and a binocular type with a larger top tube for light gathering. Binocular vision is achieved by fitting two aligned optical systems into the same tube. Because of an optical illusion, objects seen through a tube look smaller than they really are, and it is therefore necessary to introduce some magnification into a periscope system. The normal lens system gives a magnification of six, but it can be changed as required by the introduction of a diminishing telescope.

Light enters the periscope through a top window. It is reflected by a prism that directs the rays down the periscope tube, through the diminishing telescope (if inserted), and through an objective lens that brings the rays to a focal point, where a graticule is fitted. The graticule is usually cross etched into a lens to act as a sighting mark. The light then passes through another objective lens. To minimize vibration of the image in the eye lens when the submarine is moving, another telescope system is fitted that directs the image

formed at the graticule to a point where vibration has the least effect. The light then passes in parallel rays between the two main tube lenses. The bottom main tube lens focuses the rays through a prism, which reflects the rays into the horizontal and onto a field lens, where the image is observed through an eye lens that can be focused to suit the individual. In binocular periscopes, a second pair

▲ A lieutenant using the periscope on the USS *Skipjack* adjusts the left handle, which controls the top prism and thus alters the view above and below the horizon.

of prisms is fitted in the eyepiece, enabling the distance between the eye lenses to be adjusted. It is also possible to introduce another prism into the system for the purpose of mounting a camera. Only the top portion of the periscope turns, and it is moved by means of a lever or gear system.

The top prism can be pivoted vertically to scan above and below the horizon by means of a rack and pinion mechanism operated through pulleys and wires from the left training handle at the bottom of the periscope. The diminishing, or change power, telescope can be inserted or removed from the lens system in the same way, but the control for doing so is located on the right training handle.

A pair of contrarotating prisms, called the estimator, can be inserted above the bottom prism by means of a handle and gearing. When rotated, these prisms produce a ghost image. If the base of the ghost image is placed at the top of the real image, the angle subtended by this movement can be read on a scale, and if the height of the object is known, its range can be calculated. The periscope is usually equipped with a small calculator for making these calculations.

In some periscopes, a sextant is fitted. The light for this system enters through a window below the top main window. Normally, a horizon has to be visible for sextant readings to be taken, but in some cases, it is possible to take sightings when no horizon is visible by introducing an artificial horizon. This condition is achieved by a complex system of lenses, calculators, and a gyro built into the periscope.

The periscope is supported by a bracket, called a crosshead, which is attached to twin hydraulic hoists that move the periscope up or down through a gland and bearings so that it protrudes out of the submarine fin. In the crosshead are devices that transmit the bearings of objects to various computers in the submarine. The periscope tube casing must be made of thick metal strong enough to withstand the pressures found at great depths. The modern periscope is not purely for the observation of target vessels, it is designed to be an integral part of a submarine's weapons and navigation systems.

Remote-viewing systems

In cases where remote viewing is required and space is at a premium, fiber-optic systems are used to relay the image, with the considerable advantage that the light path may be curved. This advantage is offset, however, by a loss of resolution. In other cases, periscopes are being totally replaced by television systems in which the image is relayed electronically.

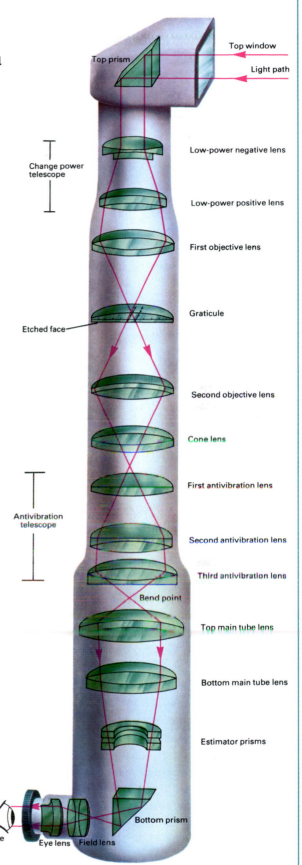

A PERISCOPE

A diagram of a typical submarine periscope lens system. (To save space the section between the two main tube lenses has been omitted.) The antivibration telescope ensures that the image remains steady when the submarine is under way. A number of telescope lens systems are usually incorporated to maintain the field of view. The normal lens system gives a magnification of six.

SEE ALSO: BINOCULARS • FILTER, OPTICAL • GYROSCOPE • HYDRAULICS • LENS • LIGHT AND OPTICS • MIRROR • PRISM • SEXTANT • SUBMARINE • TELESCOPE, OPTICAL

Pest Control

Pests include animals that attack field and plantation crops or produce, such as grain, and also those that attack farm animals and people, often transmitting disease organisms to them. About a quarter of the world's food supply is consumed or destroyed by pests, mainly insects, nematodes (for example, eelworms), and rodents (rats and mice), while much sickness and disease is spread by pests such as mites, ticks, mosquitoes, tsetse flies, and snails. Other prevalent pests include birds, millipedes, woodlice, and slugs.

In planning control measures, the first essential is an accurate identification of the pest concerned and an assessment of the amount of damage it is doing so that control measures and their benefits can be costed. After that, it is desirable to know its life cycle, periods of activity and quiescence, how it winters and whether it originates within the field attacked or migrates in from elsewhere, what other plants it attacks and whether it feeds exposed or in concealment, and if it has natural enemies. Without some of this knowledge, control measures can be only a temporary expedient to stop an attack already under way. With more information, better measures can be planned, and attacks can sometimes be forecast and steps taken to avoid or prevent them.

Indirect control

Indirect ways to control pest attack include crop rotation, choice of crop variety to avoid attack, changing the sowing date so that a critical stage of growth does not coincide with the period of activity of a particular pest, and application of fertilizer to encourage rapid early growth. Crop rotation is most effective against immobile or relatively immobile pests, such as cyst nematodes, and insects that winter in the soil, or pests that attack only one particular crop. Crop rotation, however, is ineffective against mobile pests, for example, birds, strong-flying insects, and greenflies carried by air currents; pests deriving their numbers from wild or semiwild alternative food plants (such as fruit flies from grassland that lay eggs on oat seedlings); and pests, such as wireworms, crane fly grubs, slugs, and millipedes, that are able to feed on several crops.

Sometimes crop varieties that resist attack can be bred or genetically modified: oats, clover, and alfalfa resistant to stem nematodes; potatoes and cereals resistant to cyst nematodes; and raspberries and lettuce resistant to greenflies. Often, however, indirect methods are insufficiently effective, and pesticides must be used.

▶ Spraying crops with pesticides usually increases yields, although some pests develop an immunity to the chemicals used for control.

▼ The pyrethrum (*Chrysanthemum cineariaefolium*) produces a natural pesticide that can be manufactured synthetically for use on other crops.

Direct control

Poison baits, seed treatments, and sprays, dusts, and granules containing potent pesticides are among the means of direct control. For pests in soil, warehouses, and buildings, fumigants are normally used. They are usually liquids but sometimes powders that vaporize and spread themselves throughout the infested area. In greenhouses, smoke canisters and aerosols may be used.

Chemicals were first tried against the Colorado potato beetle about 1850, when it spread from desert plants to potato patches in the United States. From then until the 1940s, almost the only chemicals that could be used were arsenic compounds or insecticidal extracts from plants, such as rotenons from derris roots, pyrethrum from flower heads, and nicotine from tobacco waste. After the discovery of the organochlorine insecticide DDT in Switzerland in 1939, things changed rapidly. Lindane (gamma BHC—benzene hexachloride) soon followed, as did the powerful soil insecticides aldrin and dieldrin. Many of these substances, known as persistent organic pollutants, or POPs, have now been withdrawn in many countries. Because of their persistence and killing power and because they kill by contact, even if an insect walked over a film left by dust or spray applied days or weeks earlier, it would be killed. These organochlorine pesticides lessened costs and revolutionized pest control in buildings, fields, and orchards. They also made possible the control of mosquito-borne malaria, for which purpose DDT is still licensed.

A parallel advance pioneered in Germany was the organophosphorus pesticides, many of which are absorbed by plant roots and leaves and permeate all parts. Usually they kill only those animals that feed on plants or suck their sap, that is, not by contact, thus sparing beneficial species. A range of these compounds is now available, persisting in plants from a few days to several weeks. While in large quantities DDT is toxic to humans and animals, organophosphorus compounds are intensely poisonous even in small amounts. The carbamates are another group of pesticides, some of which behave like organochlorine and some like organophosphorus compounds. Recently, a new range of contact insecticides has been synthesized from pyrethrum that are as potent as DDT but without some of the disadvantages of organochlorine, organophosphorus, and carbamate pesticides. Warfarin and similar poisons that prevent the blood from clotting are used in poison baits for rats, mice, and gray squirrels, while metaldehyde has proved effective against slugs.

Applying pesticides

With few exceptions, pure pesticide is rarely employed. Most are marketed ready for use, but those intended as sprays must first be diluted with water. Common diluents include inert dust, oils, solvents, water, and air, of which the last two are cheapest. Hydrated lime, diatomaceous earth, talc, and other clay minerals are common dust diluents. Granules are made from attapulgite clay, corncob grit, or coal dust.

In orchards, fairly large amounts of spray are applied (100 gallons or more per acre) to secure good coverage of leaves, buds, twigs, and fruits. Sometimes the spray is propelled by a blast of air from a powerful fan. Fields are treated with much smaller amounts of more concentrated pesticide using a low-volume spraying method. Where pesticides in granule form are considered more appropriate, they are sprayed by machines designed to cover a large area quickly. Poison baits are usually pelleted but are applied by the same machines.

Spraying, dusting, and granule-applying machinery cannot pass through tall or mature crops or through forests or dense plantations. They must be treated from the air. Fixed-wing aircraft are cheapest for large areas, but helicopters have several advantages: they are more maneuverable, they do not require landing strips, and the downdraft they generate helps to force pesticides into crops. They are, however, expensive to maintain. Light aircraft have proved essential to control locusts in remote areas. Bands of wingless juveniles on the ground can be attacked with persistent contact insecticides sprayed in a lattice pattern from the air, or poison bait can be dropped from the air. Flying swarms can be sprayed repeatedly from above at close range.

Because rats and mice are wary, killing them with poison baits must be a planned operation in which unpoisoned bait is first offered at a number of baiting points inaccessible to livestock and humans. When the rodents are feeding freely, poison bait is substituted. If further baiting is needed, the food material is changed, as survivors may shun the first bait if it made them sick.

Natural enemies

The numbers of most pests are limited by naturally occurring enemies, for example, ladybug beetles that feed on greenflies, ichneumon flies that lay eggs in the young of many insects, and predatory beetles and spiders. Unfortunately, some pesticides kill many of these beneficial species, perhaps resulting in massive outbreaks or in the emergence of new pests. The red spider mite has increased significantly since orchards began to be sprayed to control other pests and diseases, mainly because spraying kills their principal enemy, the red-kneed capsid.

To avoid these problems, growers use pesticides selectively so that they kill only the target species. The particles of pesticide can be coated with zein (an amine obtained from corn) or encapsulated and thus they do not kill by contact

▼ A ladybug eating an aphid. Pests are sometimes controlled biologically by the introduction of their natural enemies. Aphids can cause costly damage to crops, so when ladybug beetles (which eat aphids at a great rate) are released into infested fields, farmers are saved expensive spraying. Ladybugs also kill selectively in a way that most pesticides do not.

but must be ingested. Alternatively, the pesticide is applied when the beneficial species is absent or quiescent. Sometimes the pesticide can be placed only where it is needed, for example, on seeds or in the seed row. Increasingly, several methods of control are combined or integrated, with the object of decreasing or eliminating the wholesale use of pesticides and encouraging pests' natural enemies to do the job.

Resistance to pesticides

DDT resistance in houseflies was first observed in Sweden in 1946 and was almost worldwide by 1950. Since then, many insects have developed resistance to organochlorine and organophosphorus pesticides, and rats resistant to warfarin have appeared in Britain. A new rodenticide—Sorexa-CR—has been developed in its stead. It works by providing too much vitamin D (which deposits calcium in the body) and too little vitamin K, which is vital for blood coagulation. Eventually, current pesticides will cease to be effective, hence the importance of discovering new kinds of pest prevention, such as growth hormones and agents that cause sexual sterility.

Hazards to people and wildlife

Because pesticides in sprays and dust may be inhaled or penetrate the skin, most developed countries have stringent legislation that insists operatives must wear protective clothing when dispensing or applying pesticides. The accumulation of pesticides in the tissues of birds and other

◄ Rotting garbage creates an ideal environment for disease-carrying rats to scavenge and breed freely. However, rats are clever animals and soon learn to avoid bait laced with poisonous substances, such as warfarin.

animals has caused much concern among those interested in the preservation of rare species. If thoughtlessly applied, pesticides kill bees and wildlife and, if allowed to enter waterways, fish. Those applied to soil greatly change the soil fauna and consequently are heavily regulated.

Biological control

In biological control, natural enemies such as predators, parasites, fungi, bacteria, and viruses are used to control pest species. It has met with some spectacular successes. As long ago as 1892, an Australian ladybug beetle was introduced to control mealybugs in Californian citrus plantations, but it did not survive the winter. Around 1917, ladybugs were bred on potato sprouts infested with mealybugs, making possible the release of millions of ladybugs at a cost less than that of spraying. In 1929, two parasites introduced from Australia replaced the ladybugs controlling one kind of mealybug, but ladybugs are still used to control the other kind and also in greenhouses. A range of biological controls is available, such as nematode worms, used against the destructive vine weevil grub, and encarsia wasps, which lay their eggs in whitefly "scales." Pheromone traps, which mimic the scent of the female of certain species and attract males to a sticky substance, are also being increasingly used against pests such as the apple codling and pear moths.

The scale of biological control operations is sometimes very great. In Canada and the United States, many millions of species of parasites and predators are used against some 200 pests.

FACT FILE

■ Attempts to curb alfalfa aphids imported accidentally into California from the Middle East failed, as the pests quickly developed immunity to insecticides used. Effective protection was achieved by introducing wasp parasites that killed the aphids, and by strip-harvesting the alfalfa to leave an environment in which the aphid's natural enemies can live and multiply.

■ Among new weapons used against malaria-carrying mosquitoes as they become resistant to pesticides are mustard seeds that stick to larvae in water, causing them to drown or starve and the Gambusia minnow, which feeds on the larvae and is a major controller of the insect in many parts of the world.

SEE ALSO: AGRICULTURE, INTENSIVE • AGRICULTURE, ORGANIC • PARASITOLOGY • PHEROMONE • POISON • WEED CONTROL

Petrology

◄ Two scientists take measurements of the temperature and velocity of gases escaping from a vent on Mt. Etna in Italy. The gases were highly corrosive and measured more than 1800°F (1000°C), hence the red coloring in the vent's walls. Petrologists have borrowed techniques used in physical chemistry in order to gain a greater understanding of the properties and behavior of magma.

Petrology is the materials science of the geological world. Petrologists study the chemical compositions of rocks, the minerals rocks are made of, their structure, and the condition under which they have formed as well as their distribution and occurrence. These areas are assessed using laboratory experiments, thermodynamic analysis, and field observations. The subject has much common ground with materials science; someone with a knowledge of petrology is not limited in scope to geology but may also be employed on materials development in industry.

The memory of rocks

The idea of thermodynamic equilibrium lies at the heart of petrology, that is, that a rock of given composition at equilibrium, under the same conditions of temperature and pressure, should always have the same mineralogy. As a simple example, consider the chemical element carbon, which normally exists as the mineral graphite under the standard conditions of room temperature and one atmosphere of pressure. At much higher pressures, carbon is transformed into diamond, whose structure is more compact. The rocks that we collect at Earth's surface have all at some time in the past experienced conditions in Earth's interior and acquired mineralogies corresponding to conditions of higher temperature and pressure. The processes that continually reshape our planet have subsequently brought these rocks to the surface.

The structure and composition of rocks indicate the earlier conditions in which the rocks formed because mineral transformations and chemical reactions between minerals are very slow at surface temperatures, requiring geological time scales. Thus, we can mine diamonds at Earth's surface, and diamond rings and necklaces in jewelers' shops do not transform into graphite.

The three main types of rocks studied by petrologists are igneous, sedimentary, and metamorphic rocks. Igneous rocks are formed by the cooling of molten material and constitute the vast majority of rock types. Consequently, the range of specialist areas of study for these rocks is also large. Sedimentary rocks are formed by the gradual accumulation of sediment and are the most common rocks on Earth's surface. The study of sedimentary rocks is often divided into two branches—carbonate rocks, such as dolomites and limestones, and noncalcareous rocks, such as clays and sandstones. Metamorphic rocks are formed from existing rocks by the effects of heat, pressure, and the movement of chemicals. Metamorphic rocks usually cover whole regions but may also be localized.

Experimental techniques

Petrologists can actually create artificial rocks in a small capsule surrounded by strong confining materials using high pressures and temperatures. In this way, they can map out the combinations of pressure and temperature where minerals are sta-

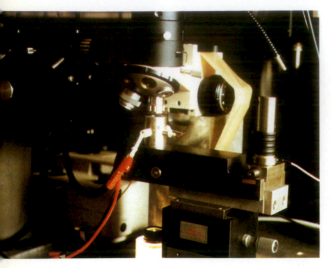

◀ A diamond anvil cell— a small amount of material is pressed between diamonds, subjecting it to a million times atmospheric pressure, emulating the conditions under which rocks are formed deep in Earth.

ble. Such a map is known as a phase diagram, the stock-in-trade of the petrologist.

Several tools are available that enable petrologists to increase our understanding of rocks. One particularly powerful tool is the diamond anvil cell invented in 1958. It consists of a press that subjects a small sample of material, confined between diamonds, to a million times atmospheric pressure. The transparency of the diamonds allows the sample to be heated by a laser beam to a temperature of several thousand degrees and allows images to be taken using X-ray crystallography under the conditions of the experiment. It is thought that these are the conditions existing deep inside Earth.

The properties of the minerals obtained in the laboratory may now be compared with, for example, a knowledge of the deep structure of the globe provided by seismology. Thus, it is possible to explore the compositions and the phase diagrams of the materials making up the deep Earth and to make contributions to the study of important problems, such as how the liquid iron outer core is slowly crystallizing to produce the solid inner core and how it is stirred by vigorous motions. These processes are responsible for the generation of the geomagnetic field, showing how the study of regions, seemingly so remote, can lead to understanding of phenomena of everyday significance, such as the direction in which a compass needle points.

Additional methods for studying the structures of rocks include the petrographic polarizing microscope, which uses extremely thin sections of rock around 0.03 mm thick. Because different rocks have different optical qualities, polarized light can be used to ascertain their structure. The petrographic polarizing microscope, however, is not able to magnify areas smaller than 0.5 µm. For higher resolution than this, the petrologist must use an electron microscope. To study the chemical structure of a rock, an electron microprobe can be used. With this technique, a beam of electrons is directed at a single rock grain, causing the grain to emit X rays. A computer measures the X rays for their concentration and intensity, and the resulting data is used to determine the chemistry of the rock sample. Other equipment used for studying rocks include the X-ray fluorescence spectrometer and the mass spectrometer—used to determine the chemical composition of a rock by measuring, for example, the proportion of isotopes of an element found in the sample.

Magma

Molten rock, known as magma, is ejected during volcanic eruptions. Petrologists have learned how to combine their measurements of the thermodynamic properties of magma with fluid dynamic models of how it flows beneath volcanoes. Small amounts of gases (mainly water and carbon dioxide) are dissolved in magma, the quantities of which may be measured using techniques from physical chemistry, such as infrared absorption spectroscopy. This technique has enabled petrologists to measure how much of these species can be dissolved in silicate melts. In addition, it is possible to determine how the solubilities of these species increase with pressure and thus predict how magma tries to degas as it rises through Earth's crust beneath volcanoes.

The process by which bubbles form in the melt as it decompresses causes a large expansion that accelerates the rising magma toward the eruption vent and, in turn, determines whether the magma is expelled as a lava flow or as a violent jet, ejecting volcanic gases and aerosols high into the atmosphere, and is ultimately responsible for the environmental impact of volcanic eruptions.

▶ A piece of material that has been subjected to extremely high pressure in a diamond anvil press. The red area has been superheated using a laser.

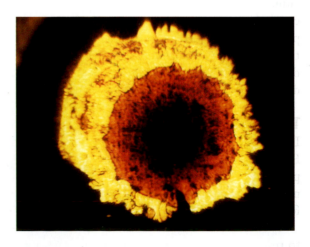

SEE ALSO: CHEMISTRY, ANALYTICAL • GEOLOGY • MASS SPECTROMETRY • MATERIALS SCIENCE • MICROSCOPE, ELECTRON • MICROSCOPE, OPTICAL • POLARIZATION • X-RAY IMAGING

Pharmaceuticals

The word *pharmaceutical* is an adjective or noun that derives from the Greek word *pharmakon*, meaning "drug," "magic charm," or "poison." Pharmaceuticals are chemical compounds and preparations intended to have a beneficial action against physiological or psychological illness. Pharmaceuticals form part of the larger family of drugs, which also includes naturally occurring substances such as nicotine in tobacco, cannabis, alcohol from fermentation of sugars, and caffeine from tea leaves and coffee beans.

Many substances that now generally are classed as controlled substances and narcotics were once used as pharmaceuticals. They include cocaine and heroin, which were once used as painkillers but have now been replaced by less addictive or more effective substances. Other substances, such as amphetamines, continue to have legitimate uses in the treatment of disorders where their beneficial effects outweigh undesirable side effects.

It is not unusual for a single drug to act in many ways—beneficial and harmful—on the human organism. Aspirin (acetylsalicylic acid), for example, is an analgesic (painkiller) and antipyretic (fever reducer). It is not a good choice of painkiller for sufferers of gastric ulcers, however, since it causes more gastric irritation and bleeding than do other painkillers, such as ibuprofen. On the other hand, a small daily dose of aspirin has been found to inhibit the formation of blood clots, and thus would benefit sufferers of certain cardiovascular disorders.

The various effects of aspirin illustrate how the choice of a remedy for the disorder of an individual must be chosen to suit an individual's susceptibility to a range of possible side effects. The prescribed dosage must also be adhered to, since the beneficial effects of a drug may occur at lower dosages than side effects do, and exceeding a dosage might cause the onset of side effects.

Types of pharmaceuticals

Drugs are often classified by their principal effect. Each class includes numerous chemical compounds, and a given compound might fall into more than one class, depending on effects. The following are some of the main types:

Analgesics relieve pain, and some can also act to reduce fever, in which case they also classify as antipyretics. The best-known analgesics are aspirin, codeine, and ibuprofen.

Anesthetics kill pain by preventing conduction of nerve impulses. General anesthetics render the

patient unconscious; local anesthetics block pain impulses from the site of an injury or surgical wound without causing loss of consciousness. Cyclopropane is a general anesthetic taken by inhalation; novocaine is a local anesthetic administered by injection close to the source of pain.

Antibiotics combat bacterial infections by destroying bacterial cells and other microorganisms. Antibiotics administered to patients before and after surgery help prevent infection. Penicillin is the best-known of all antibiotics.

Antidepressants treat clinical depression by adjusting the balance of chemicals in the brain. Anxiolytic antidepressants reduce anxiety, and so help in the treatment of bedwetting and phobias. Tricyclic antidepressants, such as nortryptyline, are so named for their chemical structures, which include three rings of atoms. Monoamine-oxidase inhibitors (MAOIs) and selective serotonin-reuptake inhibitors (SSRIs) are named for their mode of action in boosting the brain's concentra-

▲ A herbalist with a selection of medicinal herbs. Many of the pharmaceutical compounds used in conventional medicine are synthetic versions of the active components of herbal medicines or chemical derivatives of those compounds. Aspirin, for example, is acetylsalicylic acid—the acetyl derivative of salicylic acid, which was traditionally extracted from willow bark and used to fight pain and fever.

tion of serotonin, a chemical responsible for the sensation of well-being. The best-known SSRI is Prozac (fluoxetine hydrochloride).

Antihistamines alleviate the symptoms of colds, allergies, such as hay fever, and insect bites and stings by counteracting histamine produced by the allergic responses of tissues. Their effect is to reduce pain and swelling and to dry up secretions in the nose, throat, and eyes.

Antihypertensives reduce abnormally high blood pressure by stimulating receptors that inhibit stress and by dilating blood vessels.

Anti-inflammatories act to relieve swelling, joint pain, stiffness, and fever. They are useful in treating the symptoms of arthritis. Cortisone, a steroid, was used for many years, but has largely been replaced in the treatment of rheumatoid arthritis by nonsteroidal anti-inflammatory drugs (NSAIDs), such as ibuprofen and flurbiprofen.

Anorexics (appetite suppressants) stimulate the central nervous system (CNS) to suppress appetite. Commonly called "diet pills," anorexics are prescribed to people who are trying to overcome obesity. The most widely known anorexic drug is amphetamine, which is also used to treat hyperactivity in children and narcolepsy, a condition that causes sudden bouts of deep sleep.

Cardiovascular drugs are a broad class of drugs used to treat heart disease and related conditions. Their effect is to reduce blood pressure and chest pain; dilate arteries and capillaries, thereby improving circulation; control heart rate; and increase the force with which the heart beats.

Decongestants and expectorants are two types of drugs used to alleviate the symptoms of colds. Decongestants shrink swollen mucous membranes in the nose and reduce the viscosity of mucus. Expectorants promote the expulsion of accumulated mucus by coughing.

Diuretics stimulate the elimination of excess body fluids by boosting urine production. Diuretics are used in conditions such as renal (kidney) malfunction and cirrhosis of the liver. Since the elimination of body fluids helps reduce blood pressure, diuretics are also useful in the treatment of congestive heart failure.

Muscle relaxants induce temporary paralysis by inhibiting the contractions of muscles. These substances are used during surgery to prevent muscle contractions when incisions are made.

Oral contraceptives—drugs containing estrogen and progesterone—practically eliminate the risk of pregnancy by changing the balance of hormones in the female body. Low-dose "minipills" protect against pregnancy while reducing the risk of side effects, such as thrombosis, the formation of blood clots in blood vessels.

◀ In this culture dish, the antibiotic property of *Penicillium*—the disk-shaped mold—has inhibited the growth of *Streptococcus* (top), leaving a tract of clear medium between the two.

Sedatives and hypnotics are substances that induce a state of deep relaxation (sedatives) or sleep (hypnotics). This class of compounds includes the barbiturates—esters of barbituric acid.

Tranquilizers, similar to sedatives in some respects, are substances that decrease anxiety and physical tension without causing excessive drowsiness. The best-known tranquilizer is perhaps diazepam, the active principle (physiologically active component) of Valium.

Dosage

Dosage is the schedule of administration of a drug—the frequency and total number of doses and the amount of drug in each dose. An effective dosage schedule maintains a concentration of pharmaceutical that is sufficient for it to have a therapeutic effect but lower than the level associated with harmful or unpleasant side effects.

After each dose, the concentration of pharmaceutical increases as the drug is absorbed and then gradually decreases as the body metabolizes and eliminates the drug by excretion. The peak concentration depends largely on body weight—the greater the weight, the larger the quantity of drug required to produce the necessary concentration. The rate at which the drug is eliminated (and its concentration falls) depends on the age and physical condition of the patient. The length of time that a drug stays in the body is expressed as its half-life—the amount of time taken for its concentration to fall by 50 percent.

Standard dosages for adults and children over 12 are calculated for a 154 lb. (70 kg) male. The actual dosage must be adjusted for patients who deviate significantly from this description. For children between 5 and 12 years of age, the dosage is usually reduced to between one-third and one-half of the recommended adult dose.

Children under 5 years do not metabolize drugs in the same way that older children and adults do. For this reason, only a limited range of adult medicines can be used to treat children.

Administration

Administration is the mechanism by which a drug is introduced into the body. Apart from specifying a dosage, a doctor must also indicate the administration route and the form in which the drug will be administered to a patient.

The four main administration routes are by mouth (orally), in the rectum (rectally), by injection (parenterally), and through the lungs (by inhalation). The most convenient route—and therefore the preferred route in many cases—is the oral administration of pills or liquid medicine. Rectal administration is an alternative that can be used if a patient is vomiting or unconscious or cannot swallow for some other reason. Drugs may be injected intravenously (into a vein), intramuscularly (into a muscle), or subcutaneously (just under the skin). Injection is necessary when a drug must be introduced directly to the bloodstream for speed of effect or to protect the drug from the effects of stomach acid, for example. Inhalation is indicated for drugs that are intended to act on the lungs themselves, or to enter the bloodstream rapidly through the linings of the respiratory tract, as is the case with anesthetic gases. Less widely used administration routes include administration via the nasal membranes or by slow absorption through the skin.

There are various forms of drug preparations, and a single drug might be administered in various forms, depending on administration route and the physical form of the drug. Common preparations include tablets, capsules (granules of solid medicine in soluble casings), solutions or suspensions in liquids for injection or to be taken by mouth, and patches for skin absorption. Suppositories are tablets for rectal administration; pessaries are for vaginal administration.

Drug distribution

It is rarely possible to introduce a drug directly to its site of action—the part of the body that needs treatment. In most cases, the administration route causes a drug to first enter the bloodstream, directly or indirectly. Once a drug is in the bloodstream, the high speed of blood circulation ensures that the drug is transported throughout the entire body within one minute.

A disadvantage of drug distribution through the bloodstream is that only a tiny proportion of the administered drug is at the intended site of action at any one time—the vast majority is spread through other parts of the body. Consequently, the dosage must be many times greater than would be needed if it could be administered directly where needed.

The absorption and distribution of a drug are affected by its interaction with the different kinds of membranes in the body. Cell walls consist of fatty substances called lipids, so the ability of a drug to penetrate cell walls is directly related to its solubility in fatty substances. Water-soluble drugs tend to be quite insoluble in fats, so they do not penetrate cell walls; exceptions include drugs of extremely small molecular size.

A drug in the bloodstream enters surrounding tissues through pores in the walls of blood capillaries. As the concentration of the drug in the bloodstream diminishes, this is also the route by which the drug returns to the bloodstream. In most cases, the pores are larger than drug molecules, so most drugs pass back and forth through the capillary wall with little difficulty.

If a drug has to enter the central nervous system (CNS) in order to act, it must be capable of penetrating the blood–brain barrier. The capillary walls in the brain are tightly joined together,

MECHANISMS OF PAIN AND PAIN RELIEF

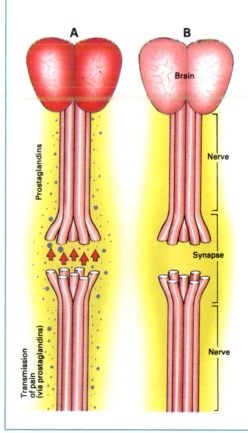

Pain is an unpleasant sensation that occurs when tiny electrical impulses from the site of an injury, for example, reach the brain. These impulses pass through nerve tissues, which consist of granular cells that connect one to another through synapses. Without painkilling treatment, natural chemicals called prostaglandins help the pain "signal" pass through synapses (A). Some analgesics, such as aspirin, are believed to reduce pain by inhibiting the production of prostaglandins in the body. When this happens, the prostaglandin that is needed to propagate pain impulses becomes scarce (B), and the pain signals that reach the brain diminish even though the source of the pain persists.

L-DOPA—DRUG OF THE AWAKENINGS

In the summer of 1969, an extraordinary series of events occurred in a hospital for the chronically ill and disabled in New York. Over a period of months, patients who had been motionless and mute "living statues"—for almost half a century in some cases—became transformed into walking, talking humans by taking a new drug: L-dopa, or *levo-d*ihidroxyphenylala-nine. The drug took effect within days—in some cases hours—of the first dose.

The illness that had afflicted the patients was an extreme and bizarre form of parkinsonism, a neurological condition, caused by a viral infection—encephalitis lethargica, or sleeping sickness—that swept through Europe and North America in the early 20th century. Between 1917 and 1927, almost 5 million people fell victim. Around one-third of the affected died, some recovered, but most fell into a motionless, speechless, timeless state. Still conscious of themselves and their surroundings—the condition does not damage intelligence or imagination—they witnessed their own suspended animation.

People with parkinsonism are unable to start, coordinate, or stop walking and talking at will—as one long-term sufferer said, "I can't start and I can't stop." Yet an event in their surroundings—the arrival of a visitor, for example—can often initiate smoothly flowing movements.

Parkinsonism affects two small tissue areas, called the *substantiae nigrae* (Latin for "black substances"), located in the midbrain. These tissues modulate streams of impulses that travel from the brain to the muscles and coordinate movement.

A simplified theory of parkinsonism proposes that the *substantiae nigrae* act to inhibit movement. If they fail to function, the nerve pathways that excite movement act unopposed. Then the nerve signals for motion are all "go"—there are no "stop" signals to keep them in check.

The nerve damage in the *substantiae nigrae* that underlies parkinsonism can stem from a variety of factors from brain injury to the side effects of some drugs. In the majority of cases, parkinsonism develops gradually in later life, when it is called Parkinson's disease.

In the 1950s, neurology researchers were investigating neurotransmitters—the chemicals that carry nerve impulses across synapses, which are gaps between nerve cells. By 1960, they knew that Parkinson's disease was associated with low levels of dopamine (*d*ihidroxyphenylethyl*amine*), a neurotransmitter produced by cells in the *substantiae nigrae,* suggesting that the symptoms of parkinsonism might diminish or disappear if levels of dopamine in the brain could be topped up.

Injections of dopamine itself do not increase brain dopamine, however, because dopamine is unable to cross the blood–brain barrier—the boundary that separates the bloodstream from the fluids in the brain's tissues. Therefore, injected dopamine stays in the bloodstream until it is eliminated by the body's metabolism.

At this point, L-dopa comes into the story: dopa (dihydroxyphenylalanine) is a precursor, or chemical starting material, for dopamine. Unlike dopamine, however, dopa can cross the blood–brain barrier.

There are two mirror-image forms of dopa: the dextro (D) form and the levo (L) form. The two forms differ in an important way: L-dopa can lock into a brain enzyme that catalyzes a reaction that converts it into dopamine; D-dopa has no such interaction with that enzyme, so it does not react to form dopamine.

By 1967, it was shown that oral doses of L-dopa quickly suppress virtually all the symptoms of Parkinson's disease. Within a few years, L-dopa became the standard treatment of Parkinson's disease and other forms of parkinsonism.

Although L-dopa was initially hailed as a miracle drug, its use in the therapy of parkinsonism is not without problems. One problem is that much of the L-dopa taken in pills never reaches the brain at all. Instead, it is converted into dopamine and other substances in the rest of the body, causing side effects such as nausea, vomiting, and heart rhythm disturbances.

These problems can be minimized by administering L-dopa with another drug that inhibits the conversion of L-dopa into dopamine. The inhibiting drug cannot pass the blood–brain barrier, so the formation of dopamine within the brain continues.

A second problem is that too high a dose of L-dopa causes a whole new set of symptoms, such as tics, obsessive rituals, the repetition of words or phrases, and hallucinations. It is therefore essential to find the optimum dose for each patient.

The third problem is that therapy with L-dopa is not indefinitely useful. Over time, the body becomes accustomed to attempts to interfere with its defective dopamine metabolism, and the symptoms of parkinsonism gradually return.

▼ The chemical structure of dopamine, a neurotransmitter. In dopa, one or the other of the hydrogen atoms on the carbon attached to the nitrogen atom (blue) is replaced by a carboxylic acid group (–COOH).

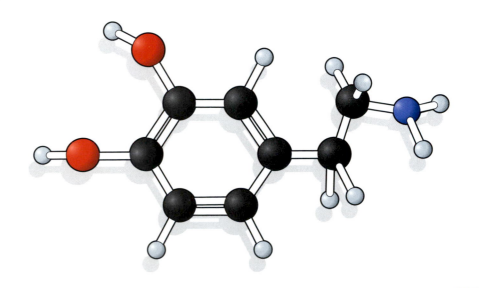

and covered in a fatty sheath; they also lack the pores present in capillaries elsewhere in the body. These two factors tend to limit the entry of many drugs into the brain. The nature of the blood–brain barrier makes it almost impossible for penicillin to enter brain tissue, for example, whereas thiopental (Pentothal, a drug that acts on the brain) enters the CNS with ease.

In pregnant women, the ability of a drug to penetrate the placental barrier and enter the fetal bloodstream becomes significant. Because the tissues of a fetus are in development, they are susceptible to side effects that do not occur in the fully developed tissues of adults. In some cases—as happened in the 1960s with the sedative thalidomide—a drug can cause malformation of the limbs of a fetus. This effect is called teratogenesis. Late in pregnancy or during delivery, drugs may cause respiratory problems, because the baby is not able to metabolize or excrete them.

Drugs that cause dependency in adults can also cause dependency in the fetus and withdrawal effects in the newborn infant as the supply of the drug from the mother ceases. Morphine and other narcotics cause fetal dependence, as do tranquilizing and sedating drugs.

Side effects

Drugs have therapeutic effects because they are able to interfere or interact with biochemical processes. Since a drug reaches tissues other than those where it is required to act, the same ability to interfere with biochemical processes can have undesirable consequences, called side effects.

Some anticancer drugs, for example, act by blocking the formation of DNA in rapidly dividing cells, such as cancer cells. At the same time, the formation of hair cells (which also divide rapidly) can be blocked, leading to temporary hair loss. This effect can be diminished if the patient wears a cooling cap during chemotherapy sessions: the cold contracts the blood vessels near the scalp, restricting the supply of drug-bearing blood to the follicles during treatment.

In some cases, such as when a drug causes minor depletion of vitamins, the patient might not be aware of the side effects unless the treatment is prolonged. In other cases, such as when a drug causes dizziness or nausea, a patient might be tempted to abandon the drug therapy entirely.

Dependency and resistance

When taking a drug over a prolonged period, a patient might develop a physiological or psychological compulsion to take a drug. This state of dependency is sometimes called addiction, especially when it arises through drug abuse.

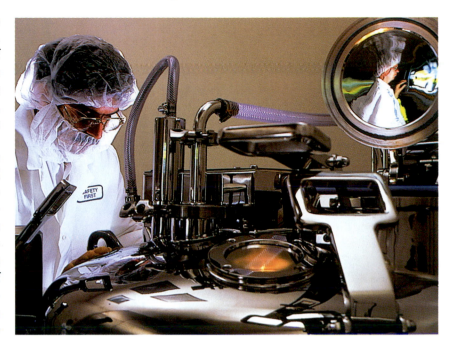

▲ A technician inspecting the contents of a stainless steel reaction vessel during the pilot production testing of a new drug. Strict hygiene must be adhered to during the manufacture of drugs to avoid contamination with any foreign substance that might affect the working or safety of the product.

Physiological dependence occurs when a drug's pharmacological properties alter the biochemical processes of a patient's body—permanently or temporarily—such that unpleasant physical symptoms, called withdrawal symptoms, occur if the dosage suddenly stops. Such symptoms can often be avoided by progressively reducing the dosage so that the biochemistry of the body has time to adjust accordingly.

Psychological dependence happens when taking the drug becomes a habit. It frequently occurs with drugs that have stimulant, sedative, analgesic, or mind-altering properties. The person taking the drug can develop a strong psychological association between use of the drug and an increased feeling of well-being, thus he or she develops a real compulsion to take it.

Both types of dependency are related to an effect called drug tolerance. Tolerance is a gradual weakening of the effectiveness of a drug caused by its repeated usage. The dosage must be continually increased to maintain a constant effect, and there is a risk of creating dependency.

Drug combinations

If two or more drugs are taken at the same time, one drug might amplify the effect of another or generate a different effect. In some cases, this interaction between drugs is useful in therapy. In others, the combination might cause unpredictable side effects or even death. Thus, alcohol, itself a drug, should be avoided by anyone receiving a course of drug treatment.

SEE ALSO: BIOCHEMISTRY • BLOOD • CANCER TREATMENT • CELL BIOLOGY • IMMUNOLOGY • METABOLISM • PHARMACOLOGY • VACCINE

Pharmacology

Pharmacology is the study of physiologically active substances, such as natural and synthetic drugs and toxins. Until the 19th century, plants and animals were the only sources of compounds that could be used as medicines. Pharmacists developed techniques to extract and purify these substances from their sources and to mix and prepare them as powders, pills, and liquid medicines. The medicinal value of a substance would often be discovered by accident.

The development of synthetic organic chemistry in the 19th century provided a new means for producing compounds for medicinal use. In some cases, such as that of quinine (an antimalarial compound from the bark of the cinchona), chemists developed methods for synthesizing natural compounds. The new synthetic methods freed pharmacists from their dependence on often rare or exotic plants as sources and made it possible to prepare medicinal substances in greater quantities than are available in nature.

In other cases, chemists used synthetic methods to prepare compounds related to natural medicinal compounds. Such compounds would then be tested for their medicinal worth using screening techniques that would go on to form the basis of modern pharmacology.

Aspirin

An early example of a medicine developed using synthetic organic chemistry is aspirin (acetylsalicylic acid, $CH_3COOC_6H_4COOH$). Salicylic acid (HOC_6H_4COOH), a compound derived from willow bark, is an effective painkiller and fever remedy; unfortunately, it is an extremely bitter substance that irritates the stomach lining.

In 1893, the German chemist Felix Hoffman used organic reactions to produce a compound in which the acidic –OH group of salicylic acid is replaced by an –O(CO)CH$_3$ group. The resulting compound is less aggressive to the stomach lining than is salicylic acid, but it decomposes in the body to form salicylic acid, which then acts to alleviate pain and reduce fever.

Prototypes

Modern pharmacology continues to be inspired by natural prototypes, or "lead" chemicals, that are known for their therapeutic value. These natural compounds often have side effects, however, and one of the goals of pharmacological research is to produce and identify new compounds that have a stronger therapeutic effect or weaker side effects (or both) than their natural prototypes.

▲ A research technician examines a thin-layer chromatography (TLC) plate during development of a new anti-inflammatory drug. TLC uses solvents to separate the components of tiny samples of mixtures produced by attempted drug syntheses.

At first, the synthesis of compounds based on natural prototypes was haphazard and strongly influenced by the limited number of synthetic approaches available. Over time, drug research became more systematic as the understanding of biochemical processes improved and the scope for synthesizing new compounds broadened.

Alkaloids

Around one-fifth of drug prototypes are alkaloids, complex organic bases that seed plants produce as a defense against foraging predators. Given that their natural function is to deter predators, often by incapacitating them, it is no surprise that many alkaloids are potentially poisonous to humans. Used in small doses, however, many alkaloids have therapeutic effects.

The traditional method for obtaining natural alkaloids is to crush the part of the plant that bears the alkaloid—often the leaves—together with a solvent, such as alcohol. The resulting mixture, on straining, yields a solution of alkaloid that can be concentrated by evaporation.

Some natural alkaloids are used unmodified in medicine. Atropine, for example, was traditionally extracted from the leaves of the deadly nightshade and dropped into the eyes to cause the pupils to dilate (dilated pupils are a symptom of sexual arousal, and this effect was used to increase allure). Purified atropine is now used to dilate the pupils prior to examinations of the eye. Another alkaloid, colchicine, is present in the seeds of the autumn crocus and is useful in the treatment of gout. Tubocurarine is present in *Chondodendron tomentosum*, a South American vine. It was traditionally used in curare, a paralyzing arrow poison, but is now used to relax muscles during surgery. Morphine and codeine are powerful painkillers that are components of opium, the dried latex secreted by opium poppy capsules.

In many cases, the therapeutic effects of natural alkaloids are accompanied by unacceptable side effects. In such cases, pharmacologists seek synthetic alternatives that cause fewer side effects. Cocaine, for example, is a local anesthetic extracted from the coca leaf. It is also highly addictive, so doctors rarely administer it to patients, preferring instead the nonaddictive synthetic drug xylocaine, which is just as effective.

Fermentation products

Another important class of drug prototypes is formed by the fermentation products produced by microorganisms. During World War II, the U.S. pharmaceutical industry produced massive amounts of the newly discovered penicillin from fungi. Since then, synthetic compounds modeled on penicillin, cephalosporin, and other natural antibiotics from fungi have saved millions of people from life-threatening bacterial infections.

Some antibiotics have other therapeutic effects. Doxorubicin, for example, is an antibiotic isolated from *Streptomyces peucetius*, a soil organism that has much in common with both bacteria and fungi. Doxorubicin is active against leukemia and a wide range of tumors, making it useful in the chemotherapeutic treatment of cancer.

Hormones

In their natural settings, hormones are chemicals that are produced in one part of an organism and that have an effect on the activity of cells in another part of the same organism. As such, they relay signals that control an organism's response to its environment. Used pharmacologically, natural hormones and their synthetic alternatives can affect cell activity as a form of therapy.

Hormones have been modified to provide medicines to treat asthma, high blood pressure, mental illness, rheumatism, and even cancer. Tamoxifen, for example, is a drug that resembles estrogen, a

▼ A laboratory technician monitors hydrogen uptake during the hydrogenation of a nitro compound. The product is expected to be an anticancer drug.

female hormone. It interferes with the participation of estrogen in the growth of breast cancer cells and can help cure breast cancer.

Human hormones can be administered to alter the balance of hormones in the body or to restore a normal hormone balance when the body ceases to produce one or more hormones as a consequence of aging or some form of illness. Insulin, for example, is given to diabetics to compensate for their lack of insulin production. The female sex hormones estrogen and progesterone are used in contraceptive tablets, and estrogen is used in skin patches to restore the estrogen levels of menopausal women and so reduce mood instability, hot flashes, and the risk of osteoporosis.

Drug mechanisms

Many drugs act by mimicking biomolecules—substances, such as hormones and neurotransmitters, that take part in processes in the body. In one mechanism, the drug induces the same reaction as the biomolecule; the drug is then said to be an agonist of the biomolecule: it boosts its effect.

Alternatively, a drug takes the place of the biomolecule but induces no reaction, so the effect of the biomolecule is neutralized. In such cases, the drug is an antagonist of the biomolecule.

In a third case, drug molecules can physically block the tiny channels in cell membranes, thus preventing physiologically active substances from reaching their normal sites of action.

Receptors

The shape of a molecule largely determines whether or not it will mimic a biomolecule and therefore have a pharmacological effect, because biomolecules and drugs interact with shape-specific sites, called receptors, formed by proteins. When the appropriate biomolecule latches into a receptor, it triggers a response that is characteristic of that molecule. In some cases, the receptor is the catalytic site of an enzyme, and the biomolecule undergoes a chemical reaction when it locks into the receptor. In such cases, an antagonist drug would lock to a receptor and stay there, blocking out the biomolecule that would normally react there.

Molecular biologists often compare the shape-selective interactions between biomolecules and receptors to lock-and-key mechanisms. In this analogy, receptors are locks, and the molecules that fit them are the keys.

ANTI-HIV THERAPY

Since the early 1980s, AIDS—acquired immune deficiency syndrome—has become a major killer. AIDS is caused by the human immunodeficiency virus, or HIV. Left unchecked, this virus causes a progressive weakening of the body's immune system, eventually making its carriers defenseless against infections that are harmless to people whose immune systems are competent. AIDS occurs when several such infections have taken hold and are starting to pose a threat to the HIV carrier's survival.

When HIV was first recognized, there was no effective means to control it. Worse, when it was realized that HIV is a retrovirus—a virus whose genetic material is RNA (ribonucleic acid) rather than DNA (deoxyribonucleic acid)—it was feared that it would evade attempts to develop an effective therapy, since other retroviruses, such as herpes, were notoriously difficult or impossible to treat at that time.

The first drug used against HIV was AZT (azidodeoxythymidine), a drug that was developed for cancer treatment. AZT is chemically related to thymidine, one of the four nucleosides that combine to form chains of DNA. The key difference between the compounds is that thymidine has two reactive sites that take part in DNA chain formation, while AZT has only one.

When HIV replicates, it does so by a process of reverse transcription: it first forms molecules of DNA that correspond to its RNA sequence; those molecules then

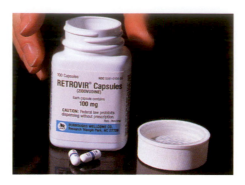

▲ Zidovudine (AZT, azidodeoxythymidine)— a nucleoside analog—was one of the first drugs used to combat HIV infection.

act as templates for the production of more RNA. If a molecule of AZT takes the place of thymidine in a growing DNA strand, the growth of that chain suddenly stops, because AZT lacks the second reactive site necessary for the chain to continue growing. The incomplete DNA strand is unable to act as a template for making RNA, so the replication of HIV is blocked. Drugs that act in this way are called reverse-transcription inhibitors, and they are all nucleoside analogs.

Therapy using nucleoside analogs has drawbacks, however, since they also block the growth of normal DNA, resulting in unpleasant side effects that limit the dosage that can be given, and often the period over which any given drug can be taken. Furthermore, the ability of HIV to mutate helps it become resistant to drugs, particularly if drug therapy is interrupted.

With time, trials showed that better results are achieved when two or three reverse-transcription inhibitors are used in combinations. The effectiveness of such therapies was measured as a greater reduction in the viral load (concentration of HIV in the body) compared with the results of single-drug therapy.

The next great advance in HIV therapy came with the introduction of protease inhibitors. As part of the life cycle of HIV, the virus produces a long-chain protein coded for by genes in its RNA. An enzyme called HIV protease then cuts that protein into shorter protein fragments that play key roles in assembling new virus and infecting cells. Protease inhibitors work by locking into the active site of protease and destroying its ability to catalyze the formation of protein fragments.

The standard treatment for HIV uses "cocktails" of two or more nucleoside-analog reverse-transcription inhibitors and a protease inhibitor. The combination varies between individuals, and the best compromise between effectiveness and side effects, such as nausea, is often found by trial and error.

In the most successful cases, the viral load is reduced to undetectable levels. The treatment does not eliminate the virus, however, and the infection becomes reestablished if the drug therapy stops. Nevertheless, therapy restores the immune system and a reasonable quality of life as well as greatly increasing life expectancy.

The shape of the receptor "lock" depends on the sequence of amino acids in the protein that forms the receptor. Interactions between adjacent amino acids determine how protein chains fold and curl up to form three-dimensional bundles. Receptors are cavities or indentations in such bundles, and their shapes match the shapes of the appropriate "key" molecules.

The physical shape of a receptor is not the only factor in deciding which molecules it will accept. The receptor also has functional groups that carry slight negative and positive charges and groups that can form hydrogen bonds with appropriate groups on other molecules. The strength of the interaction between a molecule and a receptor

therefore depends on how well a molecule fits the shape, charge distribution, and hydrogen bonding at a given receptor site.

Molecular modeling

The traditional aids for envisaging the shapes of molecules include ball-and-stick models, from which structures can be built to represent the average positions of atomic nuclei in molecules. Such models are based on typical bond lengths and angles measured in spectroscopic and X-ray-diffraction studies of many molecules.

Ball-and-stick models are of limited value, however, in assessing how well a molecule will fit into a receptor site in a protein molecule, because they do not represent the cloud of electrons that surrounds the nuclear skeleton, and that electron cloud is what one molecule "sees" as it approaches another molecule.

Advances in computing have produced new tools for molecular modeling that are more appropriate for drug design. Computerized quantum-mechanical calculations provide reasonable approximations of the relative positions of nuclei in molecules and of the distribution of electrons within a molecule. Computer graphics can produce virtual models of the shapes of electron clouds around molecules, highlighting regions of positive and negative charge.

If X-ray diffraction results are available for the target receptor of drugs research, it can be portrayed using computerized molecular modeling. This makes it possible to define the appropriate molecular profile to fit the receptor and to compare that profile with those of candidate drug molecules. The candidates whose profiles best fit the receptor would then be synthesized and tested for activity and toxicity.

In many cases, candidates for further testing are chosen by modeling a molecule that is known to have pharmacological activity and identifying molecules that have similar profiles. A slight difference from the original molecule can cause significant differences in one or more lock-and-key interactions. In some cases, these differences improve the balance between therapeutic value and side effects; in other cases, the test compound proves to be more toxic or less therapeutically active than the starting compound.

Drug targeting

Side effects are physiological reactions that occur when a drug acts on receptors other than the targets of therapeutic action or when it inhibits the action of biochemicals that are vital to healthy processes. A good receptor fit improves the likelihood that a compound will be an effective drug but is no guarantee against side effects.

Many pharmacologically active substances are optically active, that is, they exist in two mirror-image forms, or enantiomers, that rotate the plane of polarized light in opposite directions. The proteins that form receptors occur in only one of their two mirror-image forms. As a result, one enantiomer of a drug tends to fit its receptor much more effectively than the other form, so its potency is much greater. The mirror image can be more potent in causing side effects, so it is often desirable to produce pure enantiomers to increase potency and reduce side effects.

Side effects can be minimized by designing a drug so that it is preferentially delivered to its site of action or impeded from reaching the receptors responsible for side effects. The side effect of drowsiness associated with early antihistamine drugs has been overcome by the development of antihistamines that do not cross the blood-brain barrier, for example. In many cases, the transport of drugs across membranes in the body can be influenced by manipulating their fat solubility using factors such as acidity, basicity, side-chain length, or electron distribution. Judicious control of these factors can help deliver the drug to the specific cells, organs, or invading microorganisms on which it is required to act.

Drug testing

The effectiveness of a new drug can sometimes be tested on cultures and tissue samples in laboratories. Nevertheless, the only way to determine the broader effect of a drug, including its side effects, is by testing on live organisms. Animal tests lasting months or even years precede the first human tests, and statisticians evaluate the results of tests to distinguish between genuine toxic effects and chance complications unrelated to the drug.

The first human tests seek to identify safe dosage levels and side effects in healthy humans. Then, clinical studies start on small numbers of patients with the disease for which the drug is intended. At this stage, the true effectiveness of a new drug relative to established drugs starts to become apparent. Tests include a placebo—a neutral pill or other preparation that appears identical to the drug under test. Neither the patients nor the medical staff can be aware of which patients are receiving the test drug and which are receiving the placebo, because the act of taking a drug can cause some patients to feel effects—positive or negative—that are unrelated to the activity of the drug.

Once a drug has been successful in trials, it can be licensed for general use. In the United States, the organization that issues such licenses is the Food and Drug Administration (FDA). The FDA insists that all side effects be thoroughly documented and monitored for rare side effects that might only become apparent once hundreds of thousands of patients have received treatment using the drug.

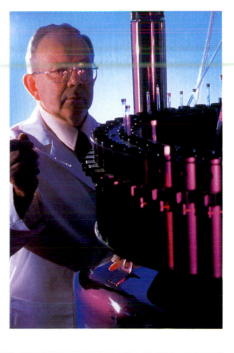

▼ Loading samples into an NMR (nuclear magnetic resonance) machine. NMR uses pulses of radio-frequency radiation to stimulate transitions of magnetic nuclei—such as those of hydrogen—within molecules. The spectrum of the radio frequencies that interact with a given molecule gives information about its structure.

SEE ALSO: BIOCHEMISTRY • CELL BIOLOGY • CHEMICAL BONDING AND VALENCY • ENZYME • MEDICINE • MICROBIOLOGY

Pheromone

ants and termites use pheromones to lay trails to sources of food that can be followed by other members of the group. They can also be used to signal danger, but most often they function as a means of attracting the opposite sex, or they trigger hormonal changes that promote ovulation.

Two categories of pheromones have been identified. Releaser pheromones have an immediate effect on behavior, while primer pheromones are more long term in effect and affect physiological processes. Although this simple definition is workable when applied to insects, it is difficult to apply to higher organisms such as mammals. The animal's psychological state interacts with the pheromone effects, making it more difficult to make predictions about the animal's reaction to a given pheromone.

Moth sex pheromones were first discovered as long ago as 1900, but science had to wait until 1961 for the first structure of a sex pheromone—that of the silkworm moth—to be determined. It is now possible to synthesize and use pheromones for human advantage owing to the huge amount of scientific effort that has been invested in the isolation and identification of these substances since that first breakthrough in the 20th century.

Pheromones and behavior

Pheromones are involved in sexual pairing in many moths. The female emits a pheromone to attract males. When a male moth senses a female pheromone, he flies upwind toward the probable source of the pheromone by keeping within the plume, which is a stream of pheromone emitted from the female.

At the beginning of pheromone research, scientists believed that they would find a unique pheromone substance for each species of moth. The idea is sensible because it is of little use, for example, for a female to attract a male from another species.

The assumption proved to be overly simplistic as the number of identified pheromones grew. In many cases related species release pheromones that are isomers (having different spatial arrangements of their atoms) of each other. In other cases, mixtures of pheromones are released, with the proportions of components differing from one species to another. Only in a few isolated instances has exactly the same substance been found in more than one species—but in these instances, the species involved do not breed at the same time of year.

Pheromones are a particular form of semiochemical—substances that carry information between organisms. Pheromones are semiochemicals that affect the behavior and physiology of others of the same species. Pheromones have been best documented in insects and vertebrates but have been identified in mammals and have been postulated in humans. No evidence of pheromones has been discovered in birds, though some species of algae and fungi are known to use them as attractants in reproduction. Pheromones are produced in special glands or can be distributed in other secretions, such as urine, mucus, or sweat.

The purpose of pheromones is primarily to draw members of the same species together, whether for social or sexual reasons. Colonies of

▲ Pigs are used to hunt for truffles because the truffle emits a chemical substance that mimics the pheromones given off by male pigs. As the relationship between pig and truffle is mutually beneficial, the chemical that attracts the pig is called a synomone.

Male pheromones

Male moths also emit pheromones. Two types have been identified: courtship pheromones and long-distance pheromones. When a male has followed a female pheromone plume to its source, he approaches her to within 1 in. (2.5 cm) before emitting his own courtship pheromone, which biologists believe plays an important role in sexual attraction. Long-distance pheromones occur in moth species where the roles of the sexes are reversed. The male emits a pheromone that the female can detect from some feet away. Male pheromone synthesis may depend on specific feeding patterns during its period as a larva.

Using pheromones

Pheromones have an important role to play in pest control. However, the vision of many researchers in the 1960s has not come true. They had hoped that synthetic pheromones could be used to bait traps to control moth populations, but in practice, the method did not work. The subsequent populations of moths were not reduced in number. Although pheromones have proved ineffective at controlling populations directly, they can be used to indicate potential pest troublespots. The number of moths caught in traps is an accurate indication of the state of the moth population in the locality. If an outbreak of pests is detected, insecticide can be used to eradicate them. This practice reduces the indiscriminate use of insecticides and the related hazards.

Synthetic pheromones have also been used to interfere with the mating patterns of moths. Synthetic pheromones can be encased in microcapsules. Distributed in high enough concentrations over an agricultural area, the released pheromones confuse males, making it difficult for them to find females. Scientists believe that the real pheromone plumes from females are masked by the synthetic pheromones or that males become habituated to pheromone—they become used to a certain level of pheromone in the atmosphere and do not respond when a pheromone plume reaches them. This interference with normal mating cycles is effective in reducing the numbers of the next generation.

Pheromones in mammals

Knowledge of mammalian pheromones is far less detailed than that of insect pheromones, the main body of research having started in the 1970s. Many pheromones are found in urine. In mice and other rodents, pheromones have been found in urine. There is considerable evidence that pheromones in their urine have an important effect on the onset of puberty in mice.

A component of male mouse urine has been found to accelerate the onset of puberty amongst immature females, acting as a primer. Exposure to urine from dominant males has a greater effect than exposure to urine from subordinate males. The exposure is effective over a long timespan, even from before weaning. Other types of pheromones, those from female urine, can also affect puberty in females—in this case, delaying the onset of puberty.

The Whitten Effect is another male mouse urine effect. This time estrus is accelerated or decelerated after exposure to urine. Pregnancy may be blocked by the Bruce Effect, when a newly impregnated female is exposed to the urine of a more dominant male.

Pheromone effects have been noted in many other animals, notably pigs, cows, sheep, and goats. Many of these animals have been found to have a structure in the nose called the vomeronasal organ (VNO) that scientists believe can detect pheromones. Some researchers have claimed to have found pheromone effects in humans, and products that claim to use pheromones to attract the opposite sex have been marketed, but the usefulness of these products has not been confirmed by scientists. Humans appear to have the remnants of a VNO in the nasal cavity, but studies have failed to find any receptors that could communicate such information to the brain.

▼ Scientists have not yet established whether humans emit pheromones, though evidence exists that chemical messaging plays a part in communicating subtle signals between humans. In fact, babies can recognize the smell of their mothers, and vice versa. Also, studies have shown that groups of women living together may develop synchronized menstrual cycles because of the influence of each others' body secretions.

SEE ALSO: CHEMISTRY, ANALYTICAL • ENDOCRINOLOGY • HORMONE • PEST CONTROL • REPRODUCTION

pH Measurement

The pH scale was introduced in 1909 by the Danish chemist S. P. L. Sørensen as a method of expressing the acidity, or hydrogen ion concentration, of a solution. The p of pH stands for the German word *Potenz*, meaning "power" (in the mathematical sense) and the H represents the hydrogen. One of the most common uses of pH is in chemical analysis, with indicators or pH meters being used, for example, to find the end point of a titration with an acid neutralizing base. Control of pH is important in many industrial processes, and the effects of corrosion can be minimized by pH control. Similarly, the pH of soil has a marked effect on its fertility, while many body processes depend on the maintenance of the correct pH—often by the use of buffer solutions.

Hydrogen ion concentration

An acid is a substance that ionizes in water to give hydrogen ions (H^+), and a base is a substance that ionizes in water to give hydroxyl ions (OH^-). The strength of an acid or a base depends on the proportion of molecules that ionize in the water. A strong acid is one in which most of its molecules are ionized, and a weak acid is one in which few molecules are ionized. Since hydrogen ions or hydroxyl ions are always produced, the strength of the acid or base depends upon the concentration of hydrogen or hydroxyl ions. The concentration of hydrogen ions depends upon the concentration of acid or base molecules in the water, the proportion of these molecules that ionize, and the temperature of the solution.

▼ Blue litmus paper turns red when it touches the juice of a lemon because the juice is acidic. The organic compounds used in litmus paper come from several species of lichen found in the Netherlands.

Sørensen defined the pH scale as the logarithm of the reciprocal of the hydrogen ion concentration:

$$pH = \log_{10} 1/[H^+]$$

$[H^+]$ is the hydrogen ion concentration. For example, if the hydrogen ion concentration of a solution was 0.03 moles per liter:

$$pH = \log_{10} 1/0.03 = \log_{10} 100/3 = 2 - 0.477 = 1.523$$

One mole of a chemical compound has a mass equal to its molecular weight in grams. For example, 1 mole of HCl (hydrogen chloride) has a mass of 36.46 g.

In pure water, which is neither an acid nor a base, very few molecules ionize. Since water is made of a hydrogen and a hydroxyl ion, their concentrations are the same. At 77°F (25°C), the concentration of both ions is only 0.0000001 moles per liter. The pH of pure water is thus

$$\log_{10} 1/0.0000001 = \log_{10} 1 \times 10^7 = 7$$

and because the higher the concentration of hydrogen ions, the lower the pH, it follows that pH values lower than 7 are acid. When the pH is greater than 7, the concentration of hydroxyl ions is greater than that of hydrogen ions, and the solution is a base—and is often referred to as being alkaline. A neutral solution has a pH value of 7.

Measuring pH

Some plant extracts and other chemicals change color when exposed to acids and are therefore useful as indicators. Three common indicators are litmus, which is red in acidic solutions and blue in basic, changing color between pH 6 and 8; methyl orange, which is red in fairly strong acidic solution, changing to yellow between pH 3 and 5; and phenolphthalein, which is colorless in acidic solutions and turns pink in basic conditions at pH 8 to 10.

Universal Indicator is obtained by mixing a number of indicators together so that the indicator changes color gradually over the whole range of the pH scale, thus enabling the pH to be measured approximately.

More accurate measurements of pH can be made with a pH meter. All pH meters are based on a method originally developed by Sørensen. He measured the potential difference between

◄ A suitable soil pH is an important factor in plant growth. Potatoes, for example, like slightly acidic conditions.

(NaOH), combine with the hydrogen ions from the acetic acid to form neutral water. Since any hydrogen or hydroxyl ions that are added to buffer solution combine with other ions, the concentration of hydrogen ions and hence pH remains constant.

the solution and a special electrode. The very small potential difference produced was proportional to the logarithm of the hydrogen ion concentration. Today, a glass electrode meter is commonly used. It consists of a thin-walled glass bulb. Inside this bulb is a solution of constant pH (a buffer) with a platinum wire dipped into it. There is also a reference electrode, usually a calomel (mercurous chloride) electrode, which enables the potential difference to be measured by an accurate potentiometer when the two electrodes are dipped into an unknown solution. The pH may be read directly from a scale on the meter.

Buffer solutions

A buffer solution is one of known pH, which does not vary with the addition of small amounts of an acid or a base. Buffer solutions are made by mixing together solutions of a weak acid (one that is only slightly ionized) and a salt of the weak acid (which will be completely ionized).

For example, acetic acid and sodium acetate form a buffer solution when mixed. Acetic acid is only slightly ionized into hydrogen ions and acetate ions:

$$CH_3COOH \rightleftharpoons CH_3COO^- + H^+$$

acetic acid   acetate ion   hydrogen ion

Sodium acetate, however, is almost completely ionized:

$$CH_3COONa \rightarrow CH_3COO^- + Na^+$$

sodium acetate   acetate ion   sodium ion

If an acid, such as hydrochloric acid (HCl), is added to the buffer solution, the hydrogen ions from the acid will combine with the acetate ions to form nonionized acetic acid:

$$H^+ + Cl^- + Na^+ + CH_3COO^- \rightarrow Na^+ + Cl^- + CH_3COOH$$

If a base is added to the buffer, the hydroxyl ions from the base, such as sodium hydroxide

▲ In this automatic titration, a substance of unknown concentration is analyzed by adding measured amounts of a known solution, which reacts chemically with it. The reaction is monitored by measuring the pH by means of electrodes immersed in the solution. The operation stops by itself at the correct point.

SEE ALSO: Acid and alkali • Chemistry, analytical • Ion and ionization • Soil research

Phonography

◄ A silver-coated lacquer master disc ready for electroplating with nickel. When the lid is lowered, the disc will be spun to ensure good contact with the electrolyte solution. Constant filtering and temperature control also help ensure an even deposition of metallic nickel over the silver. The silver-faced nickel disc that results, called the master shell, is then split from the master disc.

The word *phonography* stems from the Greek words *phone* (sound) and *graphein* (to write); it refers to the practice and technology of recording sound. The first sound recording was achieved in 1857, when the French inventor Léon Scott produced a machine called a phonautograph that drew sound waveforms on a smoke-blackened cylinder. Unfortunately, he failed to invent a device that could play back the recordings.

The first machine that was capable of both recording and playing back sounds was the phonograph, developed by the U.S. inventor Thomas Alva Edison in 1877. The phonograph used a sound-sensitive diaphragm attached to a stylus to cut indentations in tinfoil wrapped around a hand-cranked brass drum. A separate stylus and diaphragm were used for playback. It was impractical to unwrap the tinfoil from the drum, however. In 1885, the U.S. inventor Alexander Graham Bell developed the graphophone—a device for recording sounds in wax cylinders. The phonograph and graphophone both cut "hill-and-dale" grooves—the phono-cut method—whereby the varying depth of the groove represented the variations in air pressure that constitute sound waves.

The format of recordings took a step closer to modern methods in 1887, when the German-born inventor Emile Berliner developed the talking machine gramophone. Berliner's device recorded on discs, which were easier to change than cylinders, and used laterally modulated grooves—the needle cut—whereby sound was recorded and reproduced by side-to-side motion of cutting and playback styluses in spiral grooves.

Berliner began production of his gramophones in 1894, and his venture ultimately became part of the Radio Corporation of America (RCA). Until 1913, both cylinders and discs were manufactured, both hill-and-dale and lateral-cut discs were available, and playing speeds varied to a maximum of 100 rpm, each format option requiring a different player. Eventually, the 78 rpm lateral-cut disc became the standard.

Electric recording

Electric recording techniques developed and largely replaced mechanical recording between 1915 and 1925. Microphones that had originally been developed for telephony were used to convert the sounds of artists' voices and instruments into electrical signals. These signals could then be used to drive electromechanical devices for cutting master discs for pressing records.

Since the start of electric recording, the introduction of magnetic and then digital recording have made the capture of live performances more versatile. Improvements in technology, and particularly digital technology, have also increased the fidelity of the recordings.

Inputs from microphones, guitar pickups, and synthesizer output leads are recorded as separate "tracks" (channels of information). Mixing engineers then adjust the relative sound levels of the tracks to create a balanced sound. Sound effects, such as reverberation, can be added at this stage. In stereo recordings, which are now the norm, the balance of each track is then adjusted to give it a position in the perceived stereo sound image.

► Here, the mother shell, the first positive copy of a master disc, is split from the master shell. The mother shell will be used to make stampers—negative discs used to stamp records in vinyl.

Once the record producer is satisfied with the recording, all the tracks are mixed down, or combined, into two tracks: one for the left channel of stereo, one for the right channel.

Where magnetic tape is still used, 24 or 32 tracks on a 2 in. (50 mm) wide tape that travels at 15 in. per sec. (38 cm/s) are mixed down to two tracks on a ¼ in. (6.2 mm) master tape. Increasingly, these tapes are replaced by computer files.

Record manufacture

The production of many hundreds or thousands of copies of a record starts with the production of a master disc. A series of negative and positive copies of the master disc results in the molds that are used to press records for sale.

Master disc. The first positive imprint—one that could be played on a record player—is cut in a layer of nitrocellulose on an aluminum disc. Electrical signals from the recording drive a cutting head that carries the cutting tool—a heated sapphire or ruby stylus—while the disc rotates under the tool at a constant speed on the turntable of the cutting lathe. With direct-cut discs, there is no master recording; instead, the amplified and mixed outputs from microphones drive the cutting head as the musicians play.

The walls of the grooves are at 45 degrees to either side of the vertical, and the radius of curvature at the bottom of the groove is 0.0002 in. (0.005 mm). The mean depth of 0.002 in. (0.05 mm); vertical and lateral movements during cutting encode the sound in the groove.

As the disc turns, a lead screw drives the cutting head from the edge to the center of the disc. The rate at which this happens relative to the turning speed determines the pitch of the groove—the density of turns along the radius. The pitch varies from 140 to 400 turns per radial inch (approximately 55–160 turns per cm), allowing up to 35 minutes of recording on one side of a 12 in. (30 cm) 33⅓ rpm record. A suction head removes swarf (cut material) as cutting proceeds.

Master shell. The master shell is the first negative copy—one whose groove protrudes from the surface. It is made by first washing the master disc with surfactants to make it hydrophilic (easily wet), then by washing with tin (II) chloride ($SnCl_2$). Tin (II) ions are absorbed on the surface of the disc, and they act as nucleation points for subsequent chemical deposition of silver. The silver is deposited by a reaction between simultaneous sprays of silver nitrate ($AgNO_3$) in ammonia (NH_3) solution and a reducing solution.

The mirrorlike silver deposit serves as the cathode in the subsequent electrodeposition of nickel using a solution of nickel sulfamate and a nickel anode. As current passes through the cell, nickel migrates from the anode to form a layer of the metal on the silver-coated surface of the master disc. The cell is run for a short period at 95°F (35°C), followed by a longer period at 140°F (60°C). After around three hours' deposition, the master shell is approximately 0.025 in. (0.635 mm) thick. It is then separated from the lacquer disc.

Although the master shell could be used to press records, it would eventually wear out and need replacement by a new master shell made from the master disc. This process would in turn cause wear on the master disc, which would eventually become unusable. Instead, the master disc is used to produce positive shells, from which numerous negative copies for printing can be made.

Positive shell (mother shell). The positive, or mother, shell is made by electrodeposition of nickel on the printed face of the master shell. The silvered surface of the nickel master shell must first be treated to ensure that the positive shell can be separated after deposition. This treatment employs superficial oxidation using chromate salts or by depositing a fine layer of organic colloids on the surface.

After deposition and separation from the master shell, the positive shell is played and examined for defects. Small imperfections can then be removed using a manually operated engraving tool viewed through a stereomicroscope.

Matrix shell. A matrix shell, or stamper, is a negative copy of the master disc made by electrodeposition of nickel onto a positive shell. Stampers are only around 0.010 in. (0.25 mm) thick. After separation from the positive shell, the back of a stamper is polished to remove surface protrusions, and an optically centered hole is made in it. The stamper is then pressed to create the profile for the label and its raised edge.

Molding. Records are made by molding vinyl—one of a number of blends of thermoplastic polymers and additives—between two stampers. The exact molding process depends mainly on the record format.

Compression molding is the favored process, particularly for 12 in. (30 cm) long-playing records. A "biscuit" of granular polymer is squeezed, together with the labels, between two stampers mounted on mold blocks. The mold blocks have channels through which steam and cooling water can run. First, the mold blocks are

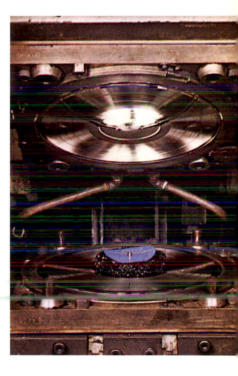

▲ A record-molding press ready for stamping. The stampers, or matrix shells, are visible on the upper and lower molding blocks. The "biscuit" of vinyl is sandwiched between two labels on the spindle.

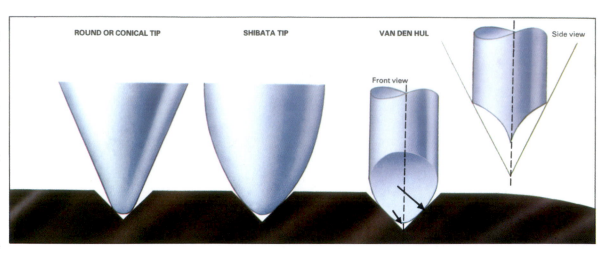

▶ Various stylus designs. The conical tip has a round end that follows the groove without causing undue wear. The elliptical Shibata stylus has a small-radius tip that fits deep into the groove and smoothly curved sides that reduce wear. The Van den Hul stylus has a tight tip radius and a straight-line footprint (far right) that improves groove following.

heated using high-pressure steam and a hydraulic pressure of around 1 ton per sq. in. (around 14 MPa). The combination of heat and pressure melts the vinyl and forms the record, and also attaches the label to the vinyl surface.

Cooling water then passes through the mold blocks to solidify the record so that it keeps its shape. The cycle is electronically controlled and takes from 15 to 25 seconds. The record is removed from the press, and the excess vinyl, called flash, is removed from the edge by rotating the record against a hot knife.

An alternative to compression molding is injection molding, which is mainly used for 7 in. (18 cm) records. In this process, hot vinyl is injected into a clamped mold. In a similar method, injection is followed by compression, the two actions occurring almost simultaneously.

Materials

Early records were made from mixtures of powdered slate in a matrix of shellac (a natural resin excreted by a type of insect). Shellac is an early example of a composite material.

In 1948, the Columbia Broadcasting System (CBS) introduced records made from plasticized polyvinyl chloride (PVC), a synthetic material. Most modern records are made from a copolymer of chloroethene (vinyl chloride, $CH_2=CHCl$) with around 14 percent ethenyl ethanoate (vinyl acetate, $CH_3COOCH=CH_2$). The copolymer has greater flexibility than does pure PVC. Traces of tin salts inhibit the decomposition of the polymer that would otherwise occur slowly in daylight. Also, a small amount (less than one percent) of lubricant helps release records from their molds and reduces wear by lubricating the passage of the stylus through the groove.

These components are blended and melted together. In most cases, carbon black is added to make the blend black and opaque; in some cases, other dyes or pigments are used to make colored

vinyls. The resulting blend is cooled and extruded as granules. Some records are molded as two clear discs and then bonded around a label.

Some vinyl blends are based on polystyrene or acrylic copolymers. They are less flexible than PVC copolymers and are used mainly for singles.

Formats

The first standard format was the 10 in. (25 cm) diameter 78 rpm disc. The high speed and large grooves (and therefore low pitch) of such records allowed only around 4½ minutes' playing time.

In the 1930s, RCA introduced a long-playing record (LP) that played at 33⅓ rpm and approximately doubled the playing time as a consequence. It was a failure, partly because the slower speed caused greater surface noise than obtained with 78s when the same materials were used.

The introduction of PVC records by CBS made possible high-quality recordings with fine grooves—microgrooves—that greatly increased playing times on 12 in. (30 cm) diameter discs. Subsequently, RCA introduced an entirely new format: a 7 in. (18 cm) diameter 45 rpm microgroove disc with a large center hole. The disc was designed for recordings of single songs. The large center hole allowed such records to be used with an automatic record changer that was launched at the same time.

The widespread adoption of the 45 rpm single made the 78 record obsolete by the end of the 1950s. During the same decade, manufacturers of 33⅓ rpm and 45 rpm records converged on a standard for microgroove records: the RIAA (Record Industry Association of America) characteristic. The RIAA standard specifies the extent to which low frequencies are attenuated to reduce groove amplitudes and high frequencies are boosted to overcome surface hiss. When played, the signal must be modified to restore the original sound, and adoption of the RIAA standard meant that all record players could be used for both formats.

Stereo

Most modern recordings are in stereo: they have two sound channels—left and right—cut into opposite walls of the groove. This system is called the 45/45 configuration, since each wall is at 45 degrees to the vertical; it was first demonstrated by Alan Blumlein in London in 1931 but was not exploited commercially until the 1950s. By convention, the signal for the left channel is carried on the wall nearest the center of the record, while the outer wall carries the right channel.

In the 45/45 system, signals are encoded as oscillations at 90 degrees to the surface of each wall. Since the groove walls are perpendicular, the modulations of the two signals are also at 90 degrees to each other. Therefore, suitable detectors in a pickup can read the two signals separately. A mono signal corresponds to a pair of identical stereo signals.

Pickup (cartridge)

Modern record players use pickups, or cartridges, to convert the vibrations of a stylus into electric signals for reproduction. Two common types of cartridges use the relative motion of magnets and conducting coils to induce currents in the coils. In a moving-magnet cartridge, a magnet attached to the stylus vibrates close to two coils, one for each channel. In a moving-coil cartridge, the coils are mounted on the stylus, and they vibrate in the field of a fixed permanent magnet.

Other cartridges use the piezoelectric effect, whereby the varying compression and relaxation of a quartz crystal produce electrical signals. Other transducer types include strain gauges, variable capacitors, and even photoelectric cells. In all cases, the output signals from the cartridge are weak, and they have to be preamplified before being fed to the main amplifier.

Stylus and tonearm

Whatever the transducer system, the quality of reproduction is ultimately determined by how faithfully the stylus follows the groove. The simplest stylus shape is conical with a tip radius of 0.0007 in. (0.0178 mm) compared with a typical groove width of 0.0025 in. (0.0635 mm). The tip material is usually diamond, chosen for hardness.

More accurate tracing is achieved using an elliptical stylus, whose major radius of 0.0007 in. (17.8 µm) provides a smoothly curved surface that causes little wear as it rides along the groove walls and whose minor radius of 0.0003 in. (7.6 µm) traces the modulations accurately.

The design of the tonearm—the pivoting support for the cartridge—is also crucial to good reproduction. An adjustable counterbalance ensures a constant weight—usually around 0.07 oz. (2 g)—acts on the stylus, and a low-friction pivot keeps the force necessary for the needle to track across the record to a minimum. A damped arm-lowering system helps prevent the stylus from jumping when placed on the record.

Tonearm designs attempt to match the movement of the cutting head that made the master, thereby reducing tracking error (inaccurate reproduction due to the angle of the cartridge relative to the groove). S-shaped tonearms help the cartridge remain almost parallel throughout the disc, and some record players have servo-driven arms that track across records in a straight line.

Drive systems

Turntables are required to maintain accurate speed while a record plays and should not transfer low-frequency motor noise, or rumble, to the stylus. In the rim-drive system, the drive is transmitted from the motor through a rubber wheel that runs along the inside rim of the turntable. This system provides a degree of isolation between motor and the turntable.

In belt-driven turntables, a rubber belt runs from a pulley on the motor shaft around a rim under the turntable. Synchronous motors lock to the supply frequency, which controls the turntable speed. Direct-drive turntables use a slow-running motor that is directly coupled to the turntable and electronically controlled to give a precise speed. Some models have pitch control—a speed control that adjusts the turntable speed within around 10 percent either side of the nominal speed. It is useful for matching beats when mixing between records on two decks.

▼ Despite the advent of compact discs and MP3 players, vinyl records and turntables have remained popular for the effects that can be created by physically slowing and sampling parts of disc while it is playing.

SEE ALSO: AMPLIFIER • COMPACT DISC, AUDIO • HI-FI SYSTEMS • LOUDSPEAKER • SOUND EFFECTS AND SAMPLING • SOUND MIXING • SOUND REPRODUCTION

Phosphorus

In its most usual form, phosphorus is a white wax-like element that ignites spontaneously in air. It is a nonmetallic element and occurs in the same group of the periodic table as nitrogen, arsenic, antimony, and bismuth. Because it reacts with air, phosphorus is normally stored underwater.

The element has about ten forms, known as allotropes, that occur in three major forms—white, red, and black. White phosphorus has two allotropes: an alpha form, which is stable at room temperature and has a cubic crystal structure, and a beta form, which is stable below −108°F (−78°C) and has a hexagonal crystal structure.

Phosphorus was first prepared in 1669 by the German alchemist Hennig Brand, who used evaporated urine residue as the source of the element. It is surprising that such a reactive element was isolated at such an early date, and its discovery aroused much interest among the alchemists of the time, who thought it might lead to the philosopher's stone, a material that would transform lead into gold. Phosphorus not only ignites in air, but it also glows in the dark because of a chemiluminescent oxidation process.

In 1775, the Swedish chemist C. W. Scheele discovered a much simpler method of preparing phosphorus from bones, and his method was used for many years. In the 1840s, a second form, or allotrope, of phosphorus, called red phosphorus, was discovered. This allotrope can be prepared by heating white phosphorus to 482°F (250°C) in a closed container, and it is much more stable than white phosphorus; it does not ignite in air at room temperature. It was the discovery of red phosphorus that led to the invention of the safety match. At very high pressures (12,000 times atmospheric pressure), white phosphorus is converted into a third allotrope, black phosphorus, a flaky crystalline substance that resembles graphite and conducts electricity.

Manufacture

Almost all the phosphorus-containing compounds used today are derived directly from the ore, from white phosphorus, or from orthophosphoric acid, H_3PO_4. The most common phosphorus mineral is fluorapatite, $Ca_5F(PO_4)_3$, which is found in the United States, Morocco, Tunisia, and the Russian Federation. To prepare white phosphorus, the ore is mixed with gravel (silica, SiO_2) and coke and heated in an electric furnace. The furnace has carbon rod electrodes, and the ore, sand, and coke are fed into the heating zone from a hopper. Phosphorus

▲ Guano, the name given to bird droppings, is a rich source of phosphate fertilizer. In the 19th century, islands that had previously been colonized only by birds for hundreds of years were mined for their thick deposits of guano. Today, this process is artificially induced—rafts are set out in coastal areas and food is used to encourage birds to visit.

vapor distills off from the reaction mixture and is condensed underwater. The calcium in the ore is converted into a molten silicate slag, which is removed periodically and converted into granules by rapid cooling with jets of water. Iron impurities are converted into a metallic iron–phosphorus compound called ferrophosphorus, which sinks to the bottom of the furnace. It is removed and cast into pigs (rough ingots), which are used for making certain iron alloys.

Orthophosphoric acid can be prepared directly from the phosphate rock ore or from white phosphorus. In the wet acid process, phosphate rock is treated with sulfuric acid to give a mixture of impure orthophosphoric acid and calcium sulfate, $CaSO_4$. Because the separation of these two components and the subsequent purification of the orthophosphoric acid is a relatively complex procedure, the acid is often made by burning white phosphorus in air to give phosphorus pentoxide, P_4O_{10}, and then treating the oxide with water.

$$P_4 + 5O_2 \rightarrow P_4O_{10}$$
phosphorus   oxygen   phosphorus pentoxide

$$P_4O_{10} + 6H_2O \rightarrow 4H_3PO_4$$
phosphorus pentoxide   water   orthophosphoric acid

Phosphorus itself does not have many uses, although it is employed in some metallurgical processes, in match manufacture, in the synthesis of certain organic compounds, and in incendiary bombs. Incendiary bombs have a highly flammable filling, such as gasoline, which is ignited by white phosphorus when the bomb bursts on impact. The phosphorus is often dissolved in carbon disulfide, CS_2, a volatile flammable liquid that evaporates quickly, leaving behind the phosphorus. As soon as the phosphorus is exposed to the air in this way, it ignites and sets off the main charge of the bomb.

Phosphorus compounds

Most of the phosphate rock mined each year is used to make agricultural fertilizers. Millions of tons of superphosphate fertilizer are made each year by treating rock phosphate with sulfuric acid; the phosphate component is dicalcium orthophosphate, $CaHPO_4$:

$$2Ca_5F(PO_4)_3 + 3H_2SO_4 \rightarrow 6CaHPO_4 + 3CaSO_4 + CaF$$
fluorapatite   sulfuric acid   dicalcium orthophosphate   calcium sulfate   calcium fluoride

A more concentrated phosphate fertilizer can be made by treating rock phosphate with orthophosphoric acid. The product is called triple superphosphate, and the phosphate component is monocalcium orthophosphate, $Ca(H_2PO_4)_2$:

$$2Ca_5F(PO_4)_3 + 12H_3PO_4 \rightarrow 9Ca(H_2PO_4)_2 + CaF_2$$
fluorapatite   orthophosphoric acid   monocalcium orthophosphate   calcium fluoride

Another use of phosphates is in water softening. It is the presence of magnesium ions, Mg^{2+}, and calcium ions, Ca^{2+}, in water that makes water hard and leads to the buildup of scale in pipes. The addition of small quantities of phosphate, for example, sodium tripolyphosphate, $Na_5P_3O_{10}$, will deactivate, or sequester, these ions and thus soften the water. Sodium tripolyphosphate is for this reason a major component of many detergent compositions. It is made by roasting a mixture of monosodium and disodium orthophosphates in a rotary converter.

There are many other applications of phosphates. Monocalcium phosphate and sodium acid pyrophosphate, $Na_2H_2P_2O_7$, are used as leavening compounds in cake mixes, flour, and baking powder. Dicalcium phosphate is used as a polishing agent in toothpastes. Metal articles, such as automobile bodies, are usually dipped in a phosphating solution prior to painting. A thin layer of insoluble phosphates forms on the surface of the metal, helping to prevent corrosion and providing a good surface for painting.

There are several chemical compounds containing phosphorus and halogen atoms, for example, phosphorus pentachloride, PCl_5, phosphorus trichloride, PCl_3, and phosphorus oxychloride, $POCl_3$. Phosphorus pentachloride and phosphorus trichloride are extensively used in organic chemistry to introduce atoms into organic compounds. Thus, acetic acid, CH_3COOH, will react

◀ Phosphorus deposits are built up by marine organisms, but their extraction from phosphate pits creates serious devastation on the surrounding area.

with phosphorus trichloride to give acetyl chloride, CH_3COCl:

$$3CH_3COOH + PCl_3 \rightarrow 3CH_3COCl + H_3PO_3$$

| acetic acid | phosphorus trichloride | acetyl chloride | phosphorous acid |

Phosphine, PH_3, a hydride of phosphorus, is a colorless poisonous gas with a faint smell of garlic. It is prepared by reacting white phosphorus with potassium hydroxide, KOH. The nerve gases tabun, sarin, and soman are organic compounds containing phosphorus. These compounds are extremely quick acting; they are absorbed through the skin and produce vomiting, diarrhea, and nausea. Their main effect is on the central nervous system and they can cause death within 15 minutes. Similar compounds, such as malathion, a powerful insecticide, have been made that were thought to be less poisonous to warm-blooded animals. These compounds, known as organophosphates, have been found in recent studies to inhibit the ability of cholinesterase, an enzyme, to deactivate the chemical acetylcholine, a neurotransmitter, which transmits impulses across nerves to muscles. The effect is to cause overstimulation of the nervous

◀ Making matches. Strike-anywhere matches contain phosphorus sesquisulfide, which is highly reactive. Friction on a rough surface triggers off a reaction between this material and potassium chlorate causing the match, made of wood or wax-coated paper, to ignite.

system; common symptoms are headaches, nausea, dizziness, and anxiety. At very high exposures, serious effects such as convulsions, respiratory paralysis, and death may occur. Organophosphates are also highly toxic to wildlife and have been associated with severe fish kills in various countries. These compounds are currently under investigation by the U.S. Environmental Protection Agency, which is reviewing allowable limits by 2006.

Phosphorus compounds are nevertheless also vital constituents of living tissue. The organic phosphates adenosine triphosphate (ATP) and adenosine diphosphate (ADP) play a key role in the storage of energy in the human body. The conversion of ATP to ADP is accompanied by a release of energy that can be used by the body to promote other metabolic processes.

Phosphorus sources

Phosphorus is not found free in nature except in a few meteorites, but it occurs in compounds that are found across the world in many rocks, minerals, and even organic matter. The main commercial source of phosphorus is phosphorite, also known as phosphate rock, which is an impure form of carbonate-bearing apatite. One improbable source of phosphate fertilizer is guano—bird droppings. Various islands that are home to large bird populations have been mined extensively for this extremely useful material.

SEE ALSO: AMMUNITION • CHEMICAL AND BIOLOGICAL WARFARE • ELEMENT, CHEMICAL • FERTILIZER • FIREWORK AND FLARE

FACT FILE

- Workers in lucifer-match factories in the 1830s were discovered to be suffering from "fossy-jaw," a form of phosphorus poisoning caused by exposure to yellow phosphorus. Symptoms included loss of appetite, anemia, and necrosis of the jawbone. The lucifer match was withdrawn around 1900.

- In World War II, U.S. and Japanese forces used millions of pounds of white phosphorus in mortar and gun shells and grenades. As well as having toxic effects, the white phosphorus releases a thick, billowing smoke. The white phosphorus grenade, as used in the Falklands War between Britain and Argentina in 1982, burns to the bone and is impossible to extinguish.

- Up to 19 lbs. of phosphorus per acre is lost by drainage and erosion from agricultural land treated with fertilizers. This loss leads to accelerated eutrophication, a process by which algae growth is unnaturally stimulated, choking waters and killing off many life forms.

Photocopier

Photocopiers are big business and can be found in most offices. During the early 1930s, the only method of copying business documents was basically photographic. This photographic process was slow and used liquid processing chemicals. Most copiers in commercial use today are of the plain paper type. They do not need special papers to copy on, or chemicals for developing and so enable ordinary commercial letter headings to be used. Most office machines take both letter and legal sized paper, and many offer magnification and shrinking.

It was Chester Carlson, a patent attorney living in Astoria, a suburb of New York, who realized the problems of using wet chemical methods and who spent a number of years developing a process called electrophotography. In his early experiments, he used a sulfur-coated plate that he charged with static electricity by rubbing it with a piece of fur. He then exposed the plate to a reflected image, and the light destroyed the static charge. Lycopodium powder was blown over the plate, and it adhered to the charged areas. This image was then transferred onto a piece of waxed paper.

This crude process was to be the basis for a multibillion dollar company, but Carlson spent six years trying to find a financial backer. He was turned down by both IBM and Kodak but eventually found support with the Batelle Research Institute and a small photographic company called Haloid, which later became the Xerox Corporation. The newly formed company decided to call the process xerography, from the Greek *xeros* and *graphe*, meaning "dry writing."

The xerographic drum

The modern process is very similar to the original but has been refined to six stages. Before discussing these stages, it is necessary to look at the xerographic drum.

The drum surface consists of a base of aluminum on which is laid a thin layer (approximately 10 atoms thick) of aluminum oxide. On top of this is a layer of selenium alloy. Selenium is a photoconductor—it will conduct only when exposed to light, and the drum coating is made especially sensitive. Thus, the drum can have an electrostatic charge placed on the surface that will remain there—provided it is kept in the dark. If exposed to light, the selenium conducts the charge away to the aluminum, where it is neutralized. The aluminum oxide is an insulating layer to slow down the rate of discharge.

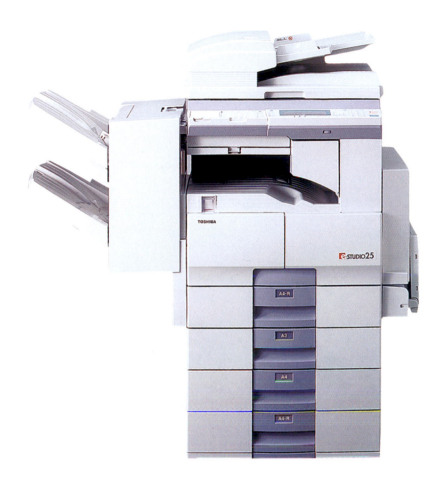

The first step of the xerographic process is to charge the whole surface of the drum electrostatically in the dark by rotating it under a corotron. The corotron is a bare wire to which a high positive voltage (approximately 7 kV) is applied. This voltage ionizes the air, and a blue cloud or corona is often seen around the wire. The charge must be uniform on the drum to produce a uniform copy, and to achieve this end the drum must pass the corotron at constant speed, the space between corotron and drum must be constant, and the corotron voltage must be constant. Furthermore, there must be a good ground connection all over the aluminum, and the corotron wire must be clean. This is a critical phase of the photocopying operation.

Exposure and developing

The next step is exposure. The image of the original to be copied is projected onto the drum by a series of lenses and mirrors. Like a photographic image, it is reversed and inverted. The white areas of the original reflect a lot of light, which destroys the charge on the drum, but black areas do not reflect and so leave the charge intact. There is

▲ Modern photocopiers are capable of many more functions than straightforward copying. Most can enlarge or reduce the size of the image, are capable of copying photographs without darkening the image too much, and can make double-sided copies. In addition, many have automatic feeders and can sort copies as complete documents.

THE XEROGRAPHIC PROCESS

Most modern photocopiers use a dry toner process that works on the principle of electrostatic attraction to attract toner powder to specific areas of the paper and seals it to the page using heat.

▶ The first stage of the xerographic process is to give an electric charge to the surface of the drum.

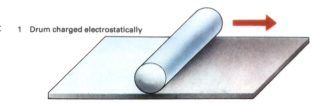

1 Drum charged electrostatically

▶ The image of the original is then projected onto it by a series of lenses and mirrors. The white areas neutralize the charge on the drum, whereas the black areas preserve it.

2 Image projected

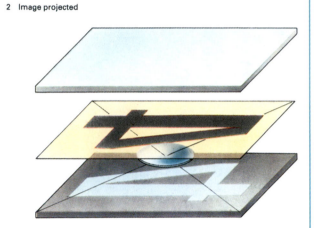

▶ Next, toner is poured over the drum and it adheres to the charged areas, which correspond to the black areas of the original.

3 Toner powder applied

▶ The image on the drum is then transferred to paper that has been given a greater charge.

4 Paper charged

5 Image transferred

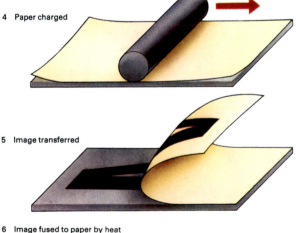

▶ Finally, the image is fused onto the paper by heating.

6 Image fused to paper by heat

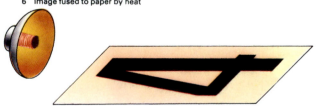

thus an image in static electricity on the drum; it is a latent image in that it cannot be seen and would be destroyed if totally exposed to light.

During the next step, developing, a special dry developer is used. This developer is a mixture of a carrier and toner powder. The carrier consists of a mass of tiny glass beads (sometimes sand or metal shot) coated with plastic about 0.0098 in. (0.25 mm) in diameter. The toner is a fine black powder composed of a thermoplastic resin and carbon. The toner particles are extremely small —in relation to the carrier, they are like a pea to a football.

Both the toner and the plastic-covered beads are triboelectric, that is, they generate static electricity when rubbed together. The carrier receives a positive and the toner a negative charge. Thus, the carrier beads become covered in a layer of toner. The developer is poured over the drum, and the toner-covered carrier beads roll over the surface. The positive charge of the latent image is greater than that on the carrier, so the toner adheres to the charged areas of the drum. (This area corresponds to the black areas of the original.) Thus, there is now a real image in toner on the drum.

Transfer and fusion

The next step is transference. The toner is held on the drum by the positive charge. To remove it and get it onto paper, the paper must have a higher positive charge, which is achieved using another corotron. It charges the paper as it is pressed against the drum, and the toner now clings to the paper.

The copy is almost finished. It now passes through the fifth step: fusing. The toner is a thermoplastic resin, that is, it melts with heat. The copy is therefore passed under a radiant heater or through heated pressure rollers. The result is that the toner melts into the fibers of the paper to give, when cool, a permanent dry copy.

The copy is now finished, but because the transfer of toner is never achieved completely, the drum must be cleaned before the next copy can be made. Cleaning, the sixth and last step, is achieved in three stages. First, the drum is discharged by means of a negative, or AC, corotron; this step is followed by wiping and exposure to light. Exposing the drum to light neutralizes any charge left on it.

Using color originals

So far, it has been assumed that black-and-white originals have been used in the copying process. However, when producing black-and-white copies from color originals, there are complica-

◀ ▶ A photograph of a daredevil biker and its copy from a color copier (left and right respectively). The copier can make copies of colored originals or, with the help of a special projector, prints from slides. However, because the original must be reproduced using only three colors—magenta, cyan, and yellow colored toner powders are used—the colors in the copies tend to be less true.

tions because of the color sensitivity of the selenium-alloy drum. Blue light causes rapid discharge of the selenium, whereas red, at the other end of the spectrum (longer wavelength), causes little discharge. As a result, blue print is difficult to copy, because it has the same action on the selenium as the white background on which it is printed. Red, on the other hand, behaves as black and copies well.

Color copying

Color xerography has now been developed that can provide copies with a range of six or more colors and black. The technique is similar to that used in color printing and involves separating the original into three color images. The colors are magenta, yellow, and cyan—the primary colors of the subtractive color system. Red, blue, and green can be produced by overprinting two colors: magenta and yellow for red, cyan and yellow for green, and cyan and magenta for a darker blue than cyan alone. Overprinting all three colors gives black.

To obtain the color magenta, for example, all areas on the drum must be discharged except those corresponding to magenta in the original. A magenta toner will adhere to these charged areas. Because magenta is a combination of red and blue, a green filter is used, allowing only green light to reach the drum; consequently, the drum will be discharged at all areas corresponding to where green is present in the original (including white, which contains green). As green lies in the middle of the spectrum, the charged areas correspond to the remaining parts of the

spectrum—red and blue, which is magenta. The other two primary colors necessary for color printing are produced in a similar fashion. The yellow color is produced from a yellow toner after exposing the drum through a blue filter. For cyan a red filter is used.

These three colors are added one after the other, exposing the drum through each filter in turn and developing at each stage with the correct toner. The composite is then fused to give the color copy.

Stabilization

Some older copiers use a toner and a developer in a process called stabilization. The reflex method uses a negative and a positive, one sensitized paper, and two solutions. The original is exposed to strong light while in contact with a sheet of copy paper. The copy paper is then passed through the baths of developer and stabilizer in the processor to form a paper negative, which is then exposed with another sheet of copy paper to give a positive print. For many applications, however, the negative may be the end result.

The direct positive method does not require a negative to be made. A different type of copy paper is used in which the white parts of the original reflect light onto the copy paper and cause it to be exposed as white, leaving the image areas dark and giving a direct positive. This technique is not suitable for double-sided originals.

SEE ALSO: COMPUTER PRINTER • LENS • LITHOGRAPHY • OPTICAL SCANNER • PHOTOGRAPHIC FILM AND PROCESSING • PRINTING

Photoelectric Cell and Photometry

Photoelectric cells are light-sensing devices useful in a variety of applications ranging from simple counting to the control of street lighting. The simplest counting device consists of a beam of light that is directed across the path of the moving objects at a photoelectric cell, which is connected to a counter. The photoelectric cell senses when the beam is interrupted and activates the counter. Other applications for photoelectric cells include their use as automatic door openers and in measuring the density of smoke from chimney stacks and in ensuring the correct alignment of an elevator when stopping at a particular floor.

The photoelectric effect

Under certain conditions, the current flowing in an electric circuit may be affected by the action of light falling on part of the circuit. This influence of radiation on electric behavior is termed the photoelectric effect, and various photoelectric cells, or photocells, have been developed that take advantage of this phenomenon. Photoelectric cells are divided into three categories depending on their action: photoemissive cells (the normal photoelectric effect), photoconductive cells (such as selenium), and photovoltaic cells, which are used widely in solar cells.

Photoemissive cells

Photoemission is the emission of electrons from the surface of a material illuminated by light or other electromagnetic radiation.

The German-born physicist Albert Einstein explained the effect by postulating that radiation consists of numerous "packets" or quanta, now called photons. Light striking the surface of a metal does so as a stream of photons, each having a discrete amount of energy. This energy can be transferred to an electron associated with an atom of the bombarded metal. If the emitted electrons are made to flow in an electric circuit, the resulting electric current can be used as a measure of the light intensity.

A typical cell consists of an evacuated glass envelope containing two electrodes. One of them, the cathode, is coated with a photoemissive material. An alloy of antimony and cesium works well with daylight. The other electrode, the anode,

▼ Photovoltaic cells are less sensitive than other types of photoelectric cells but need no outside power supply. Photoemissive and photoconductive cells change their conductivity in the presence of light but do not themselves generate a current.

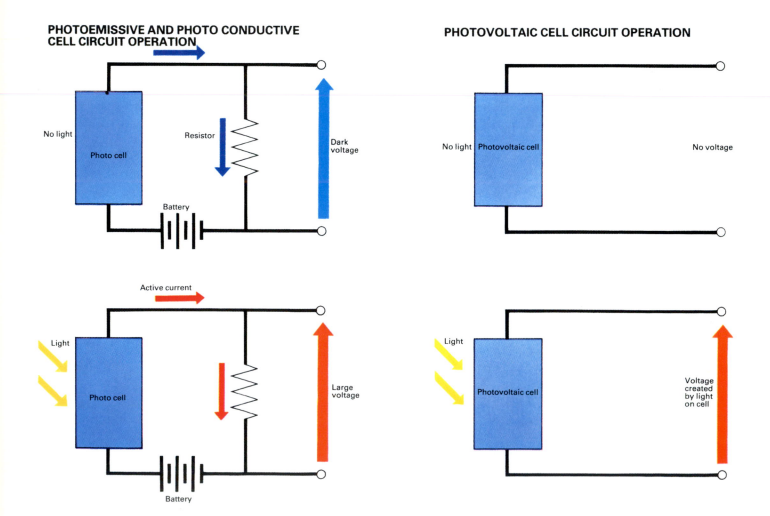

PHOTOEMISSIVE AND PHOTO CONDUCTIVE CELL CIRCUIT OPERATION

No light — Photo cell — Resistor — Battery — Dark voltage

Light — Photo cell — Active current — Battery — Large voltage

PHOTOVOLTAIC CELL CIRCUIT OPERATION

No light — Photovoltaic cell — No voltage

Light — Photovoltaic cell — Voltage created by light on cell consists of a straight wire or wire gauze. Radiation striking the photosensitive cathode causes electrons to be emitted. A positive voltage is applied to the anode, attracting these electrons, and a current is established. The main uses of this type of cell include the reading of film soundtracks in a projector and the conversion of optical signals to electric signals in television cameras.

Photoconductive cells

Changes in the intensity of light falling on certain materials cause changes in the ability of these materials to conduct electricity. This effect is known as photoconductivity.

When radiation strikes a photoconductive material such as selenium, absorption of photon energy sufficiently excites a certain number of electrons to enable them to overcome the influence of their atoms and become free to move in the electric field established by the voltage.

Thus, if selenium is connected in an electric circuit containing a battery and a meter to indicate current flow, the current flow will increase when light strikes the selenium cell, that is, the electric resistance falls. Such cells respond to a wide range of radiations and are used in switch-on relays for street lighting and in instruments for low-temperature heat-radiation measurements.

Photovoltaic cells

When light strikes the junction between certain materials, a small voltage is produced. This is the photovoltaic effect. It produces an electron flow in the circuit, and the current recorded by the meter is proportional to the illumination on the cell. This device is very efficient and has the advantage of requiring no external power supply.

Photovoltaic cells are widely used in exposure meters for photographic work and as electric eye detectors for the operation of relays, but they are less useful than photoemissive cells as accurate quantitative measuring instruments.

Photovoltaic cells (PV cells) are often used as solar cells, which convert energy from the sun into electricity that may then be used to power small devices, such as calculators and watches. On a much larger scale, PV cells may be used to create solar arrays that are capable of generating enough electricity for domestic use or industry.

Photometry

Photometry is the measurement of quantities of light, and has many more practical uses, from making sure that offices and work floors are adequately lit to determining the visibility of a lighthouse beam. The exposure meter is a simple example of a photometer used to measure light.

There are four types of measurement involved. Candlepower is one well-known type, referring to the luminous intensity in a particular direction of, for example, a car headlight. The total light output, or luminous flux, of the source itself is another quantity; there are also brightness, or luminance, of a bright surface and the illumination, or illuminance, falling on a factory bench or an office desk.

Photometers

The old Bunsen photometer had mirrors by which both sides of a white disk were seen as if side-by-side, and two lamps to be compared were set on opposite sides but at different distances, so as to make the two sides equally bright. Portable luminance meters worked similarly, but the white comparison surface, with a small variable-distance lamp to illuminate it, was built in. The same instrument was used to measure illuminance by placing a white disk on the spot in question and measuring its luminance. The illuminance could then be calculated using the previously known reflection factor of the disk.

The modern photocell can accurately compare unequal lights, and its spectral response can be matched with the curve for the standard photometric observer by a suitable color filter in front of it.

For intensity comparisons, two sources may be placed successively at the same distance from the filtered photocell, and two readings are taken. For luminance measurements, a telescope system images the desired small area on the photocell. The luminance for calibration is produced by a standard white reflecting surface, such as magnesium oxide, placed at a known distance from an intensity standard. For luminance measurements, a photomultiplier tube is often used because the amount of light available is small. For illuminance, a selenium or silicon photoelectric cell is used.

▲ Attaching a selenium cell to a streetlight. The photocell is preset to switch on the light at a specified external brightness level.

SEE ALSO: Burglar alarm • Camera • Conduction, electric • Electricity • Electromagnetic radiation • Light and optics • Road systems and traffic control • Solar energy

Photogrammetry

Measurements for the production of maps and plans are normally made by direct methods, but increasing use is being made of indirect techniques, such as photogrammetry, in which the measurements are taken from photographs. This approach is commonly used in the production of maps and plans from vertical aerial photographs, but horizontal photographs can also be used. The instantaneous nature of photographs effectively allows measurements to be made of rapidly changing situations such as floods.

Aerial photography

Measurements can be made from single photographs, but the analysis of stereoscopic pairs of photographs allows height information to be obtained in addition to basic plan positions. With aerial surveys, a series of photographs is taken in a strip along the area concerned, successive photographs along a strip being overlapped by at least 60 percent. Successive strips are overlapped by at least 30 percent with these overlaps ensuring that full stereo coverage is obtained even if slight positioning errors occur. Registration marks are made on the photographs during exposure, along with such details as the time and date, aircraft height, and exposure number. Reference, or fiducial, marks are also placed on the film at the time of exposure.

Photographs are generally taken with the camera axis approximately vertical to give an image that is similar to a map, with most of the ground area being visible. An oblique camera

▲ A photogrammetric plotter in action. Relief surveys of areas of land are often carried out by photogrammetry. This involves collecting aerial photographs of an area, then correcting them by plotting relative positions of certain points on the ground by means of field survey. Overlaps in adjacent photographs must occur to provide the necessary stereoscopic image.

axis—which gives a more immediately recognizable viewpoint—may also be used. However, important details can be hidden in oblique photographs, and the relative scale varies across the photograph.

Mosaics

One of the simplest uses of such aerial photographs is in the production of a mosaic built up from a series of prints to give a composite image of the area concerned. Generally, sections from the central areas of prints are used to form the mosaic, joints between adjacent sections being arranged to lie along irregular features, such as hedge lines or road edges, so far as possible to disguise the joint. Owing to the fact that successive photographs may be taken at slightly different heights and camera tilts it is impossible to obtain a perfect match between sections. Better matching is obtained by the use of rectified prints, which are produced by projecting the original photograph onto a tilting screen to allow compensation for camera tilts and for the effects of camera height. Mosaics formed from such rectified prints are known as controlled. Mosaics can be produced rapidly and generally contain more detail than can be recorded on a map but need care in interpretation. Mosaics also suffer from height distortion.

Plotting

A number of different techniques are used to obtain measurements from the photographs for map production with the most accurate method involving the production of a stereoscopic model by the fusion of a pair of overlapping photographs in a stereo-plotter or photogrammetric plotting machine. Prints of the photographs are made on film or glass slides and viewed through a binocular system to form a stereo image or space model. To obtain an accurate model the photographs have to be orientated relative to one another to allow for differing camera alignments, tilts, and heights. For absolute measurements the stereo image has also to be lined up with ground control points that have known positions and heights. Although such orientation can be achieved by using two points of known position along with three points of known height it is common to use several more calibration points to give increased accuracy and minimize the risk of errors creeping in. Bridging or aerial triangulation techniques may be used to form a control network over a series of images between known control points.

With the stereo model established and aligned the operator uses a set of control wheels (handwheels for plan movements and a footwheel for height) to move a floating mark image around the model. Successive positions of the mark are read off as a series of coordinates to give the required measurements of the stereo model and scaled to give the equivalent ground measurements. The plotting operation may be automated.

The movements of the plotting mark can be directly linked to a plotting table to produce a line map. The operator guides the mark along the required detail lines—for example road edges or building outlines—which are reproduced on the plotting table. Height contours are produced by setting the floating mark to a known height and then tracing round the surface of the model at that height. Alternatively the output from the stereoplotter may be directly digitized into coordinates to give a digital terrain model. Another use of the stereoplotter is in the production of orthophotographs with the original photographic image being scanned in strips and rephotographed to give a true vertical picture free from height distortions but containing all the original information.

Mapping other planets

Similar techniques to photogrammetry have been used to determine relief maps of the rocky planets in the Solar System, particularly Venus and Mars. Orbiting spacecraft used radar to make early maps of Venus because the thick clouds that cover the planet preclude optical measurement. The first clue to the surface came from the Pioneer probe in 1978, which revealed a large upland known as Ishtar Terra and mountains up to 7 miles (12 km) high. In 1983, the Russian spacecraft *Venera 15* and *16* were put into orbit together, four degrees apart. For eight months they surveyed an area between the north pole and a 30 degrees N latitude using a radio altimeter and a synthetic aperture radar (SAR). Data sent back were fed into a computer and mosaics produced that gave a better indication of the heights of some surface features.

The latest mapping mission to Venus, *Magellan*, launched in 1989 managed to survey 98 percent of its surface, again using SAR, before communications ceased in 1994. At resolutions better than 330 ft. (100 m) Venus was found to show no signs of plate tectonic movement or significant erosion of structures other than wind streaks.

Detailed mapping of the surface of Mars began in 1999 when the Mars Global Surveyor (MGS) settled into a polar orbit over the planet. On board is the Mars Orbiting Laser Altimeter

(MOLA), which will also measure seasonal changes in the polar ice masses and the formation and evolution of volcanoes, basins, and channels. MOLA works by transmitting short (8 nanosecond) laser pulses toward the surface, which trigger a time clock in the detector. A telescope focuses the scattered light that is reflected back from the surface onto a silicon avalanche photodiode, which outputs a voltage proportional to the rate that photons are received. At a certain noise threshold the counts are recorded by the time interval unit. As the height of the spacecraft is fixed, the time taken for the laser pulse to reach the surface and be reflected back gives a good indication of the distance and therefore the height of the surface.

The good resolution of the MOLA instrument has enabled topographers to plot some areas of the surface down to 6½ ft. (2 m) per pixel. By combining information from MOLA with other instruments on board MGS, controversial features such as the "face" in the Cydonia region have been resolved into a series of hills and valleys and not the alien artifact it was once believed.

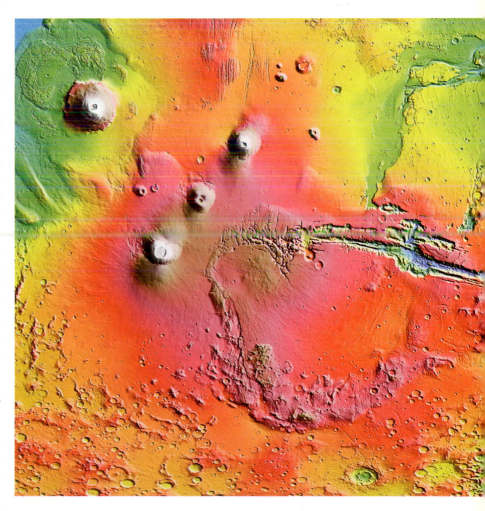

▼ Topographical relief map of the surface of Mars obtained using data from the Mars Global Surveyor. In the upper left hand corner is Olympus Mons, the tallest volcano in the Solar System. This latest survey of Mars has revealed surface features in areas that were previously believed to be smooth rock.

| SEE ALSO: | AERIAL PHOTOGRAPHY • CAMERA • LASER AND MASER • MAPMAKING TECHNIQUES • RADAR • STEREOSCOPY |

Photographic Film and Processing

Conventional photography captures images on photosensitive film when the film is exposed to light in a camera. After exposure, film is processed with chemicals that make it insensitive to light and then used to produce permanent images on transparent film or on photographic paper.

Early processes

The earliest direct predecessor of modern film photography was the calotype process, introduced in 1839 by William Henry Fox Talbot, a British inventor. (Other processes had already produced photographic images, such as daguerrotypes and heliographs, but they were incapable of producing copies of images.)

Silver iodide (AgI) was the photosensitive material in the calotype process, decomposing to iodine and microscopic black grains of silver when exposed to light. Silver nitrate ($AgNO_3$) and gallic acid ($C_6H_2(OH)_3COOH$) boosted the sensitivity to light for exposure, and solutions of these substances were soaked into paper prior to exposure. A solution of sodium thiosulfate ($Na_2S_2O_3$), or "hypo," eliminated the photosensitivity of the paper when exposure was complete.

The initial image in the calotype process was negative, since areas that had received the greatest exposure to light were darkest in the image. Positive images were obtained by shining light through the negative onto another sheet of photosensitive paper. The images had a distinctive graininess owing to the fibrous texture of the paper.

The next developments sought to eliminate the graininess of calotype images by using clear emulsions coated on glass. In 1847, the French physicist Claude Niépce used an emulsion of potassium bromide (KBr) suspended in albumin, a protein gel derived from animal products. Niépce applied the emulsion to glass plates and impregnated it with silver nitrate before exposure.

In 1851, the British photographer Frederick Scott Archer introduced a glass-plate process that used collodion to suspend the photosensitive chemicals. Collodion is a viscous solution of nitrocellulose, or guncotton, in a solvent blend of ether and alcohol. On drying, collodion gave a tough transparent nitrocellulose film from which excellent prints could be made. Since the developer solution could not penetrate the dry nitrocellulose film, however, plates had to be exposed and developed within minutes of being made, thus the system was rather unwieldy.

In 1871, Dr. R. L. Maddox replaced collodion with gelatin, a water-based gel made from the

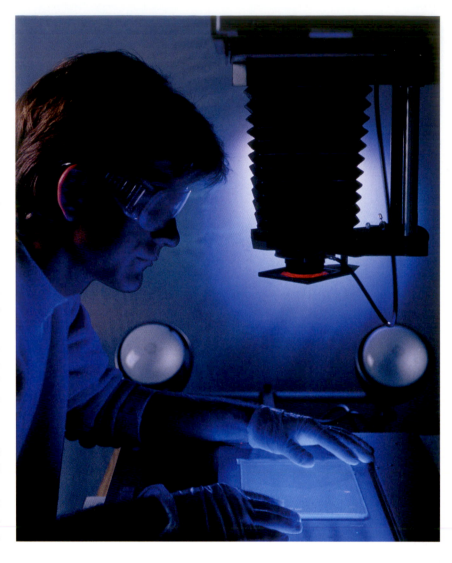

hides and bones of animals. Like collodion, gelatin forms a tough film when dry; unlike collodion, the dry film swells in contact with water and can be penetrated by water-based developer.

The gelatin process was much more flexible than the wet collodion process, since plates could be made well in advance of exposure, exposed while dry, then developed whenever convenient. In 1889, the U.S. inventor George Eastman improved the process yet further by using a flexible nitrocellulose film in place of a glass sheet as the support for the photographic emulsion.

Monochrome photography

Monochrome (black-and-white) film is a flexible plastic strip coated with a thin layer of gelatin emulsion. The emulsion contains light-sensitive crystals of silver halides—silver chloride, bromide, or iodide. The halide crystals, or grains, vary in size from around 5×10^{-7} in. to 10^{-4} in. (around 0.01–3 μm); the thickness of the emulsion is a few thousandths of an inch (a few hundred microns).

▲ An enlarger projects light through a developed negative onto a sheet of photographic paper. The distance between the lens and the paper determines the size of the image.

Exposure. When light strikes a crystal, it converts silver halide near the crystal's surface into silver and free chlorine, bromine, or iodine. The halogen reacts with gelatin or other materials in the emulsion. At this stage, the amount of silver formed is invisible to the naked eye. It forms a latent image to be revealed by development.

Developing. Developers are chemicals that convert a silver halide crystal into silver metal, provided exposure to light has already liberated some metallic silver from that crystal. During development, exposed grains are completely converted to metallic silver, which forms as a tangled mass of fibers and appears black; unexposed grains remain unaffected. Each grain acts individually, either turning completely into silver or not changing at all; in areas of intermediate tonality, a limited number of grains turn completely to silver, rather than all grains forming some silver.

Developers. Development is in effect a reduction reaction that is catalyzed by silver. The reaction proceeds as follows:

$$AgHal + e^- \rightarrow Ag + Hal^-$$

where Hal^- represents any halide ion. Developing agents are organic reducing agents: 4-aminophenol ($C_6H_4(OH)NH_2$), 1,4-diaminobenzene (*p*-phenylenediamine, $C_6H_4(NH_2)_2$), and 4-hydroxyphenol (hydroquinone, $C_6H_4(OH)_2$) are typical members of three classes of developers.

The reducing power of developers is boosted by an alkali such as borax (sodium borate, $Na_2B_4O_7$), sodium carbonate (Na_2CO_3), or sodium hydroxide (NaOH). Sodium sulfite (Na_2SO_3) preserves the developer and extends its shelf life by reducing dissolved oxygen from air.

Sensitivity. The sensitivity of a film depends on the size distribution of its halide crystals, because any crystal—large or small—will release all its silver on development provided at least four to ten silver atoms have been released by exposure to light. Large crystals release proportionately more silver than do smaller crystals for the same amount of exposure. This property is helpful when photographing dimly lit subjects. The exposure amplification that occurs during development is enormous: the most sensitive grains can be made developable by the formation of just four silver atoms, and they yield around 100 billion silver atoms when developed.

The disadvantage of large crystals is that the large clumps of silver they form can appear as grains in the final image, particularly when an image is enlarged. This graininess can reduce the quality of an image by obscuring its finer details. To achieve good sensitivity to light and produce acceptably grain-free images, grains in a range of sizes are used. Smaller grains preserve image detail, while larger grains boost sensitivity.

Color sensitivity. Light sensitivity depends on the types of halides in the emulsion. Silver chloride, for example, reacts only to ultraviolet light and does not form silver when exposed to purely visible light. Silver bromide and iodide decompose at lower frequencies, yet they are still sensitive only to high-frequency blue light. As a result, a blue dress might appear light gray, while a red dress would appear black, since none of the light from it would affect the emulsion.

Silver halides are sensitized to frequencies lower than blue light by the inclusion of certain dyes in the emulsion. The dyes absorb photons of low frequency light and pass their energy to halide crystals, making them decompose. Black-and-white film dye-sensitized to green light is called orthochromatic film; black-and-white film sensitized to the whole visible range is called panchromatic. Certain dyes make film sensitive to infrared light, a useful property in astronomy and for heat-sensitive photography.

Fixing. After developing, unexposed silver halides must be removed to make the film stable to light. Washing with pure water would be pointless, since silver halides are water insoluble. Instead, solutions of ammonium or sodium thiosulfates are used. Thiosulfate ions ($S_2O_3^{2-}$) form water-soluble complex ions with silver:

$$Ag^+ + 2S_2O_3^{2-} \rightarrow [Ag(S_2O_3)_2]^{3-}$$

and these ions wash away in the fixing solution. Fixer also contains acid, which neutralizes the alkalinity of any developer in the film and cuts its

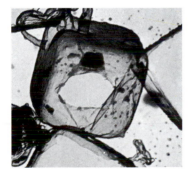

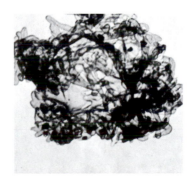

◀ Silver halide crystals (left) play a key role in photography. When exposed to light, they decompose to form some metallic silver (center). Development converts more of the exposed silver halide crystal into atoms of metallic silver (right).

developing power. The fixing solution and any remaining developer are removed by washing with purified water, then the film dries.

Dye images. Some black-and-white films designed to work across a wide range of exposures form final images in dye rather than in silver. As with conventional films, the first step is exposure of silver halide grains to form a latent image. Then, during development, the oxidized form of the developer reacts with a transparent compound to produce a black dye. Since the oxidized developer is formed by reduction of silver halide, the dye forms in those parts of the film where silver forms. The silver is then removed by oxidation using a bleaching solution.

Color photography

Color films capture a color image in three separate images that correspond to the red, green, and blue components of the image. These images form in three layers of emulsion. A latent silver image forms by exposure to light of appropriately sensitized silver halide; then development produces a corresponding image in dyes.

The top layer of a color film is sensitive to blue light. Since blue light can darken silver halides without requiring sensitizing dyes, it is prevented from reaching the other color layers by a yellow filter, which absorbs blue. The other two layers contain dyes that make one layer sensitive to red light and the other layer sensitive to green.

Development. Besides photographic grains, the layers of a color film may contain color couplers, compounds that react to form dyes with the oxidized forms of certain developers, such as 1,4-diaminobenzene (*p*-phenylenediamine). The formation of silver during development is accompanied by the formation of a corresponding amount of oxidized developer, which reacts with the coupler to form a dye image.

The coupler in the red-sensitive layer is chosen so that the dye formed absorbs red light and thus appears as the complementary blue-green (cyan) color. Similarly, a red-blue (magenta) dye is formed in the green-sensitive layer and a yellow dye in the blue-sensitive layer. Couplers are prevented from diffusing through the gelatin—and blurring the image—by the bulk of their molecules or by being trapped in tiny oil droplets.

Bleaching. Color photography differs from most types of black-and-white photography in that the silver produced by exposure to light and subsequent development is not required in the processed film. Once the developer has formed

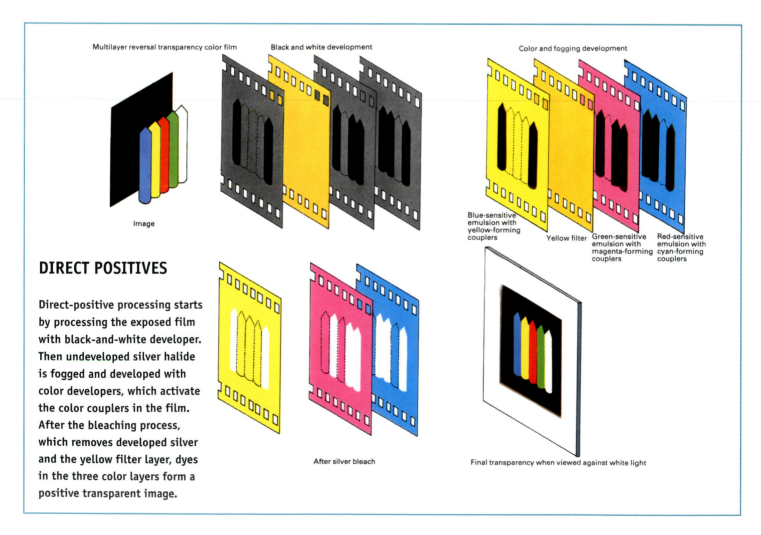

Multilayer reversal transparency color film

Black and white development

Color and fogging development

Image

Blue-sensitive emulsion with yellow-forming couplers

Yellow filter

Green-sensitive emulsion with magenta-forming couplers

Red-sensitive emulsion with cyan-forming couplers

DIRECT POSITIVES

Direct-positive processing starts by processing the exposed film with black-and-white developer. Then undeveloped silver halide is fogged and developed with color developers, which activate the color couplers in the film. After the bleaching process, which removes developed silver and the yellow filter layer, dyes in the three color layers form a positive transparent image.

After silver bleach

Final transparency when viewed against white light

the image dyes, metallic silver must be eliminated to leave the film transparent. Bleaching is a process that removes silver from films.

Simple bleaches include solutions of potassium dichromate ($K_2Cr_2O_7$) in sulfuric acid (H_2SO_4). They act by oxidizing metallic silver and producing a moderately soluble silver salt (silver sulfate, Ag_2SO_4) that can be washed out of the film. The image dyes and undeveloped silver halide crystals are left unaffected, but the yellow filter layer, which contains tiny crystals of silver, is eliminated by the bleaching process.

Rehalogenizing bleaches combine a mild oxidizing agent, such as potassium hexacyanoferrate (III), $K_3Fe(CN)_6$, with potassium bromide (KBr). The mixture oxidizes silver atoms to silver ions, which then form insoluble silver bromide. The silver bromide is subsequently removed together with the undeveloped silver halide.

Fixing. The fixing of color film is often identical to the fixing process used for black-and-white film: it consists of washing the film with a solution that contains thiosulfate ions, which form water-soluble complexes of silver ions. In the bleach-fixing process, an oxidizing agent converts the metallic silver to silver ions. These ions are complexed by thiosulfate, along with the silver ions in undeveloped silver halides, and washed away. The bleach-fixing process therefore eliminates one of the steps in color processing.

Direct positives

Direct-positive films and developing are used for amateur movie film and color transparencies. The film has a layer structure like standard color film, but the processing sequence is different.

In the first stage of direct-positive processing, exposed film is treated with a developer that does not react with the color couplers in the film. This stage produces a negative silver image but no dye. Then the undeveloped grains of silver halide are made developable by exposing them to light or by reacting them with a suitable fogging compound—a chemical that initiates the conversion of silver halide to metallic silver. Subsequent treatment with a standard color developer yields a positive dye image, and the metallic silver formed in the two development stages is removed by one of the standard bleaching processes.

Color masking

The dyes used in most films are impure colors, resulting in imperfect rendering of some colors. In negative films, this effect is avoided by tinting each of the color couplers with the same imperfections as those that will be present in the dyes that they form. This masking means that the

COLOR PHOTOGRAPHY—STEP BY STEP

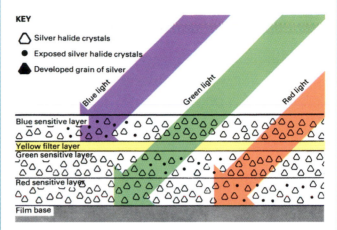

KEY
△ Silver halide crystals
● Exposed silver halide crystals
▲ Developed grain of silver

▲ EXPOSURE: Silver halide crystals become partially converted to metallic silver by incoming light in the frequency range to which each layer is dye sensitized. A yellow filter layer prevents blue light from reaching the green and red sensitive layers.

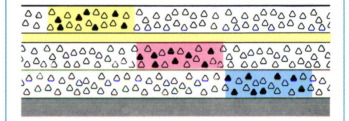

▲ DEVELOPMENT: A developer reduces silver halide in exposed crystals to form metallic silver, oxidizing the developer, which reacts with color couplers to form yellow, magenta, and cyan dyes in the different layers of emulsion.

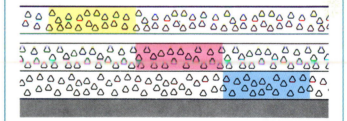

▲ BLEACHING: An oxidizing agent eliminates metallic silver while leaving the dyes intact. In some cases, the metallic silver is converted back into silver halide crystals.

▲ FIXING: A complexing agent solubilizes silver halides, which then wash out of the film, leaving it stable to light.

imperfections are evenly distributed throughout all colors and can be corrected by using suitable color filters during printing. Corrective color masks are responsible for the orange appearance of most color negatives.

Color masking cannot be used in the direct-positive process. For high-quality work, films that incorporate pure dyes are used. Excess dyes are destroyed during development, and the resulting images are accurately colored and durable.

Printing processes

Printing is the production of positive images on light-sensitive film or paper. The processes are similar to those of film exposure and processing, but printing media tend to be much less sensitive to light than is photographic film.

Exposure for printing can be done by contact or projection. In contact printing, processed film is held in close contact with the photosensitive film or paper. Light is shone through the negative image to form a positive latent image on the printing medium. The length of exposure and the light intensity determine the degree of exposure of the film and can be adjusted to give lighter or darker images in the final image. Contact prints are identical in size to the original negative, and they are often used to preview the contents of a roll of film before enlarging selected images. Cinematographic film may also be produced by contact printing from a negative processed film.

Enlarged prints are obtained by projection. The negative is mounted in an enlarger that shines light through the film then through a lens that focuses the image onto a table below. The enlargement factor depends on the height of the enlarger lens above the table, and the size, focus, and cropping of the image are set by projecting onto a white surface. Once the image has been tuned in this way, the printing medium is put in place and subjected to a timed exposure.

Final positive images are produced from the latent images on exposed printing media by using the same chemical processes that are used to process exposed films. The intensity of the image

▼ A film-coating line for applying gelatin-based emulsions to film base. After coating, the film is chilled to set the gelatin during the initial stages of drying. The drying process is completed using a draft of warm air to evaporate the last traces of water.

increases visibly in the development bath, and the process can be halted at any point by immersing the print in a stop bath, which contains chemicals that neutralize the developer.

Stabilization

Stabilization is an alternative to the fixing process when printing on paper. Whereas fixing removes undeveloped silver halides from film, stabilization transforms them into light-stable salts that stay in the emulsion after processing. Typical stabilizing agents include thiourea, $CS(NH_2)_2$.

The products of stabilization are colorless crystals that detract from image quality to some extent and can darken with time, making stabilization less satisfactory than fixing. Nevertheless, stabilization is faster and more convenient than fixing, which is why it is used when convenience and speed outweigh the quality of the final image.

Monobath

The monobath process uses a single solution that contains both a highly active developer and a fixing agent. The high activity of the developer is necessary to ensure that development is complete before the fixer has removed much silver halide. Since the process goes to completion in one step, it lacks the time control that can be used to adjust image intensity in conventional processing.

Image transfer

Image transfer is a derivative of the monobath process that is used for instant picture development in black-and-white Polaroid pictures. It uses a monobath-type solution sandwiched between photographic film and a receiver layer. When the film has been exposed, developer in the monobath solution develops the photographic film as a negative in the usual way. The fixer extracts the unexposed silver ions from the negative, but instead of those ions being washed away, they form a positive image on the receiver sheet, because the receiver sheet is coated with silver atoms that act as nuclei for the developer reaction to proceed. Dark regions form on the receiver where it is in

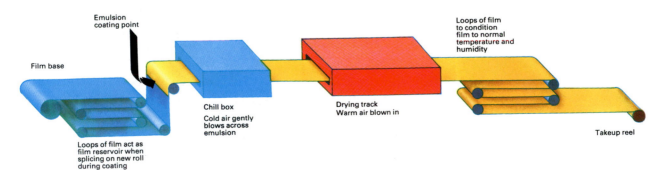

Emulsion coating point

Loops of film to condition film to normal temperature and humidity

Film base

Chill box
Cold air gently blows across emulsion

Drying track
Warm air blown in

Takeup reel

Loops of film act as film reservoir when splicing on new roll during coating

◄ This machine cuts coated photographic paper into strips. Exposure to light has fogged the green-sensitive emulsion, turning it magenta. The machine would normally operate in darkness to preserve the light-sensitive emulsions.

mixed just before use to prevent oxidation. The scarcity of sulfite ions allows quinone to concentrate where it is produced by the oxidation of hydroquinone by the first grains to be developed. The quinone stimulates nearby grains to develop faster, so rapid development occurs in areas that have had heavy exposure, whereas less exposed areas develop much more slowly. Development spreads from the highlights of the picture, which is why it is called infectious development.

Copying

Numerous combinations of techniques exist for making copies of images. The choice of technique depends on the original format of the image, the required end format, and whether there is an image reversal (negative to positive or positive to negative) from the original to the copy.

When a printed photograph is used to make an enlarged copy or several copies at the same size, two processing steps are necessary. First, a photograph of the original must be taken so as to provide a negative. Then the required number of copies can be printed using an enlarger.

contact with unexposed parts of the negative, since that is where there is more silver halide to act as a source of silver ions. The image-transfer process goes to completion and is insensitive to processing time.

Automatic processing

On a small scale, images can be processed and printed individually or in small batches. Each step of the processing sequence can then be modified to get the best from each image or to create effects by under- or overexposure, for example. On a larger scale, such an approach would make film processing prohibitively time consuming and expensive, thus, film-processing laboratories use highly automated procedures.

Roll films are spliced together in a dark environment to form a continuous strip of film for development. That strip then travels on a pulley system that dips it into reagent and washing tanks in sequence. The length of each processing stage depends on the rate of travel of the film and the length of the path through each processing tank.

Negative images on the processed films are then projected onto photographic paper in strips that can be several hundreds of yards (meters) in length. The photographic paper is then processed in strip form and cut into individual images and packed into envelopes after processing.

On a smaller scale, automatic photo booths are self-contained cameras and processing laboratories. They produce images for passports and other uses within five minutes of exposure.

Lithographic development

Lithographic, or lith, development is a specialist process used to prepare high-contrast negatives. It is used for printing processes that can represent only black or white, so grays have to be printed as dots of black on a white background that appear gray when viewed from a distance.

The developer used for this process is hydroquinone with a low concentration of sulfite ions and is usually supplied as two solutions that are

▼ A darkroom for black-and-white film processing. Red light is safe in such a darkroom, since the materials used are stable to red. Darkrooms for color processing must be totally dark, since color film is sensitive to red light.

Film copying is done by contact printing. Positive copies can be obtained by two steps of contact printing with reversal at each stage or by direct-positive printing. If direct-positive printing is used, its increased processing complexity compared with normal processing is compensated for by elimination of one photographic step.

Film manufacture

Photographic emulsions are prepared by mixing solutions of silver nitrate ($AgNO_3$) and of sodium or potassium halides in a hot solution of gelatin. The appropriate silver halides then precipitate as crystals suspended in the gelatin. The size distribution of the crystals—and therefore the sensitivity of the emulsion—depends on factors such as the rate of mixing, temperature, and the absence or presence of solvents, which help smaller grains redissolve and reprecipitate on larger grains.

The presence of dissolved salts makes the gelatin coagulate into lumps or curds that also contain the photographic grains; the nitrates remain dissolved in the water, which is discarded. The gelatin and the photographic grains are then redispersed in clean water.

The grains are made more sensitive by adding small quantities of sulfur or gold compounds to the emulsion and heating it to about 120 to 130°F (50–55°C). This step leads to the formation of small quantities of silver and gold sulfides on the surface of the grains, increasing their sensitivity. Then sensitizing dyes, color couplers, and emulsifiers are added along with compounds that reduce fogging and harden the gelatin. The emulsion is then ready for coating.

The base material for films can be any of a number of polymeric films, provided the material is nonflammable, flexible, stable, and impervious to water so that its dimensions do not change during processing. The base is cast in sheets with extremely even surfaces that may be several yards wide and hundreds of yards long. Film base is shipped and stored in rolls.

For coating, molten emulsion is pumped through a narrow slot and allowed to flow evenly onto the film base as it is drawn past the coating point. The film is then chilled to set the gelatin. This step is important, as the set gel cannot flow, so the layer remains evenly spread while drying.

X-ray films are coated exceptionally thick to absorb sufficient radiation and are usually coated on both sides of the base; color films receive several layers on top of one another, and most film materials are given a dark antihalation layer on the back to absorb light that passes through the film. Without such a layer, light could be reflected from the back of the film, causing haloes

◀ Coin-operated photo booths are essentially self-contained photographer's studios and processing laboratories. The whole process—from the flash photograph to the delivery of finished prints—lasts only a few minutes.

around bright lights in images. The film is then cut into strips of the required width, perforated (if necessary), chopped to size, and wound on spools before being packed in cassettes or wrapped.

Besides films for normal use, special films are made to record X rays or the tracks of nuclear particles. Films with particularly fine grains are made for microphotography and for use in the manufacture of integrated electronic circuits.

Photographic paper

The range of photographic papers is limited in comparison with the range of film materials. They are, however, available in a range of contrasts and finishes—matt, satin, and gloss, for example. The bases of most types of photographic paper are coated with white pigment in gelatin, which improves contrast in the overlying emulsions.

The bases of most color printing papers and some black-and-white printing papers are coated on both sides with layers of plastic, which make the base impervious to chemical solutions and allows quicker processing, since less washing is required. Such papers are called resin coated.

Traditional papers, called fiber based, are completely porous and therefore require more thorough washing. The lack of a plastic backing also makes them difficult to dry flat and liable to be damaged by rough handling when wet.

SEE ALSO: Camera • Camera, digital • Instant-picture camera • Light and optics • Lithography • Oxidation and reduction

Photomicrography

When the compound microscope was first introduced at the beginning of the 17th century, the image could be recorded only by sketching or tracing. Such records were called micrographs. Nearly 250 years were to pass before advances in photography enabled microscopists to produce a permanent record of the magnified image. The word *photomicrography* was coined to describe the production of such a record. A precise definition would be photography through a microscope.

Confusion often arises between the terms photomicrography and microphotography, but the latter refers exclusively to the recording of an object as an image greatly reduced in size.

Apparatus

The basic apparatus consists of an illuminating source, a compound microscope, and a camera. The camera has no function other than to contain the photographic recording medium, usually film. No lenses or diaphragms are required, since these parts are already present in the microscope. A shutter can be located in either the camera or the microscope. The most sophisticated cameras used in photomicrography are specially designed, but ordinary cameras may be adapted for this function. In cameras with removable lenses, the lens is simply replaced with a cylindrical extension tube, which in turn connects to the microscope eyepiece. A variety of adaptors are available for different models of cameras and microscopes.

A requirement of a photomicrographic system is that it should be supported and clamped so that it is absolutely free from vibration effects, since long exposure times are often necessary, especially when opaque objects are photographed using reflected light or when high magnifications are employed.

Modern apparatus tends to be designed on a modular basis, permitting components and accessories to be added, substituted, or adjusted with the minimum of inconvenience.

Photographic film

There are many factors to consider when selecting the photographic film that will give optimum results with a particular specimen under given lighting conditions. It is normal practice first to decide upon the combination of light source and color filters (if any) required to reveal the details of interest in the specimen and then to select the appropriate film to record the range of the visible spectrum being used.

The brightness range of the image will determine whether the film is to be of high or low contrast. If the range is short, then a high-contrast material may be used.

The color output of a light source varies with its temperature, and this factor is of importance in color photomicrography. The lower the temperature of a source, the richer the light is in the red end of the spectrum. Color films are manufac-

▼ Photography using a scanning electron microscope (SEM) is sometimes included as a form of photomicrography. Because this technique produces images in black and white, color is often added artificially to aid comprehension and to make the images more interesting. Here, a SEM image of a fly has been tinted by hand to resemble its true color.

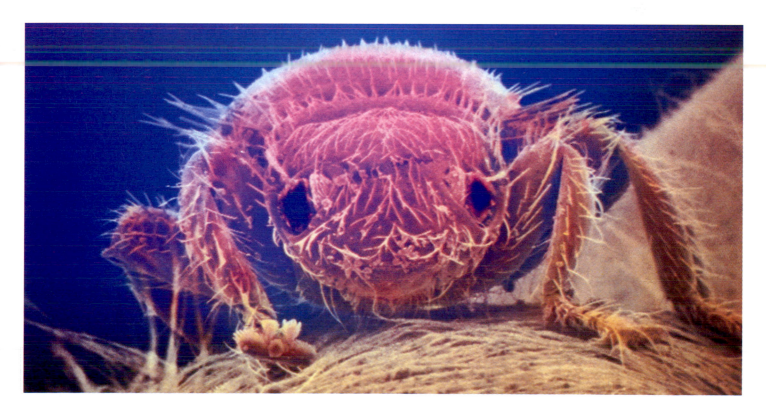

tured to give a true color rendering of a subject with light of a specific color temperature. Where it is necessary to match the light source with the color film, color-correcting filters are employed to absorb the red or blue region of the spectrum. Many other types of filters are available catering for the wide range of demands made by different types of microscope specimens and different photomicrographic techniques. Biological specimens that have been stained with methyl blue, eosin, or fuchsin, for example, have a tendency to look washed out in photographic images. This problem may be corrected using a special didymium filter that removes some of the orange portion from the visible spectrum. These filters are made using rare earth metals dissolved in glass. Filters are also available that cut out ultraviolet light, which tends to give images a blue cast, and filter out heat by removing the infrared waves produced by the microscope's electric bulb.

In addition, the microscope must be configured using Köler illumination, a method named after the German scientist August Köler, who introduced this technique in 1893. Köler illumination involves aligning and focusing the condenser and adjusting the iris diaphragm in such a way that an evenly illuminated field is created, enabling the specimen to be viewed with a minimum of heat and without glare, thus, producing a clear bright image.

Resolving power

The resolving power (RP) of a system is a measure of its ability to reveal or record very fine detail. The higher the RP, the smaller is the detail revealed or recorded. The maximum RP of the optical microscope is fixed by the wave nature of light at about 1,500 angstroms (0.00015 mm), and under good viewing conditions, the eye can resolve 0.1 mm. Therefore, provided the highest quality lenses are used, a magnification of about 700 times will reveal the smallest detail resolvable with an optical microscope.

The size of the smallest detail in the image at 700 times magnification is therefore 0.1 mm. All photographic films are capable of recording detail of this size, so resolution in photomicrography does not depend on the RP of the photographic material.

Applications

Nearly all branches of science have benefited from the application of photomicrography. In medicine, it is used as a tool for routine analysis. The examination of cervical smears for the early detection of cancer and the study of chromosomes are just two examples of its usefulness.

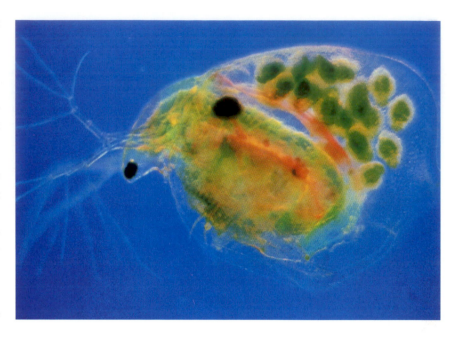

Highly accurate photomicrographic images are also presented as evidence in legal proceedings, where it is necessary to leave no room for ambiguity. The photographing of fingerprints, signatures, fibers, bullets, and so on, must be done as accurately as possible. Forensic photography is therefore regarded as one of the most exacting photomicrographic techniques. Metallurgy, biology, and geology also make wide use of photomicrography.

Recent developments

Today, photomicrography includes the use of video cameras to capture movement in microscopic samples, such as single-celled organisms during the process of cell division. Photomicrographs are also increasingly being taken using digital cameras, such as the Olympus DP-10 or the Nikon Digital Eclipse DXM 1200, which have both been specially designed for the purpose of photomicrography. These cameras may be connected to a computer so that the images can be viewed immediately on screen, thus allowing the photographer to adjust the sample, the microscope lenses, and the lighting quality to obtain the optimum image quality. The computer may in turn be connected to a specialist printer capable of producing high-quality images similar to those resulting from a conventional photographic process. Computer techniques also enable the photographer to artificially manipulate the image to correct any aberrations and highlight important details.

▲ A photomicrograph of a live daphnia. The rich colors were achieved by using polarized light and a blue filter. The magnification here is x 100. Using high quality lenses, a magnification of x 700 is possible with an optical microscope. Photographic film can easily record the minute details revealed at this magnification.

SEE ALSO: CAMERA • CAMERA, DIGITAL • FORENSIC SCIENCE • LENS • LIGHT AND OPTICS • MICROSCOPE, ELECTRON • MICROSCOPE, OPTICAL • PHOTOGRAPHIC FILM AND PROCESSING • VIDEO CAMERA

Photomultiplier Tube

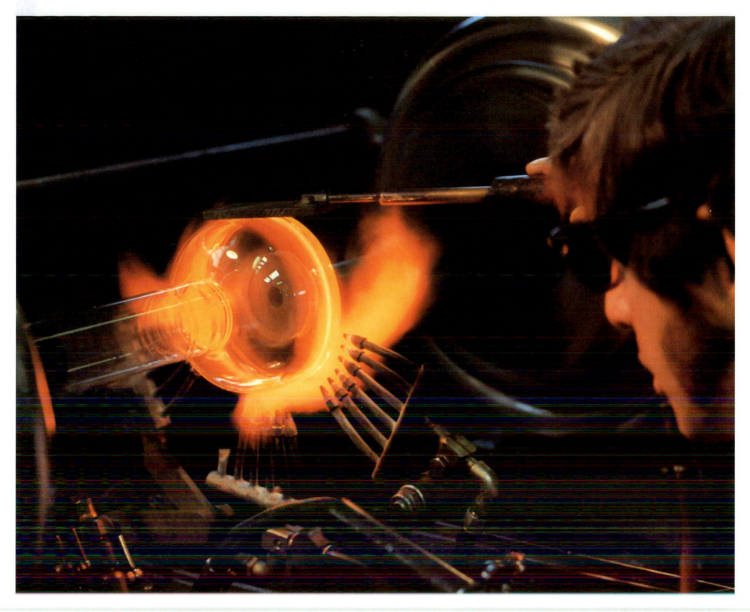

The intensity of a beam of light can be measured using photoelectric cells in which the energy associated with light radiation is converted into electric energy. An important type of photoelectric cell is that which operates on the principle of photoemission—the emission of electrons from the surface of a material as a result of incident light. The output current of such a cell is, however, low, and substantial electronic amplification is required. Photoelectric cells are often used in situations where a circuit is operated by the interruption of a beam of light, such as in alarm systems.

Because photoelectric cells produce only a low output, they have a limited range of detection. The photomultiplier tube has been developed to overcome this limitation. In this device the initial photoemission is increased, or multiplied, by a secondary emission process. When an electron moving at a sufficiently high velocity strikes a

surface, the emission of further electrons from that surface can occur. This process is called secondary emission.

Basic principles

When a beam of light (photons) strikes certain materials, the energy associated with the beam raises the energy of the electrons of the bombarded material, enabling them to overcome the influence of the atom that they are associated with. These electrons are thus emitted from the atom and can then be induced to flow in an electric circuit resulting in an electric current proportional to the intensity of the incident light beam. This is the principle of the photoemissive cell.

A typical photomultiplier consists of a metal plate, the cathode, coated with a photoemissive material contained in an evacuated glass bulb. An alloy of cesium and antimony is an example of a

▲ Welding a faceplate onto the glass envelope of a photomultiplier tube. A typical photomultiplier consists of a metal plate, the cathode, contained in an evacuated glass bulb, and a second (positive) plate called a dynode. This arrangement is backed up by a series of secondary dynodes, each one set at a progressively higher voltage.

photoemissive material suitable for the monitoring of visible light. The electrons liberated at the cathode by photoemission are attracted toward a second (positive) plate called a dynode. Each electron striking this dynode gives rise to the emission of a number of electrons by secondary emission.

A series of such dynodes is arranged in the photomultiplier tube, and the negatively charged electrons released from the first dynode, by secondary emission, can be attracted toward the next plate by the application of a higher positive voltage to this next plate. This process continues throughout the series of dynodes, each one being at a higher voltage than the previous one.

Amplification

If each electron striking a dynode causes 4 electrons to be emitted by secondary emission, then at the first dynode, 4 electrons will be released; at the second dynode, 4 x 4 (4^2), or 16, electrons will be released; and at the third dynode, 4 x 4 x 4 (4^3), or 64, electrons will be released. If the cell contains 11 such dynodes, the number of electrons available to produce an electric current in an external circuit is 4^{11}, or just over four million times the number of photons striking the cathode. The greater the number of secondary electrodes, the larger will be this multiplication effect, or amplification.

All the multiplied electrons are attracted finally to the last plate in the system, the anode, from which they are passed to the external detecting circuit. The sensitivity to light of such a system is extremely high, and a typical photomultiplier can detect and respond to very much weaker light intensities than can be detected by the human eye.

The dynodes are usually arranged in the form of slats making a Venetian blind type of structure. The voltage difference required between each successive dynode to sufficiently accelerate the electron motion is approximately 100 volts. With the number of dynodes usually incorporated into such a device, the overall operating voltage is high, and consequently, there are certain hazards associated with its use. Accordingly, the use of a photomultiplier tube is generally confined to situations where adequate sensitivity for light measurement cannot be achieved by other means. The high sensitivity also requires that ambient light be rigorously excluded from striking the system.

Applications

One of the most important areas of application of photomultiplication is the detection and quantitative assessment of radiation emitted from radioactive materials. The radiation to be measured is

arranged to strike a glass screen coated with a phosphor, a material that emits light when irradiated. The screen is placed in contact with a photomultiplier tube, and the emitted light from the phosphor is arranged to strike the photocathode. This impact gives rise to one or more photoelectrons. The photomultiplying action then increases the electron flow by a factor of a million or more.

The resulting current is measured, and by scaling this figure down by an amount related to the amplification of the photomultiplier, the quantity of radiation originally striking the phosphor can be assessed. Each flash of light produced by radiation striking the phosphor is called scintillation, and the device is called a scintillation counter.

▲ Photomultiplier tube with a dynode secondary emitting surface made from cesium and antimony.

▼ Diagram of a photomultiplier tube showing the increase in the number of electrons produced at each dynode; by the time the anode is reached, the current is large enough to be easily measured.

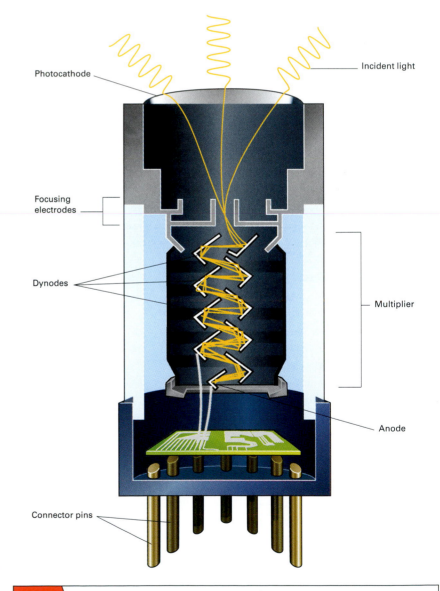

Photocathode

Incident light

Focusing electrodes

Dynodes

Multiplier

Anode

Connector pins

SEE ALSO: ATOMIC STRUCTURE • LIGHT AND OPTICS • OPTICAL SCANNER • PHOTOELECTRIC CELL AND PHOTOMETRY • RADIOACTIVITY

Photosynthesis

Plants, unlike animals, do not need to eat other organisms to obtain food. Instead, they manufacture their own food in the form of glucose using a process called photosynthesis. In order for photosynthesis to take place, four elements are needed—light, carbon dioxide, chlorophyll, and water. Deprived of any one of these factors, photosynthesis is impossible.

Photosynthesis also has important broader implications for life on Earth—photosynthesis produces the oxygen in the atmosphere that animals breathe. Without a plentiful supply of vegetable matter as food, animals would soon become extinct. Even carnivores depend, ultimately, on photosynthesis, since their prey, somewhere along the food chain, eat vegetable matter.

The overall reaction in photosynthesis is as follows:

$$6CO_2 + 12H_2O \rightarrow C_6H_{12}O_6 + 6O_2 + 6H_2O$$

Carbon dioxide and water react in the presence of light to produce glucose, oxygen, and water—overall, water is consumed in the reaction. The absorbed light energy is needed to break the chemical bonds of the highly stable carbon dioxide and water molecules so that the somewhat less stable glucose and oxygen can form. It is this energy that ultimately provides the food (caloric) value of vegetable matter. The overall effect of

▲ Algae producing oxygen as a by-product of photosynthesis. Plants obtain their own food by manufacturing glucose sugar from carbon dioxide and water.

photosynthesis is to fix carbon from carbon dioxide. It has been estimated that some 100 billion tons (90 billion tonnes) of organic carbon are produced each year by plants. It has also been estimated that every molecule of carbon dioxide in the atmosphere gets fixed into glucose once every 200 years, and each oxygen molecule every 2,000 years.

The reaction does not stop at this stage; most plants convert the glucose into carbohydrates (starch), amino acids, proteins, lipids (fats), pigments, and a range of components found in green plant tissue. These further reactions consume elements such as nitrogen, phosphorus, and sulfur, for which plants need a supply of minerals.

The reactions involved in photosynthesis have been summarized in the following generalized equation:

$$aCO_2 + bH_2O + cNO_2 + dSO_4 + \text{other minerals} \rightarrow$$
$$\text{compounds} + eO_2$$

Carbon dioxide, water, nitrate, sulfate, and other mineral-derived materials yield organic compounds and oxygen.

The structure of the leaf

Most photosynthesis occurs within the leaf in a layer of long thin cells called the palisade mesophyll. These cells contain many organelles, called chloroplasts, that are responsible for the processes of photosynthesis. Other plant cells also contain chloroplasts, but the main site of photosynthesis is the palisade mesophyll.

The palisade mesophyll is protected by an upper surface of epidermal cells that prevent moisture loss while allowing light to pass through to the layers below. Under the palisade mesophyll is the spongy mesophyll, which consists of cells separated by air spaces that allow the diffusion of carbon dioxide and oxygen as well as water vapor. Within the spongy mesophyll is the plant's vascular system, which consists of tissues called the xylem and the phloem that together form veins. Beneath the spongy mesophyll is an epidermal layer that includes cells called stomata that allow the passage of gases and water vapor and open and close to regulate water loss.

Light harvesting

Light harvesting occurs within any plant cell that contains chloroplasts. The chlorophyll molecules are arranged in groups of several hundred that together are called an antenna complex. There

PHOTOSYNTHESIS REACTIONS

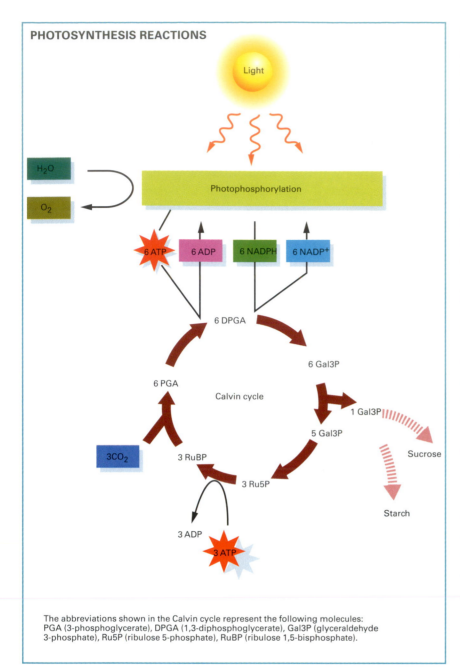

The abbreviations shown in the Calvin cycle represent the following molecules: PGA (3-phosphoglycerate), DPGA (1,3-diphosphoglycerate), Gal3P (glyceraldehyde 3-phosphate), Ru5P (ribulose 5-phosphate), RuBP (ribulose 1,5-bisphosphate).

Light-dependent stage

An electron is first raised to a higher energy level in photosystem II and is received by an electron acceptor. The electron passes down a series of electron carriers and in the process releases energy that is used to convert ADP (adenosine diphosphate) to ATP (adenosine triphosphate). ATP is the main energy-carrying molecule used to power cellular processes in both plants and animals.

The electron then arrives at photosystem I, where light energy raises the electron to an even higher energy level. Once more, the electron is received by an electron acceptor. This time, the electron is used to make another energy-carrying molecule by combining with hydrogen protons, which then combine with NADP (nicotinamide adenine dinucleotide phosphate) to form NADPH.

To replace the electrons that have been lost from the chlorophyll molecule, electrons are taken from a water molecule causing the water molecule to split into O_2 and $2H^+$. The O_2 is released from the plant by diffusion through the stomata, and the $2H^+$ are the hydrogen protons used to make the NADPH.

Light-independent stage

The light-independent stage is also known as the Calvin cycle after the U.S. chemist Melvin Calvin, who first determined the biochemical processes involved. When Calvin investigated the light-independent stage, he discovered a very complex cycle of reactions that convert carbon dioxide into glucose by using up the ATP and NADPH produced by the light-dependent reactions. The net reaction of the Calvin cycle is as follows:

$$6CO_2 + 18ATP + 12NADPH + 12H_2O \rightarrow C_6H_{12}O_6 + 18ADP + 18 \text{ pyruvate molecules} + 12NADP^+ + 16H^+$$

In more detail, the Calvin cycle starts when carbon dioxide reacts with ribulose 1,5-bisphosphate. The reaction yields a transient intermediate molecule that rapidly reacts with water to yield two molecules of 3-phosphoglycerate. Following this reaction is a series of reactions that yield intermediate products, such as 1,3-diphosphoglycerate and glyceraldehyde 3-phosphate, some of which are used to produce sugar and starch. Further steps in the Calvin cycle use the remaining glyceraldehyde 3-phosphate to produce a five-carbon sugar, ribulose 5-phosphate, which is then converted using ATP to ribulose 1,5-bisphosphate, thus completing the cycle.

Each round of the Calvin cycle reduces one carbon atom. Thus, to synthesize glucose—

are two slightly different kinds of photoreceptor chlorophyll, known as chlorophyll a and chlorophyll b, with differing sensitivities to ranges within the absorption spectrum. Photons arrive at the reaction center chlorophyll molecule, where the effect of the photon is to raise an electron to a higher energy level.

The reaction center molecules exist as two different types, known as photosystem I and photosystem II. The complexes involved in the photosystems consist of a number of chlorophyll molecules bound to a specific protein. The complex involved in photosystem I consists of 14 chlorophyll a molecules bound to a 100-kDa protein (where 1 Da, or dalton, is a measurement of mass equivalent to 1 atomic mass unit), while the complex involved in photosystem II consists of three chlorophyll a molecules and three chlorophyll b molecules bound to a 28-kDa protein.

▲ Photosynthesis occurs in organelles called chloroplasts. The first stage uses light to produce the energy carrying molecules ATP and NADPH. These molecules are then used in the light independent stage where CO_2 is converted via a series of intermediate reactions into sugar and starch.

$C_6H_{12}O_6$—six rounds of the cycle are needed. Three molecules of ATP and two molecules of NADPH are consumed in converting a single carbon dioxide molecule in the reactions that eventually lead to that carbon dioxide molecule becoming incorporated into glucose.

Rate of photosynthesis

The rate at which plants photosynthesize can be judged by measuring the rate at which oxygen is produced. Figures are usually quoted as rate of oxygen production per unit area or unit mass. A single gram of chlorophyll can produce many liters of oxygen per hour.

External factors such as light intensity, temperature, and to a lesser extent, carbon dioxide concentration affect the rate of photosynthesis.

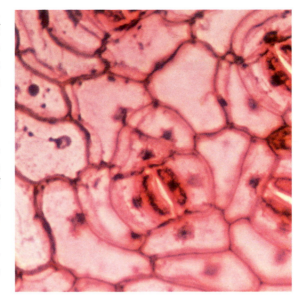

◀ A section taken from the thin outer layer of a lily leaf. Viewed at high magnification, the internal structure of plants is clearly revealed.

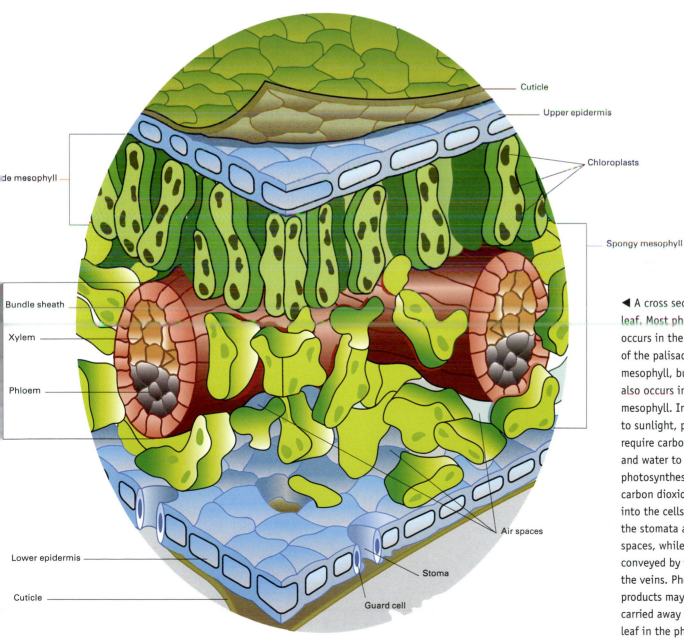

◀ A cross section of a leaf. Most photosynthesis occurs in the chloroplasts of the palisade mesophyll, but some also occurs in the spongy mesophyll. In addition to sunlight, plants require carbon dioxide and water to carry out photosynthesis. The carbon dioxide diffuses into the cells through the stomata and air spaces, while the water is conveyed by the xylem in the veins. Photosynthetic products may then be carried away from the leaf in the phloem.

◄ This lamp suspended above a group of indoor plants mimics the Sun's light to boost photosynthesis and encourage growth.

Chloroplasts and chlorophyll

Photosynthesis takes place in chloroplasts, sub-cellular structures discovered in 1940 by the British biochemist Robert Hill that contain the green pigment chlorophyll. Chloroplasts are spheroid in shape and measure some 5 μm (microns) by 2.5 μm and have a number of distinct structural features. The stroma area mainly contains dissolved enzymes, some of which are involved in converting carbon dioxide into glucose. Thylakoids are approximately 0.01 to 0.15 μm thick and contain the photosynthetic pigment or pigments. The thylakoids form stacks called grana that may be connected to other grana via tubular extensions called intergranal lamellae. The light-dependent stages of photosynthesis occur on the thylakoids.

Chlorophyll is not the only photosynthetic pigment, but it is the only one that is essential to the process. The structure of the chlorophyll molecule features a hydrophobic (water-hating) "tail," which is embedded in the thylakoid membrane. The opposite end of the molecule consists of a series of porphyrin rings containing carbon and nitrogen. The structure is doughnut shaped with a hole in the middle, and the hole is filled with a single magnesium atom.

The ring structure has a series of alternating double and single chemical bonds. When a photon of the appropriate wavelength is absorbed, an electron is promoted to a higher energy level, starting a series of related chemical reactions. The energy is passed through a system of over 300 chlorophyll molecules to a slightly different kind of chlorophyll molecule, where the energy is concentrated.

At this stage, the end chlorophyll molecule can pass on an electron to a set of intermediate carriers. From here, the electron is passed on to an NADP molecule. The central chlorophyll molecule is therefore oxidized and is reduced by accepting an electron from the hydroxyl group in water.

Photoreceptor systems

Close investigation of the relative quantum efficiency of photosynthesis—the photosynthetic rate divided by the number of quanta observed at each wavelength—led scientists to the discovery that there were two kinds of photoreceptor systems.

If there was a single kind of photoreceptor, the quantum efficiency would be expected to be independent of frequency across the entire absorption band of the system. What scientists found was that quantum efficiency drops very sharply after a wavelength of 680 nm—a surprising phenomenon considering that the absorption spectrum extends to 700 nm. The sharp decline is known as the red drop.

The case for more than one photosystem was further reinforced by the discovery of the enhancement phenomenon. The rate of photosynthesis brought about by long-wavelength light can be enhanced by adding light of a lower wavelength. For example, the rate of photosynthesis brought about by a combination of wavelengths of 600 nm and 700 nm is greater than the sum of the rates produced by the two wavelengths individually.

Scientists concluded that the only explanation for these two phenomena was that there were two photosystems at work, photosystem I and photosystem II. Both systems could react to wavelengths of 680 nm, but only one could react to the wavelengths up to 700 nm. Photosystem I, which leads to the formation of NADPH, reacts to wavelengths up to 700 nm. On the other hand, photosystem II will form oxygen only in response to wavelengths shorter than 680 nm. The interaction of the photosystems to produce ATP is known as photophosphorylation.

It has been discovered that the two photosystems are structurally distinct. For example, if chloroplast membranes are treated with detergent, photosystem I particles are released. More careful investigation using density-gradient centrifugation techniques has isolated complexes involved in photosystem I and photosystem II activity.

SEE ALSO: BOTANY • CARBOHYDRATE • CARBON • CELL BIOLOGY • ENERGY, MASS, AND WEIGHT • LIFE • LIGHT AND OPTICS • OSMOSIS • OXYGEN • PROTEIN • WATER

Phototherapy

Phototherapy, or photodynamic therapy, is the use of light to treat a number of medical conditions, particularly skin diseases. The technique was first investigated in 1893 by a Danish physician, Niels Ryberg Finsen, who used red light to prevent the formation of pustules in smallpox patients. Realizing that sunlight can kill bacteria, Finsen developed other radiation treatments including the use of ultraviolet light on patients suffering from *Lupus vulgaris*, a form of skin tuberculosis. Ultraviolet lighting is now used regularly in hospitals, microbiology research laboratories, and food preparation areas to prevent bacterial growth.

Light treatment

The ancient Egyptians used a common weed, *Ammi majus*, to treat a condition called vitiligo, in which patches of skin lose their pigment. The same weed is used today to provide the psoralen compounds, which together with ultraviolet light, form the basis of the PUVA treatment of skin complaints. Patients are dosed with psoralen-based drugs or the affected area is soaked in a dilute solution and then subjected to varying exposures to light of a particular wavelength.

The PUVA treatment has been widely successful on psoriasis sufferers, though an unfortunate side effect is that they run an increased risk of skin cancer. However, phototherapy can also be used to treat skin tumors. A new treatment under development makes use of chemicals that occur naturally in the body called porphyrins, which are found in the hemoglobin in the blood of humans and animals and in the chlorophyll of plants. When activated by a laser light, the porphyrins release electrons that can be taken up by nearby molecules. In the bloodstream, these molecules are most likely to be oxygen molecules, which form a highly reactive molecule called singlet oxygen. Because singlet oxygen is toxic to most cells in the body, it is useful for killing skin tumors. To prevent healthy cells from being destroyed, researchers have developed a porphyrin called verteporfin that reacts only to light of a certain frequency. By targeting light in the area required, only diseased cells are affected.

Porphyrins can be useful in diagnosis of disorders as well as in treatment. If porphyria victims should visit a discotheque with ultraviolet lights, their teeth would glow deep red. Under blue light porphyrins fluoresce dark red, and diagnosticians can use this fact to pinpoint tumors. By injecting porphyrins and waiting for the healthy tissue to

▲ Brown eggs contain porphyrins, which make them fluoresce under ultraviolet light. Though absent from white eggs, porphyrins occur in many life forms—in the chlorophyll of plants and in hemoglobin in the blood of animals, including humans. If the concentration of porphyrins becomes too high, disease can result, but porphyrins can also be used to destroy cancerous tissue.

rid itself of them and then subjecting the patient to doses of ultraviolet light, the position of infected tissue can be mapped.

Sometimes, owing to metabolic malfunctioning, the porphyrins build up to dangerous levels of concentration, resulting in the porphyria diseases. Light waves, including those from sunlight, activate the metal-free type of porphyrins, causing them to convert oxygen molecules into singlet oxygen. Sores form, the flesh disintegrates, and even death may follow. However, these porphyrin explosions can be of much use if surgeons can safely harness the energy in them.

Internal phototherapy

Phototherapy can also be extended to treating internal tumors and disorders such as atherosclerosis. Clinical trials are now underway using synthetic porphyrins that can be activated by light from fiber-optic cables or by X rays. Atherosclerosis is an inflammation of the blood vessels that results in lesions and thickening of the walls, which restricts blood flow. Conventional treatment of this condition is by angioplasty, which may itself cause more damage to the wall linings. By injecting patients with lutetium texaphyrin and then threading an optical fiber through a catheter to the vessel to be treated, researchers

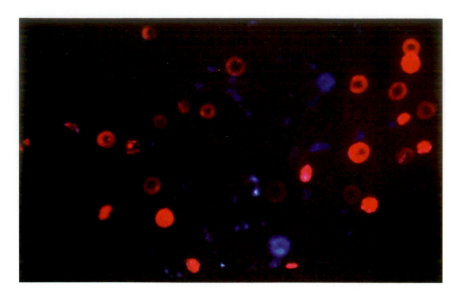

have found that they can shrink lesions by at least 10 percent. Lutetium texaphyrin is activated by red light, enabling light to shine through the blood without damaging it.

A related compound, gadolinium texaphyrin, is being tested on tumors deep in the body that catheters cannot reach, such as the brain. Short bursts of X rays are used to generate singlet oxygen and kill the cancerous cells. The procedure may also prove useful in treating cancers of the pancreas, prostate, and neck.

Other treatments

In conjunction with porphyrins, light can be a powerful weapon in the surgeon's armory. In other circumstances, it becomes a gentle healer, though no less efficient. Neonatal jaundice is a common disorder of babies in the first days of their life, before their livers are fully operational. Bilirubin is a red pigment in bile, and its function is to join up with worn-out blood cells so that they can be excreted via the liver.

In babies, particularly premature babies, the bilirubin sometimes builds up to a high level, causing jaundice and putting the victim in danger of neural damage and even death. However, if the babies are bathed for up to a week in high-intensity blue light, the jaundice retreats. The light acts in such a way on the bilirubin molecules that they become susceptible to absorption by the bile and can be excreted by the liver.

In many cases of neonatal jaundice, exposure to sunlight is probably sufficient. For the 10 percent of newborn babies needing treatment, phototherapy using light in the blue part of the visible spectrum is the only effective alternative to exchange blood transfusions. The light treatment of neonatal jaundice is a true phototherapy; it does not use any chemical photosensitizers. Photochemotherapy uses light in association with

▲ Photomicrograph of blood from a porphyria victim, under ultraviolet light. Some red blood cells fluoresce bright red, because the porphyrins make sufferers sensitive to light, leading to painful sores or even death.

▶ Photochemotherapy uses light and sensitizing agents to alleviate and even cure some illnesses such as psoriasis, as seen on the hands and legs of this patient. The affected areas are soaked or painted with psoralen-based solutions and exposed to ultraviolet light. The drawbacks to this type of treatment are severe sunburn, sensitization of the skin, or even cancer.

▶ This deep-sea jellyfish is colored red-brown by the porphyrin it contains.

sensitizing agents and is probably the most widespread use of light in medicine.

Seasonal affective disorder (SAD) is a form of depression that has been linked to low levels of light and the shortening of the day as winter approaches. Sufferers experience a lack of energy, depressed moods, and a tendency to sleep too much. Daylight regulates production of a hormone, melatonin, that regulates the body's clock. Without daylight, the body switches to a 25-hour cycle. Exposing sufferers to fluorescent light daily for 30 minutes at 10,000 lux from September to early spring has been found to alleviate many of the symptoms. Light therapy has also been used to treat those with jet lag, sleep disorders, and changing shift-work schedules.

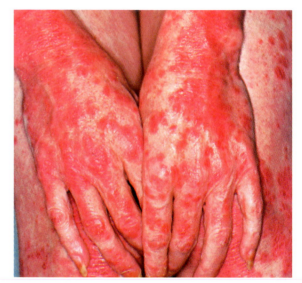

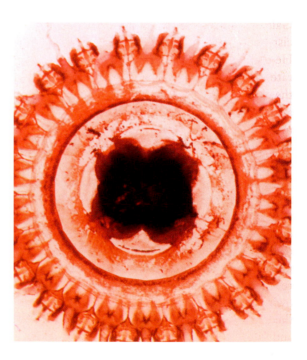

SEE ALSO: BLOOD • CANCER TREATMENT • ELECTROMAGNETIC RADIATION • FIBER OPTICS • LASER AND MASER • SKIN

Physics

Physics is the science of energy and matter and of their behavior and properties. It is the most fundamental of the physical sciences, and its models, theories, and equations are tools for scientists in other fields, such as biology and chemistry.

The scope of physics is enormous, since it encompasses the behaviors of vast systems—galaxies and the Universe, for example—while also describing atoms and their constituent electrons, neutrons, and protons. Much current physics research is concerned with detecting and understanding the fundamental particles of which all matter—even protons and neutrons—is composed and understanding the nature of the fundamental forces: electromagnetism, gravity, and nuclear, at work in the Universe.

Classical mechanics

Mechanics attempts to understand the behavior of matter in motion. It is the branch of physics that was studied in a scientifically mature way before all others.

Ancient Roman and Greek philosophers believed that an object would stay in motion only if constantly pushed or pulled—a notion based on experience with carts and other everyday objects. Weight—the force of gravity on an object that has mass—was a baffling force, since it caused free-falling objects to drop with increasing speed, apparently with nothing to push or pull them.

The Italian philosopher and astronomer Galileo Galilei—arguably the first true physicist—set about changing the concepts of forces. He demonstrated that objects fall with the same rate of increasing speed (acceleration), provided the effects of air resistance are eliminated. Galileo also proposed that an object would continue moving indefinitely provided no force acted on it, an early example of a *Gedankenexperiment* (German for "thought experiment").

Galileo considered what happens when a ball rolls down a groove in one inclined plane and then up another. The ball gains speed as it rolls downhill and loses speed as it rises up on the other side, eventually rolling back down, and back up the first incline. Galileo reckoned the height reached by the ball became less on each return owing to some resisting force: friction. Take away the friction, and the ball would roll endlessly back and forth, always reaching the same height.

Galileo then considered what would happen if one of the frictionless slopes were more gently inclined: the ball would travel farther to reach the initial height, and it would lose speed at a much lower rate. Taken to the extreme of a flat "slope," the ball would travel an infinite distance without ever slowing down from its maximum speed.

This and other observations by Galileo laid the foundations for three laws of motion that would be proposed in 1687 by the British scientist Isaac Newton, who was born in the year Galileo died. Newton's First Law states that a body will remain in uniform motion until a force acts on it. In other words, a body in motion will move at constant speed in a straight line, and a body at rest will stay at rest, unless forces act upon it.

Newton's Second Law states that the acceleration of a body is proportional to the net force that acts on it divided by its mass. Using appropriate units of measurement, this law can be expressed as $F = ma$—(force = mass x acceleration).

The third law states that, for each action, there is an equal and opposite reaction. That is, if one body exerts a force on another—during a collision, for example—the first body will experience an equal and opposite force (the reaction) from the second body.

These three laws are sufficient to derive equations that describe all forms of motion of macroscopic (large) objects. They explain the curved trajectories of cannonballs, the motions of the

◄ The Dez Dam at Dezful, Iran. Dams such as this hold water in a state of high potential energy due to the ability of the water, if released, to accelerate under the influence of gravity and acquire kinetic energy. In a hydroelectric plant, some of that kinetic energy is transferred to turbines that drive generators and produce electrical energy.

planets as they orbit around the Sun, and the movements of colliding pool balls.

Newton's laws of motion also apply to systems that rotate, such as flywheels and spinning tops. In describing the rotation of extended bodies, the concepts of torque, moment of inertia, angular displacement, angular velocity, and angular acceleration obey relations exactly analogous to those governing force, mass, displacement, velocity, and acceleration of nonrotating systems.

Gravitation

Circular motion is the orbital motion of a mass around a central point. To stay in a circular path, the mass must experience a centripetal force—one that acts toward the center of its orbit. When two objects orbit one another, they rotate around a point called the center of mass, which lies closer to the more massive object. Equal forces act on both objects, and those forces both point toward the center of mass of the rotating system—a manifestation of Newton's Third Law.

When two orbiting masses are planets, the force that acts between them is gravity. The origin of that force is an effect called gravitation, which is a property of objects that have mass. Newton coupled his law of motion with observations of celestial bodies to produce an expression for the force (F) due to gravity:

$$F = \frac{Gm_1m_2}{r^2}$$

where m_1 and m_2 are the masses of the two objects, r is the distance between them, and G is the universal gravitational constant. For an object of mass m on Earth, this expression becomes the much simpler $F = mg$, where g is acceleration due to gravity—the same acceleration that Galileo had proposed would be identical for all objects.

Conservation of momentum

The conservation of momentum is fundamental to physics. It states that the total linear momentum of a system must remain constant, as must its total angular momentum. (Linear momentum is the product of the mass and velocity of an object: mv; angular momentum is the product of moment of inertia and angular velocity.) If a system consists of two objects that collide, for example, the total momentum must be the same throughout,

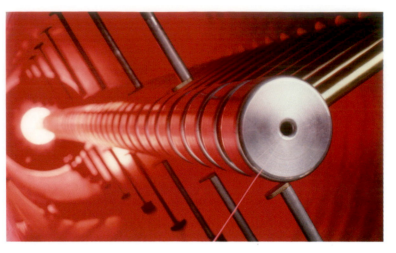

▲ The Drift Tube Linear Accelerator at Los Alamos National Laboratory, New Mexico. Linear accelerators use electrical fields to promote charged particles, such as electrons, to high velocities and therefore high kinetic energies. In particle colliders, the kinetic energies of such fast-moving particles is absorbed in collisions with other particles. The energy contents of such collisions are sufficient to split colliding particles into subatomic species. The paths of such species in electrical and magnetic fields yield data about their charges and masses.

even though each object's momentum changes.

The principle of conservation of momentum has countless applications ranging from macroscopic to submicroscopic scales. It helps in the analysis of road-traffic accidents as much as in the detailed study of the traces left in cloud chambers by the fragments of decaying subatomic particles.

Work, energy, and power

When all the linear forces and all the torques that act on an object are in balance, there is neither a net force nor a net torque, so the object stays in uniform motion (constant linear and angular velocity). Such a state is called equilibrium.

When an object is out of equilibrium, the net force, or torque, that acts on it causes it to accelerate. In this case, the force does work on the object. If the force is constant, the amount of work (W) done is related to the force (F) and the distance (d) the object moves in the direction of the force: $W = Fd$. If the force varies, the work done is the force integrated over distance.

Work has energy units—a typical unit being the joule (J)—since it is the amount of energy transferred by the action of the force. For example, the work done by the net force of a train's traction engines—subtracting drag and rolling resistance—will be equal to the increase in the train's kinetic energy, provided the track is perfectly straight and level.

Energy is the capacity to do work. If the train in the example caught up and coupled with another slightly slower-moving train, the first train would do work on the second as the velocities of the two trains became equal. What allows it to do work in this way is the kinetic energy it possesses by virtue of its speed and mass.

Power is the rate at which work is done—in other words, the rate at which energy is transferred. A typical unit of power is the watt (W), and 1 W is equal to 1 J/s.

Conservation of energy

In classical mechanics, the law of conservation of energy demands that in any process where work is done, the total energy after the work is equal to the total energy before. In most cases, the form of energy changes as a consequence of the work. In the case of an electric motor, part of the electrical energy consumed by the motor will end up as heat as a consequence of friction and electrical resistance. The rest will be converted into mechanical energy, such as the kinetic energy of a vehicle or the increased potential energy of a mass on a hoist driven by the motor.

Thermodynamics

Thermodynamics concerns the transfer of energy—in particular heat energy—and the work that can be done during such transfers. Its pioneers include the British physicists James Joule and William Thomson (Baron Kelvin): Joule described the rate at which an electric heater converted electrical energy into heat, thereby establishing the equivalence of heat and energy, and Thomson invented a temperature scale whose zero—absolute zero—is the temperature at which objects have minimum heat energy.

The first law of thermodynamics is identical to the law of conservation of energy. It states that energy can neither be created nor destroyed. The second law states that entropy must increase for a process to occur spontaneously.

Entropy is a measure of energy that is unavailable for doing work and an indication of the disorder of a system. It is intimately related to concepts of high-grade (low-entropy) energy, such as electrical energy or the chemical energy of a fuel, and low-grade (high-entropy) energy, such as the thermal energy of tepid water: the former readily does work, the latter less so.

Whenever high-grade energy is produced from a lower grade energy, the second law requires that yet lower grade energy must also be produced. For example, in the case of a thermal power engine, which converts less than half the energy of high-pressure steam into low-entropy electrical energy, the rest of the energy becomes the low-grade heat energy of cooling water.

Thermodynamics developed at first in connection with steam engines, since it addressed the efficiency with which they perform mechanical work. Thermodynamics later became useful in understanding chemical processes.

Electrostatics

Electrostatics is the study of accumulated electrical charges, rather than of electrical currents. The French physicist Charles Coulomb established that the forces between two point charges behave in a similar way to gravitational forces: the magnitude

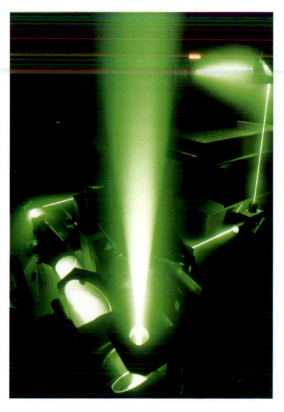

▼ This Twyman-Green interferometer uses green light from an argon laser to measure distances less than 1,000 angstrom (100 nm). Such devices are used to examine high-precision mirrors for telescopes. The invention of the laser was made possible by the understanding of quantum energy states and the rules of nature that govern changes between them.

of the force is proportional to the product of the two charges and the inverse of the square of the distance between the two point charges. The force is attractive if the two charges are of opposite signs—positive and negative—and is repulsive if they are of the same sign, either positive or negative.

Electrostatic forces are explained in terms of the electrical fields that charged objects create in the space that surrounds them. Any charged object experiences a force in an electrical field, and field strength is defined as force per unit charge. Charged objects have potential energy as a result of being in an electrical field.

Electromagnetism

Electric fields are one aspect of the electromagnetic force. The other aspect—magnetism—is a property of charges in motion.

An electrical current will flow whenever charged species are able to move in an electrical field. In most electrical circuits, the moving charges are free electrons in conductors, such as metals. In semiconductors, such as doped silicon, the charge carriers are either electrons or electron vacancies, called holes. In electrolytic cells, the charge carriers are ions—individual or grouped atoms that carry negative or positive charges.

When a steady current flows in a straight wire, it can deflect a compass needle near the wire. The deflection is caused by a magnetic field that encircles the wire. The field is described in terms of circular flux lines that have the wire at their center. If the wire is coiled, the same current produces a toroidal (donut-shaped) field around the coil, with straight flux lines along the central axis of the coil. This property is the basis of the operation of electromagnets—electrical coils that project magnetic fields when energized by a current.

Permanent magnets are made from materials that contain unpaired electrons that are considered to spin, forming magnetic fields. In most substances, electrons exist in pairs whose spins are opposed, so their magnetic fields cancel out. Where there are unpaired electrons, such as in iron, the spins of the unpaired electrons can be made to line up together by exposing the substance to a magnetic field. When the external field is removed, the spins stay aligned and produce their own magnetic field.

Each of a pair of parallel current-carrying wires produces its own contribution to the local magnetic field and experiences a force that is analogous to the force between two charges. This type of force underlies the action of motors.

When a conductor moves through a magnetic field, the changing magnetic flux causes electrons to flow in the conductor. The current is called an induced current, and the effect is called inductance. Changing magnetic flux also exists around conductors of varying currents, such as the alternating currents of most supply networks. When a coiled conductor is placed next to a coil through which alternating current passes, the oscillating magnetic field around the second coil induces an alternating current in the first. This phenomenon is the basis of how transformers work, since the peak voltage of the induced current is proportional to the number of turns in the coiled conductor.

Photons and light

Modern physics explains the communication between conductors—the mechanism that causes effects such as conductance—in terms of the exchange of photons between conductors. Photons are massless packages of oscillating electrical and magnetic fields that carry energy in those fields. In a vacuum, photons travel at 186,000 miles (297,000 km) per second. Their energy is proportional to the frequency of oscillation, and the constant of proportionality is h (Planck's constant) whose value is 6.626×10^{-34} J/s.

Radio and television signals are streams of photons that oscillate thousands to billions of times per second and can communicate between transmitting and receiving antennas separated by enormous distances. Microwave radiation oscillates at high radio frequencies, and infrared radiation and light oscillate at yet higher frequencies.

Radio, microwave, infrared, and visible light are all part of the electromagnetic spectrum, which also includes ultraviolet, X-ray, and gamma-ray radiation. The properties of such radiation—diffraction, interference, reflection, and refraction—are described by wave optics.

Quantum physics

While light is traditionally thought of as being propagated as waves, photons have some properties of particles: they are quanta (packages) of energy rather than continuous waves, and they have finite amounts of angular and linear momentum. Conversely, particles have some wave properties: electrons and neutrons can be diffracted, for example, and they have frequencies that are proportional to their energies.

In the early 20th century, acceptance of the wavelike properties of electrons led to the devel-

◀ The Diablo Canyon Nuclear Power Plant at Avila Beach, California. The energy released by chains of fission reactions has been harnessed for the generation of electricity since the mid-20th century, when physicists worked out how to control fission reactions. The reactors occupy the two containment domes in the background. The tower in the foreground is part of a transmission network that takes power to its users. The transformers and switchgear of such networks are designed according to equations developed by physicists in the 19th century.

opment of a quantum theory of atomic structure. In this theory, electrons in atoms oscillate around nuclei in well-defined states that differ by exact quantities of energy and angular momentum. An atom can jump between states by absorbing or emitting a photon whose energy and angular momentum exactly correspond to the difference between the initial and final states. The model has been confirmed by atomic spectra.

Powerful computers help produce models of the electronic structures of molecules, which can also be confirmed by spectroscopy. These models account for the structures of chemical compounds and explain their chemical properties.

The quantum picture of molecules also extends to their translational motions, vibrations, and rotations. The energies associated with these motions can be calculated using relatively simple mechanics, but they are confined to specific speeds and frequencies. Hence there are sets of allowed energy levels for each type of motion of a molecule, with the spacing between allowed levels reflected in the observed molecular spectra.

Statistical mechanics examines how collections of atoms or molecules distribute themselves among the allowed energy levels. The distribution takes the form of a bell-shaped curve, called a Boltzmann distribution, that trails off slowly toward high energy. This distribution explains the heat capacities of materials, since the heavier occupation of higher energy levels requires a heat input as temperature increases. Analysis of the distribution of gas molecules among their translational energy levels also explains the relationship between the pressure, temperature, and volume occupied by a sample of gas.

Other quantum theories include quantum chromodynamics, which explains the structure of nuclei in terms of fundamental particles called quarks and leptons. Combinations of these fundamental particles also occur in cosmic rays and can be produced in high-energy particle colliders.

SEE ALSO: ASTROPHYSICS • ATOMIC STRUCTURE • ENERGY, MASS, AND WEIGHT • LIGHT AND OPTICS • RELATIVITY • SPECTROSCOPY

Index

Page numbers in **bold** refer to main articles; those in *italics* refer to picture captions.